D1608952

The Parents' Handbook of Grammar and Usage

The Parents' Handbook of Grammar and Usage

William F. Russell

STEIN AND DAY/*Publishers*/New York

First published in 1982
Copyright © 1982 by William F. Russell
All rights reserved
Designed by L.A.Ditizio
Printed in the United States of America
Stein and Day/*Publishers*
Scarborough House
Briarcliff Manor, N.Y. 10510

Library of Congress Cataloging in Publication Data

Russell, William F., 1945–
    The parents' handbook of grammar and usage.

    Includes index.
    1. English language—Grammar.   2. English
language—Usage.   I. Title.
PE1112.R8   428.2   81-5288
ISBN 0-8128-2821-6   AACR2

To my parents
for caring so much,
and with so little return

CONTENTS

The Parents' Handbook of Grammar and Usage

1. WHAT IS THIS, A GRAMMAR BOOK?

On your last day of high school you turned in your grammar book along with all your other textbooks, right? And now you can't remember whether the comma goes inside or outside the quotation mark, so you put it directly underneath just to cover yourself in case your reader actually knows or cares which is correct. Or you find yourself in a cocktail chat with the company president, and you are just about to use the word *who* in a sentence when you realize that in this case you should use *whom*—or should you? So you slur the words into an indistinguishable mixture and resolve to learn the difference so that this problem never embarrasses you again. But where do you find out which is correct? You turned in your grammar book, remember?

If these problems sound familiar to you, believe me, you are not alone. The most common idea that American adults express about their own education is that they wish they had acquired more skill in English. The principles that govern the use of spoken and written English were taught to all of us, over and over, year after year. Our grammar textbooks had different covers each school year, but the material inside seemed to be identical: the same old rules presented in the same old way. And yet we never believed that the sub-ject would be of much importance to us as adults.

Do you remember hearing, saying, or just thinking those common teenage excuses for your lack of interest in language study? "I won't need to know how to spell or punctuate: I'll have a secretary to do that." Or, "Why should I have to learn how to write a thank-you note when I can just pick up the telephone?" Today we look back on these notions that seemed so sound to us in our youth and wonder how we were ever allowed to be so misinformed. We hear our own children expressing similar ideas, and we know that old chestnuts like "I believed that when I was young, too" will have as little impact as they did on us.

While almost all parents believe that the most important skill a child can acquire is the ability to speak and write well, very few parents feel confident enough in their own skill with language to help their children toward this goal. So there are actually two reasons that parents universally lament their own failure to appreciate and take advantage of the language lessons given them in school: Skill in written and spoken English is prized in the adult world, and parents who do not have this skill are unable to help their children acquire it.

1

I honestly believe that if the people who really wanted to be in high-school English classes could actually be there, the average age of those classes would be 40 or 50, at least. It is unfortunate, but very few such classes are available to adults. Schools commonly feel that it is unwise to have adults and children in the same classroom and that studying the basics of English would be "beneath" most adults anyway. Rubbish—on both counts. The fact is that most adults will never have that second chance for classroom instruction in the use of written and spoken English. However, many problems that adults commonly have with language do not require personal interaction with a classroom teacher. Many errors can be corrected and many embarrassments prevented by referring to that old, high-school grammar book. But you don't have that book anymore, and most schools don't make textbooks available for purchase by the public. Perhaps by now you are beginning to think, as I do, that grammar books, like love and youth, are wasted on the young.

Having a textbook on English grammar and usage would help you in two ways. First, for those occasions on which you want your writing to reflect well upon you (a letter to the in-laws, who are eager to detect every flaw; the mid-year report to your supervisor; the written-response section of your child's report card), the text could serve as a reference book that would allow you to identify and correct your mistakes before your readers merely identify them. Additionally, a grammar textbook could serve as a means for self-improvement. By acquainting yourself with the principles of English and by developing an awareness for common usage pitfalls,

you can prevent many of the language blunders that happen simply because there is no time for reference or reflection. You can develop a confidence about your use of spoken English that will allow you to be at ease in conversations with people whose speech you admire. You can call upon, when necessary, one of those little verbal niceties that separate you from the uneducated in the eyes of others.

As adults, our primary goal is not to acquire a skill in language that will impress other people. We might dream about someday having the power to persuade others with our use of language, but our immediate goal is much more important and much easier to achieve. We simply don't want our misuse of language to be an embarrassment to us. Is it fair that our teenage sin of ignoring what we were taught should brand an indelible mark on everything we say or write for the rest of our lives?

The Parents' Handbook of Grammar and Usage can be viewed as that much-maligned grammar textbook that you have rather recently learned to appreciate. It contains all the rules about the various forms that words can take depending upon their position in a sentence, and it covers the "do's and don'ts" of traditional English usage as well. So, one of the functions of this book is to replace that old grammar textbook. By reading the chapters that concentrate on the structure of the English language, you can refresh your memory of those important principles; you can restore to your vocabulary the terminology that is used to describe the classes of words and the positions of words in a sentence.

But this book does not demand that you understand (or even read) the more theoreti-

2

cal material on language structure. It contains very practical information that can have an immediate impact on your use of language. It not only includes hundreds of examples of common words and phrases that are frequently misused, but it can also help you solve common problems in punctuation and spelling, too. It is a reference book that is unlike any other in your home. Most homes, in fact, have only one language reference book: a dictionary. It is a wonderful tool for both correcting and selecting the words you use in speaking and writing, but it can't offer much help toward improving the structure of what you say and write. You can't just run to the dictionary to decide whether to use *who* or *whom;* nor can it tell you where the comma should be placed. But *The Parents' Handbook of Grammar and Usage* can tell you how to solve these and countless other language problems as well. It is a textbook and a reference book in one.

The fact that the title of this book employs the word "parents," rather than just "adults," suggests that this handbook intends to be more than just a textbook and a reference book. It is a teacher's manual for those parents who want to augment the language study their children receive in school. It contains information and suggestions about how to teach various language concepts to children of various ages. It provides general guidelines for those parents who would like to help their children improve their use of language but who don't know whether they are capable or how they should begin. It identifies both the language problems that are common with children and the problems that are shared by many adults. It also provides answers to those "Why should I learn this?" and "What

difference does it make?" questions that children commonly ask, but that parents and teachers are all-too-frequently unable to answer.

It is a textbook, a reference book, and a teacher's manual rolled into one. Whether you choose to use it in just one or in all of these ways, this book will start you looking at language again—both your own usage and that of others. It will spark your curiosity about words, and your curiosity will make you intensely aware of every new or different usage that you hear or read.

The more you learn about words and their use, the more you will want to know, and the more you will want others to experience this same excitement. We all wish that we had caught this spark when we were in school, and we all hope that our children will catch it while they are in school. But what we must realize is that school is not the only place in which curiosity can be ignited. And school is, after all, one of the last places in which curiosity can find practical application and reward. We are in a better position today to begin a program of language study than we were during our school years. We not only have an honest desire to learn, but we also are painfully aware of the consequence for failing to learn.

For each of us, a lifetime of *using* language lies ahead—a lifetime of listening, speaking, writing, and reading that will both teach and test us at the same time. *The Parents' Handbook of Grammar and Usage* is merely an introduction to this lifetime of language study. It is a grammar book, to be sure, but you will not have to—or want to—turn it in when you are finished.

2. SOME PRINCIPLES OF HOME EDUCATION

It has been an all-too-common belief among teachers that parents are an obstacle to education. I remember hearing, on more than one occasion, a colleague lament that all his efforts in the classroom were destroyed in the living room. The feeling has traditionally been that children somehow "unlearn" everything they have been taught as soon as they go back home for a summer, a weekend, or even a night.

It is not difficult, then, to understand why parents have felt left out of the educational process. Rather than provide materials to parents that would help a child's day become constantly educational, teachers and textbook publishers have devised programs such as "new math" and "new grammar" that have had the effect (if not the intent) of eliminating any possibility of the parents' interfering with their own children's education. Parents have been viewed by their children as failures because the parents couldn't multiply in the base four. That they could balance a checkbook and determine which sizes and brands were the better values was deemed of little importance, and the parent-child relationship suffered as a result.

Today, the attitude of teachers toward home education has changed and is continuing to change. It is safe to say that by now a vast majority of teachers has recognized how helpful a concerned parent can be. The vast majority of parents now has recognized that the schools alone—in spite of their best efforts and intentions—simply cannot provide a thorough education for every student at every grade level. The forces of parents and teachers—both equally concerned with the educational welfare of the child—are finally recognizing each other's capabilities and limitations, and are finally beginning to cooperate because they know that it is in their own best interest to do so. Through teaching, the parent becomes a better parent. By strengthening the role of the parent, the teacher is able to be a better teacher. The child, of course, prospers doubly from this cooperative effort, and that fact alone certainly justifies the effort itself.

The only thing that is remarkable about this change in educational direction is that it was so long in coming. School-age children spend many more hours at home than they spend at school. Even discounting the time spent sleeping (which is done to varying degrees in both realms), the home wins hands down. Why did it take us so long to realize that every waking hour is educationally precious and irreplaceable? How could we have deluded ourselves into writing off the major-

5

ity of those hours just because they weren't spent in the "proper" place or in the company of "trained" personnel? Why did we as parents turn over to people we barely knew the total responsibility for giving our children a better education than we, ourselves, had been given?

Perhaps parents just never felt confident in their own abilities as teachers. The excuses of "It's hard enough just being a good parent!" and "Isn't that what I pay taxes for?" are common masks for the all-too-common worry many parents have that the knowledge they acquired in school has suffered some erosion over the years or that they simply won't know *how* to teach a certain concept.

Those very real fears on the part of parents have stood in the way of meaningful home education for a long time. But the concerns about making factual errors in subject matter and tactical errors in method should be viewed in light of the extraordinary advantages that parents have as teachers. They should also be viewed in light of the actual tasks that are involved in home education.

Let's begin by understanding that the intent of home education is not to have parents replace teachers. On the contrary, home education depends upon teachers to establish the framework of the curriculum and to provide the ever-increasing challenges that students need in order to learn. Parents merely augment the efforts of the teacher. To do this effectively and to ensure that parents and teachers are not working against each other, there must be coordination and communication between the two. If parents and teachers cannot meet on a regular basis, then parents must at least be aware of what the teacher is trying to accomplish, of what ground the teacher will cover in the near future, and of what areas the teacher knows it is best to avoid. In short, teachers and schools are necessary and integral parts of home education.

Not only do teachers provide the overall framework for a child's education, they also provide the precise knowledge of the subjects in which they were trained. This is the role that frightens parents most, but it is one role that parents simply should not play. Parents have been far too busy learning a trade and raising a family to compete with teachers in a test of facts or formulas. Home education does not demand that parents acquire any more knowledge than they have right now.

This book covers only the study of language, but the basic principle of home education applies to mathematics, art, science, and every other subject as well: *Whatever knowledge parents have that is useful to their children's education should be transferred from parent to child.* Sounds simple, doesn't it? You see, there should be no fear about not having all the factual knowledge of a highly trained teacher, because home education only involves the transfer of "whatever knowledge parents have ... " If it is important for a child to know that Edgar Allan Poe was born in 1809 and died in 1849, then the child will simply have to learn that in school. Home education in English concerns itself with other matters entirely—matters about which parents already have a working and practical knowledge.

I will grant you that your knowledge of practical grammar and usage may not be as complete or as precise as it once was. But you did have several years of training in this area, and you have also had years of speaking, listening, reading, and writing experience on top of that. The facts about grammar and usage that are in this book will not be new to you. Indeed, this book depends upon your having a certain amount of that knowledge already. That knowledge, however, lies a little below the surface and will require scraping away some topsoil before it is apparent to you that you have applied this knowledge for years, and that you probably have a better understanding of grammar and usage today than at any other time in your life.

The principles and topics in this book that do prove a bit troublesome to you can be studied and mulled over for as long as you wish before you decide to present them to your children. You will be the teacher and you will be the one to decide when you understand a point sufficiently well enough to pass it along. ("Staying a chapter ahead of the students" is not a method wholly unknown to classroom teachers, either.)

So, you need not fear making factual errors, but what about the fear of making tactical errors? Parents are not trained in the art and science of teaching. How can they be expected to know the best ways to convey their knowledge to their children? This book will help. I have included many tried and tested techniques for teaching various lessons to children of various ages. Later in this chapter I will also set forth some guidelines and suggestions that will help you teach and reinforce whatever concepts you choose to stress. These methods will help you get the process started and will provide a general structure or overview to your teaching.

A far greater help than this book, however, is for you, the parent, to realize your inherent value as a teacher and the extraordinary advantages that you have over the classroom teacher. Once you accept the fact that no teacher-training program in the world can ever hope to give its graduates the tools that you have at your command, you will have the confidence that is essential to good teaching.

Consider for a moment the built-in benefits that you have as a teacher. First of all, unlike the classroom teacher, you will have only a very few students to teach. It would be an unusual family, indeed, that would compare in size with a teacher's average class-size. Therefore, the amount of time and special attention that you can give to each of your "pupils" is far greater than that available to the most conscientious classroom teacher.

But the advantages you have extend beyond mere numbers. The fact is that you know your children better than anyone else possibly could. You understand their strengths and weaknesses; you know what makes them happy and sad; you are able to recognize immediately when they are having difficulty; and you are aware of the illnesses, traumas, and other circumstances that might contribute to that difficulty. Classroom teachers try as best they can to gain an understanding of every student, but secondary-school teachers see their students less than an hour each day, and even elementary-school teachers must start all over with a new "family" after only nine months.

Even more important, though, than your knowledge of your children is your love for them. You simply care more deeply and feel more strongly about your own; it is an undeniable and irreversible fact of nature. This love makes your teaching meaningful because you truly care that your children learn; you feel the elation they do when they succeed, and

7

you agonize with them as they struggle to succeed. Don't for a minute think that you are too close to your children to be a good teacher. This advantage you have is yours alone and should be prized as well as used. You will discover, as many parents already have, that home education actually brings families closer together. The bond between parent and child is strengthened because both understand that they are working toward a common goal. They learn to know each other better if only because they are spending more time together than they ever have before.

So, although most parents are justifiably worried about their lack of training as teachers, their fear must be tempered by the gifts they bring to teaching and by the opportunities that teaching brings to them.

GUIDELINES AND GROUND RULES

One of the educational advantages that a school has over a home is that there is (or should be) an atmosphere of learning in a school. The students recognize that a school is a building in which learning takes place, and so they expect to be challenged and broadened by new ideas when in school. The home, on the other hand, is generally viewed as a place to eat, sleep, and play. The mere idea of being challenged and broadened at home would be dismissed by most children as unlikely and an unwarranted invasion upon their "free time."

Home education does not demand that parents try to create a school-like atmosphere in their home. Some parents who have spent large sums on multi-volume encyclopedias and unabridged dictionaries understand all-too-well that merely having books around the house is no assurance that those books will be read. Although creating a quiet place for a child to study can be a marvelous benefit to any student, there is certainly no guarantee that any sacrifice of floorspace will contribute to learning. Books and rooms may help to duplicate the physical atmosphere of a school, but creating a learning atmosphere is something else entirely.

Parents must realize before they embark on any program of home education that they are making a long-term commitment. To "try it out for awhile" simply will not work, and the reason is that the intent of home education is not merely to transfer facts, but also to promote positive attitudes. The success of any attempt at home education is ultimately measured by the way in which a child looks at learning.

One of the healthiest attitudes that a parent can instill in a child is curiosity. Perhaps the word "instill" is a bit misleading because children are innately curious. All-too-many children, however, lose that curiosity, or at least they lose interest in applying that curiosity. If a parent can direct a child's inquisitive nature and if a parent can inspire that child to long for the thrill of discovery and understanding, then educational success for that child will be assured.

Directing this curiosity toward the study of language is made easier by the fact that there is always something to learn about language. The study is never completed because, first of all, there is more to learn than anyone can possibly know. The most learned speakers and writers of our time, for instance, have vocabularies that include, perhaps, 30,000 words. But there are more than 600,000 words in the English language! Obviously, persuasive speaking and writing depend more upon the quality of the words in one's vocabulary than upon their quantity. Still, one would think that there must surely be some words in the remaining 570,000+ that would prove useful on certain occasions.

The second reason that the study of language is endless is that language is constantly changing. While technology and slang serve to enrich the word stock by creating new words and new usages, language itself is increasingly called upon to function in new ways: to describe wholly new phenomena or to communicate the complex ideas that are part of our increasingly complex world.

In addition to channeling their children's curiosity, parents can help their children see that knowledge can be useful and rewarding. Children are more likely to adopt this attitude if they perceive that it has been adopted by their parents. If a parent's view toward learning a fine point of language or mathematics is that such knowledge is "impractical and a total waste of time," then the child is likely to excuse anything he does not know as being unnecessary for real life. But parents who introduce a new concept—even a new vocabulary word—to their children by conveying the idea "I used something new today that might prove useful to you" also convey clearly that learning is a continuing process that is continually rewarding.

By pointing out a particular use that was found for a new kernel of knowledge, the parent instills the idea that learning can be applied. The child, however, has a much more limited opportunity to apply the knowledge he happens to acquire—especially any newly acquired knowledge about language.

The world in which the child moves does not make many demands upon, or offer many rewards to, those of polished skills in language. *Therefore, it is essential that parents make those demands and offer those rewards.* If a child is to realize the thrill of applying a new skill in language, the proving ground must be in the home. It is the duty and the responsibility of parents, then, to challenge their children in language and to recognize and appreciate their every attempt toward meeting that challenge. Children simply must have the benefit of knowing that they can try out a new word or audition a complex sentence at home without being criticized for "showing off" or "being the family dictionary." Even if the usage is inaccurate or inappropriate, the home is still the appropriate place for the attempt. What is the purpose of a proving ground, anyway?

The learning atmosphere that parents create in their home does not have to be filled with "great literature" and "wise conversation." In fact, one of the most important ideas that parents can instill in their children is that all listening and all reading can be sources for learning about language. Radio and television, for example, can have a great educational value if a child begins listening for *how* things are said as well as for *what* things are said. News programs and interview shows can be a rich source for vocabulary, and even the standard situation comedy occasionally demonstrates a witty turn of phrase. Most children (and most adults as well) consider radio and television to be passive media. They want only to be entertained and bombarded by words and pictures without having to give anything of themselves. But we could all become active participants in this entertainment without diminishing our pleasure a bit.

One way of making television a more positive contributor to education is to keep a dictionary near the set at all times. The dictionary should not be one of those ponderous, bigger-than-a-breadbox, unabridged versions, although such dictionaries are quite valuable for other uses. Huge dictionaries are just not "friendly" books. People tend to fear them and to avoid the difficulty of locating a specific word or a specific meaning from among the millions that are, for the moment, useless. The type of dictionary that should be handy during viewing times is a type that is, itself, handy to use. Both parents and children should be able to hear an unusual word, locate it in the dictionary, and understand its meaning before they forget the exact way in which they heard it used. A pocket dictionary will serve this purpose, but the larger collegiate style is almost as easy to use and contains a more complete set of words and definitions. Some dictionaries of this type even include usage notes and remarks about the precise difference between words that appear to have the same meaning.

Merely having this dictionary close at hand, however, is no guarantee that your children will use it. You must create the learning atmosphere yourself by reaching for the dictionary whenever an unfamiliar word or phrase comes over the air. Don't wait until the next commercial, and don't fool yourself into believing that you will be able to recall the word and its use later when it is more convenient for you to examine them. You probably won't even remember that you had something to remember, much less the specific word or how you heard it used. But by

going to the dictionary immediately, you not only help your memory, you help convey to others the idea that a curiosity and thirst for knowledge are too important to be governed by mere convenience. Placing a dictionary near the television, using that dictionary yourself, and even keeping a written list of words you learned from television are practical, effective steps that you can take right now, and are steps that will have a practical effect on both you and your children.

Newspapers and magazines can be read not only for entertainment and information, but for knowledge about how words are spelled (and misspelled) and how sentences are punctuated. New words can be easily learned from these sources because each unfamiliar word is used in context, and so the reader already has a clue about its meaning.

Just as all reading and listening should be viewed as sources for learning about language, so all speaking and all writing can serve as applications of that learning. Parents who can get their children to see that the purpose of "good English" is not just to please a teacher will begin to see their children taking advantage of conversations with friends, visits by relatives, and "thank-you" notes to demonstrate their speaking and writing skills. Once a child realizes that his use of language is always on parade, he will begin to care about how his language makes him appear to other people. Once he understands that in order to become comfortable with a new word or a new usage he must get through that first uncomfortable use of it in public, he will look upon every conversation as an opportunity to somehow weave in that word or usage any way he can.

When a child considers all listening and all

reading to be sources for learning about language, his curiosity gradually grows into vigilance. This vigilance—this alertness and watchfulness for errors and beauties in everything that is said and written—can stay with the child for life. Teaching a child to be vigilant about language, and encouraging a child to practice that vigilance, go hand in hand. When you, the parent, make an error in usage during a conversation, and when your child spots the error and brings it your attention, your dedication to home education will be severely tested. It is very difficult, indeed, to accept correction or criticism from a child. But you must allow yourself to be criticized. You must summon up the inner strength necessary to view that criticism as a learning experience for your child. This is a very difficult thing to do; I am well aware of that. But it will be only a temporary difficulty if you will just use it to help your child even further.

Ask your child how he feels when his own mistakes are pointed out in school. Ask your child what he thinks about his classmate (there is one of this type in every class) who is always correcting everyone else. "But you told me to always watch for mistakes in language, didn't you?" is the common reply. "Yes, but being watchful does not mean being critical" would be a proper answer. You are now applying some fine tuning to the education of your child. You are not teaching about substance, but about feeling. This will take time, but gradually your child will understand that he can be watchful without letting his subjects know that they are being watched. He can learn from the language of others without being personally responsible for the correctness of their speech.

Once the child understands that others will

not view his criticism lightly, you can begin again to encourage vigilance and to encourage error identification *in the home*. Children will understand that their parents are encouraging this practice as a means of helping the children learn. When a parent points out a language error made by a child, or when a child points out a language error made by a parent, it no longer has the negative effect of stern criticism. Rather, it has the positive benefit of instruction and reinforcement.

You should always remember, however, that children learn more from their successes than they do from their failures. It is important to point out a child's language errors because you want the child to be aware of those errors. But it is far more important, and far more effective, to point out a child's successes with language. If a child uses a difficult word such as *lie* or *whom* correctly in a sentence, let him know that you noticed his accomplishment. Don't be hesitant at all about offering praises like "I am proud of you for telling that whole story without saying 'you know' once." Such praises are deserved and go a long way toward ensuring that the successes will continue.

When the feeling of mutual respect and concern becomes firmly established, dinner table conversations and all the other family speaking situations can be both amusing and challenging. Everyone is aware that his sentences are expected to be complete and error free. The degree of inspection grows as everyone's knowledge of language grows. This tends to tie the family more tightly together, for it is only within the home that these inspections and challenges have the benefit of mutual understanding and an established set of ground rules.

Remember, though, that these ground-rules, too, have their place and time. There will always be occasions when *what* a person says is far more important than *how* it is said. The serious heart-to-heart talks between a parent and a child are surely not the times for language study. Vigilance must simply take a back seat to the far more weighty concerns that affect the parent, the child, and the family. Knowing the difference between when scrutiny of your child's language will have a beneficial effect and when it will prove disruptive is not a matter that can be taught; it can only be learned. Children gradually come to know when their own critical observations will be tolerated and encouraged, and when they are out of place. Parents are more quick to learn precisely where this fine line is, but even knowing their children as well as they do, their timing is not always perfect.

A few final observations about home education in general, and then we'll move along to *what* you can teach your children and *how* to go about teaching it.

As anyone who has ever been a teacher can attest, the very best way to fix an idea in your own mind is to teach that idea to someone else. This truism applies not just to classroom teachers and to academic subjects, but to business people and to everyday life-skills as well. In order to teach your trade or a specific facet of your business to a new employee, you have to prepare yourself to answer the many questions that will arise—questions that you no longer ask yourself because you are so familiar with the subject. But by anticipating the problems that a new worker will face and the questions he is likely to ask, you are forced to re-examine the entire operation, and you cement all of its workings in your mind.

When you teach someone else how to prepare a favorite recipe, you prepare yourself as well as the dish at hand. Your answers to "Why?" and "Why not?" may demonstrate that you don't know certain things as well as you thought you did. You will find them out, however, before you teach this recipe again.

So it is with teaching language and usage to your children. The concepts become fixed much more securely in your own mind after you have been through the trial of teaching these concepts to others. Keep in mind that this reinforcement through teaching works as well for your children as it does for you. The very best way to instill a principle of language in your children is to have your children teach that principle themselves. This can be accomplished in two ways. After one parent has presented a lesson to a child, the child can teach what he has learned to the other parent. The parent who acts as the student in this case, can heighten the reinforcement by making a few calculated errors and by asking for frequent explanations. The child will gain even more experience and reinforcement by writing out a short test for the parent to take. The other way to apply this method is to have the child who has just learned a principle teach that principle to a brother or sister. This technique is especially effective when the two children later act together as a team in a language game that covers the principle in question. Having one child teach another, of course, is not possible in all families, but where it is possible, it should be tried at every opportunity.

One of the most common difficulties that parents have when they embark on a program of home education is a general inability to cope with their children's failures. When a child's speaking or writing contains the errors that his parents have spent considerable time teaching him to avoid, the parents view this failure as their own. They believe that their teaching is at fault, and they abandon the program in a belief that this will avoid any further harm they might do.

The simple fact is that children will fail in their use of language in spite of their parents' best efforts. What is more important to realize, however, is that children will fail *because* of their parents' best efforts. This may sound strange, but it is only the very best teaching that will produce failure. A child's misuse of a speaking or writing principle indicates that he is trying something new. If an absence of error is the only goal for a child, he will revert to the simplest and safest forms of expression he can find. He will not make any noticeable errors, but he will not have challenged himself or grown in any way, either. Failure itself must be viewed in a positive way—as an indication of both self-imposed challenge and of growth. We all have known people whose vocabulary is forever stilted because they fear either misspelling or mispronouncing the words they would like to use. Children must be appreciated for the attempts they make at expanding their use of language. Their little failures can, and will, be corrected in time, but the stifling of a child's growth in language by not allowing him these failures will endure forever.

No matter what decision you make about teaching standard English to your children, keep in mind that using standard English in the home is the greatest language benefit that your children can possibly have. Numerous studies have shown that children who come from homes in which usage standards are

important and observed have a decided advantage in school—not only in their language classes, but in all phases of their education. These children are not necessarily more intelligent or more "gifted" than other students. But, almost by osmosis, they have acquired the gift of being able to use the forms most often employed in clear, effective communication. They bring this talent *to* their education because they have already absorbed the standards in their homes. These standards, in fact, become so much a part of what the child hears that they do not interfere with the child's speaking and writing.

One final word about home education, and this is, perhaps the most important idea of all: *Good teaching, like good parenting, takes time and practice.* Human beings are the only species on earth that needs to be taught how to raise its children. This can be argued, of course, but a case can be made for the idea that we simply perform this task more poorly than any other creature. But we have our successes, and we do improve with experience. We look back on the mistakes that we made with our first child, vow that we won't make those mistakes with our next, and discover that, indeed, we haven't: We have made an entirely new set of mistakes, instead.

We learn from all of these mistakes, and it can be fairly said that our children are the beneficiaries as well as the causes of our many trials. Just as you cannot expect to be a master parent right from the beginning, neither can you expect to be a master teacher. Just as your skill at parenting is honed to a finer edge with each year of being a parent, so will your teaching improve with each attempt at being a teacher.

The "perfect parent" and the "perfect

teacher" are romantic goals at best. However, being a *better* parent and being a *better* teacher tomorrow than you are today are goals that can be reached and are, as Little Orphan Annie sings, "only a day away."

3. WHAT IS GRAMMAR?

One reason that young children ask "Why?" about practically everything is that they know the question is impossible for parents to ignore: It will always generate a response. But as children grow older, their questions demand not just a response, but an understandable explanation as well. Even their *why?*'s grow more difficult and complex, and responses such as "Because that is just the way things are done!" or "Because I said so!" just don't satisfy their desire to know.

All of us feel more comfortable when we know the *why?* of things. Granted, there are certain notions that we accept on faith alone, but we search for reasons whenever we can. For anyone who wishes to teach a concept, knowing the reasons behind it is an absolute necessity. Not only does this knowledge allow the teacher to give understandable answers in response to questions, but it also allows the teacher to understand and reveal how this one concept fits into the whole of the subject. If a plumber who teaches an apprentice how to connect a certain valve doesn't also convey the theory behind *why* the procedure is performed as it is, the apprentice will not be able to transfer his knowledge to any other situation: He will know only how to connect that particular valve under those particular conditions.

Coming to grips with the *why?*'s that abound in the study of grammar and usage allows you to construct a set of personal standards for your own speaking and writing —standards that are logical, practical, and acceptable to you. Usages that are new to you can then be tested against these standards to see which you reject and which you accept for your own use. The result is not just a greater understanding of the structure of English, but a greater confidence in your own use of English as well.

If you choose to help your children with their language study, adopting a position on usage that is acceptable to you will prove to be invaluable, for it can carry you through many difficult situations. You will not only be able to make well-founded judgments in response to wholly unexpected questions, but you will also be able to offer reasoned explanations and acceptable answers to all those *why?*'s that are certain to arise.

You may have your own beliefs and explanations about why certain uses of language are "right" or "wrong," even about why you and your children should study language at all. But if you do not, or if your own explanations are not firmly fixed in your own mind, or if those explanations are not quite acceptable or defensible, I will offer you a few of my own. A good place to begin, I think, is with a

15

brief discussion of what "grammar" is and, more importantly, what it is not.

Most people have a general idea about what they mean when they say "grammar" or when they accuse someone of using "bad grammar." Few people, however, could offer a concise explanation of precisely what they mean, and fewer still are aware that "grammar" itself is only casually related to the idea they have in mind.

It is not necessary, here, for me to delve into a long explanation of the various branches of language study. But I do think it is worth noting that, many years ago, the word *grammar* generally referred to everything connected with the science of language. More recently, however, language study has become increasingly specialized and has many separate branches such as semantics, etymology, and rhetoric. The term *grammar,* itself, now has a much narrower meaning than it had before, and today refers only to the changes in the forms of words and to the arrangement of words in a sentence. For example, the grammar of English tells us that most speakers and writers convey the idea "more than one book" by adding an *s* to the end of the word *book:* books. English grammar does not say that we should do this, only that this is how the meaning is generally communicated in the language. Similarly, it is because of the grammar of English that we understand who gave what to whom in the sentence *Bill gave Jim a watch.* If we switch the positions of *Bill, Jim,* and *watch,* the sentence can have a different meaning or no meaning at all (*Watch gave Bill a Jim)*[1] The grammar of English tells us that the meaning of a sentence depends upon the order of the words in that sentence. The grammars of other languages describe different word orders; the grammars of some languages tell us that word order is of little or no importance at all.

The most important thing to realize and remember about the meaning of *grammar* is that a grammar is not a set of rules that a society has invested to govern its language. Rather, a grammar is a set of observations that have been discovered about a language. If you choose to think of these observations as rules, try to remember that these rules are made "after the fact." They would be similar to the rules of football if those rules had been developed by allowing groups of players to do whatever they wanted with a pig bladder, and then groups of researchers wrote down only those things that the vast majority of players actually did.

So, if using the word *ain't,* for example, is not a case of bad "grammar," what is it? It must, after all, be a case of bad something! The question of *ain't* (and practically every other construction we have been told to avoid) is a question of *usage.* This distinction between "grammar" and "usage" is not just another case of educators' developing a new "buzz word" to use in place of a well-known word that means exactly the same thing. The terms "grammar" and "usage" will be very useful to us in discussing language, but only if their meanings are not blurred. If you will allow "grammar" its most narrow definition, (the form and arrangement of words) and

---

1. An asterisk (*) is used throughout this book to identify words, phrases, and sentences that do not conform to the principles of standard usage.

apply "usage" to all questions of correctness and appropriateness, you will see that although the grammar of our language does affect our usage, the constant changes in the way our language is used rarely have an effect on our grammar.

Most of us grew up believing that there was a "right" and a "wrong" to everything that involved language. Words could be misspelled, mispronounced, and certain words were "wrong" no matter how you wrote or said them. When our vocabularies increased and we discovered some words that could be spelled or pronounced in two different ways, we were told that only one of the forms was "preferred." The obvious questions of "Preferred by whom?" and "Why is the other one in the dictionary?" received the same vague explanations as did our inquiries about the language "errors" committed by the great authors in our textbooks. Besides, what possible difference could it make whether you used *who* or *whom* when they mean exactly the same thing?

The whole idea of applying "right," "wrong," "correct," and "incorrect" to uses of language is just as difficult to justify to students today. It seems to have so many holes and contradictions in it that it is neither defensible nor practical. So, in a classic example of "throwing out the baby with the bath water," most students reject the entire idea and replace it with one that requires much less skill and effort in plugging up the holes. The replacement generally takes the following form: "What does it matter how I say or write something as long as I get the meaning across? After all, the purpose of language is to communicate."

This notion does seem to have the appear-ance of good sense to it. It is somewhat similar to the explanation offered by many high school history and science teachers for only grading student research papers according to their "content." "After all," the teachers explain, "*what* you say is much more important than *how* you say it." And it is difficult to argue, for instance, that anyone in the country would fail to understand who is being referred to when a person says "between you and *I*" instead of "between you and *me*." No, based on their "content" alone, that is, based on the meaning of the words they contain, the two phrases are identical. The problem is not with the meaning of the words, but with the other meanings that the phrases convey— meanings that the user may not have intended or even known were possible.

To say that the purpose of language is to communicate is like saying that the purpose of the wind is to blow. Language always communicates. Even grunts and groans transmit an idea from the sender to the receiver. The one fact that is absolutely vital to realize, however, is that language communicates or transmits information about the speaker or writer at the same time it transmits the meaning of the words he (or she) uses. That is, while you are trying to convey your intended meaning to the person you are speaking or writing to, you are also conveying information about who you are—your beliefs, background, education, etc. Your use of language can communicate these hidden ideas just as crisply and forcefully as it can your more obviously intended meaning.

For example, when a person fills out a job application and misspells several rather common words, the meaning of those words may be quite clear to whoever reads the application. But the reader will, very likely, also judge the applicant as being unfit for a position that requires written communication. No business that cares about its image can allow its correspondence to convey an impression of carelessness to others. Similarly, an applicant who speaks only in an urban black dialect during an interview conveys to the interviewer that he may have difficulty communicating orally with people who speak "standard" English, and that, therefore, he may not be able to effectively represent his employer in those situations.

Now, do these "hidden messages" tell interviewers, or anyone else, that the applicant is unemployable, or do they make the applicant a lesser human being in any way? Absolutely not. But the more important question here is whether the applicant *wanted* to convey the messages he did. Almost certainly, he did not, but he was powerless to do anything else.

If you think that it is unfair to judge a person by the way he speaks or writes, let me say that the manner in which a person expresses himself allows others to make observations, not judgments. Granted, some people actually do condemn or respect others solely on the basis of the form of their communication. But that is a flaw and a weakness within those who adopt this practice, not in the use of language as a basis for making observations. Besides, basing observations about people on their use of language is not different from basing observations on their dress or their table manners. All of us have made these observations and will continue to do so. Everything we do—including everything we say or write—says something about us, and because we have the ability to control

what we say about ourselves, it is unquestionably in our own best interest to do so. Once we become conscious of all the ideas we are communicating—those that pertain to our intended meaning and also those that characterize ourselves—we will begin to choose those usages that convey only the ideas we intend.

Now, in order for these ideas to be communicated, the person to whom you are speaking or writing must be able to recognize the differences between various usages. When you are conversing with a very close friend, you may be able to know with some surety that your friend won't recognize any difference between the phrases "neither of the boys *was* in school" and "neither of the boys *were* in school." It is much more difficult, however, to know whether a person who is able to recognize these differences will care about them. Friends are likely to tell you that the usage errors they detect in your speech or writing don't matter to them at all. But just because the errors were detected is an indication that they do, indeed, matter. Besides, how many people with whom you communicate do you actually know well enough to be able to say whether or not they can recognize errors or will care about them? Your husband or wife, your children, your parents, a very close friend or two, and that's about all. You simply don't know enough about all the rest of the people in the world to make a valid judgment. Therefore, whenever anyone other than your few close friends and relatives hears you speak or reads what you have written (even if you are not speaking or writing to that particular person), the way that you use language will very possibly be saying things about you that you do not intend and that you would just as soon other people did not know.

You may think that I am promoting the employment of one set of usages for communicating with people you know, and still another set for communicating with strangers. In fact, I am, but this should not seem so unusual, for you already use this system anyway. The vocabulary and sentence structure you use when speaking informally to your closest friends is different from the way you speak when addressing a group, a prospective employer, or your child's teacher. You know that certain expressions are appropriate for casual conversation and decidedly inappropriate for more formal discussions. If you stop to think about why you make these decisions, you will discover that the reason is to aid you in communicating. A distinctly inappropriate usage—*either one that is too informal or one that is too formal*—can divert your listeners' attention away from the idea you are trying to convey. If they are shocked or threatened—either consciously or subconsciously—by the way in which you express an idea, they are far less likely to understand or agree with the idea you are expressing.

Which usages are "appropriate," then, depend entirely upon your audience. It is quite common, in fact, to hear teachers and linguists talk about "levels of usage"—that is, usages that have been separated into groups and are appropriate for different audiences. These levels of usage apply almost entirely to spoken English only, and they take into account the many spoken dialects that exist in the language. A dialect is a variation of a language that is shared by a group of people.

Dialects differ in their vocabularies, pronunciations, and phrases; different dialects are employed by different regional groups, economic groups, professions, races, and other groups as well. No dialect can be called the "right" one, and no dialect is any "better" than any other. One dialect may very well be better suited to a *certain situation* because it is appropriate *in that situation,* but it will never be appropriate *in all situations.* For example, the dialect (or level of usage) a person employs when speaking to his minister or to his company's president is simply inappropriate for conversing with his basketball teammates in the locker room. It is inappropriate because it stands out, and it gets in the way of communication. The converse would be equally true, and for precisely the same reason.

Although there are many spoken dialects of English, there is only one dialect for writing. No matter how differently two people may speak the language, the way they write what they want others to read will be almost identical. I am not referring to their handwriting, of course, but to the forms they use when their writing has a general audience: business letters, school projects, letters to the editor of a newspaper, etc. (Authors who write dialogue occasionally try to convey how a dialect sounds when spoken, but the writing I am concerned with now is the general writing we do to express ourselves.) Why, if you overlook certain minor variations in spelling and vocabulary, you cannot tell whether the writer of a book spent his entire life in London or Atlanta. But have the author read aloud a mere sentence or two and all doubt will quickly vanish.

This universal form for writing the English language is called Standard Written English. It has rules and conventions that are rather concrete and are accepted by those who write as well as by those who read. These conventions include spelling, punctuation, capitalization, sentence structure, and precise meanings of words and phrases. If a person wants to communicate in writing and doesn't want his ideas to be obscured by the unusual form of his writing, he will write in Standard Written English.

Because there is a standard form for writing, there can be very little argument about the need to learn this form. Questions about appropriate levels of usage do not, for the most part, pertain to writing. There is not a standard of spelling that should be employed in the locker room and another in the board room. You simply cannot select and control the audience for your writing because, unlike speech, a piece of writing can endure long after the person for whom it was intended has finished reading it. The people who read your writing expect to read Standard Written English, and any deviation from that form signifies that you do not have the knowledge or the ability to understand or employ it. You don't have the luxury, as you do in speaking, of being able to choose the form that would be appropriate. On the other hand, your task should be simpler just because there is only one appropriate form.

Earlier I said that no spoken dialect is "correct" or "better" than any other all the time. There is, however, one spoken dialect that is more frequently used than any other. The reason that this dialect, called Standard Spoken English, is used so often is that it is considered appropriate for occasions when the speaker does not or cannot know what other dialect would be better. When speaking before an audience that is composed of people from diverse groups, a speaker will use Standard Spoken English. Newscasters and announcers on nationally televised programs realize that their words will be heard in many different regions and by many different groups, and so they use Standard Spoken English in order to communicate with all. Many regional radio personalities, on the other hand, can speak in the dialect most common within that region because they know that this dialect is preferred by the vast majority of their listeners.

No matter what dialect we prefer to use or to hear, we all understand Standard Spoken English. In fact, when we hear Standard Spoken English, it does not sound like a dialect. We can't place the speaker as being from any region or belonging to any specific group. The purpose of this dialect, then, just like the purpose of any other dialect, is served because it does not stand in the way of communication. It allows the speaker to convey an idea without causing any listener to be concerned about, or even aware of, the way the idea is being said.

Standard Spoken English is also used in situations that have much smaller audiences. Even when the audience is just one person, if you do not know that person well enough to communicate in any other dialect, then Standard Spoken English is the one to use. A single conversation with a stranger may very well begin in the standard dialect, and may change when the parties realize that each is more comfortable speaking and hearing another form. Some rather small conversations are almost always in Standard Spoken English:

job interviews, discussions with a teacher, polite discourse at somewhat formal business or social gatherings, etc. But the larger your audience, the more likely it is that your choice of the standard dialect will be the right one. Standard Spoken English is the "common currency" of spoken communication in the United States. You may (and should) deviate from it when the occasion demands, but you simply cannot expect to ignore the dialect entirely and not suffer for your ignorance.

So, the English language has a standard form for all written communication and a standard form for most spoken communication. Usages that deviate from these standard forms are called "nonstandard." Nonstandard usages are not necessarily "wrong"; they are simply "not standard" or "not customary in the standard forms of written or spoken English." Some of these usages may, in fact, be very "right"—that is, very appropriate for use in a particular situation even though they are considered nonstandard. But we must recognize that nonstandard usages are only appropriate when they are intended. As speakers, we may choose to use nonstandard forms in certain situations because we believe these usages are better able to convey our ideas than the standard ones would be. We must, however, avoid the trap of using nonstandard forms without realizing that they are nonstandard.

If our general goal is to be able to communicate our ideas efficiently and effectively in all situations, then we should begin by learning our language's standard forms because they are appropriate in more situations than are any other forms. The rules and conventions for Standard Spoken English are somewhat less rigid than those that govern Standard Written English, and so understanding the standard written form would seem to be adequate preparation for understanding and using the standard spoken dialect. In fact, for most of the history of public education in America, teachers have believed that having students practice the standard written form would ensure their adopting the standard spoken form for their speech. I think that this whole method should be turned around in order to take advantage of what we all know or feel is involved in the process of writing. When we are faced with the task of setting something down in writing, all of us, initially, try to "write what we want to say." That is, we try to record in writing the way we would express an idea in our most polite, most considered speech. Therefore, it would seem that if we understood how to speak in Standard Spoken English—if this dialect became second nature to us—we would have a much easier time writing our ideas in Standard Written English.

This is the reason that it is so important for parents to understand the standard dialect and use it for conversations in the home. Children who hear this dialect constantly, consider it a natural form of expression and are much more likely to try to represent this form in writing. Because there are so many more occasions for speaking than there are for writing, the opportunities for constant reinforcement and application of Standard Spoken English are far greater than the opportunities for cementing the rules for writing. A good case can be made for teaching these forms as though they were separate languages, but if one form can be learned by practicing the other, then I think that practicing the spoken form is the better of the two alternatives. It is also the method by which parents can have the most noticeable impact on their children.

Being knowledgeable about both standard forms allows us to decide when and where we will deviate from these forms. We know that we can, and should, deviate from the standard spoken dialect when doing so enhances our chances of being understood. We also know that any deviation from the standard form in writing will almost certainly decrease those chances and will convey a less-than-favorable impression to our readers.

One very common form that is quite different from the standard dialect is Urban Black English, which is commonly referred to simply as "black English." This dialect is not a different language but, rather, a different form of the English language; it is a dialect just as Standard Spoken English is a dialect. It differs from the standard dialect in its vocabulary, pronunciation, and sentence structure, and it is generally used by blacks who live in urban areas or who learned the dialect there.

Although black English is spoken by a large number of people and has a rather consistent grammar all its own, it is just one of many dialects used in the United States. Like other dialects, black English works very well *in certain situations.* In some situations it is the only dialect that will allow the speaker to be accepted by the listener, and, therefore, the best dialect for effective and efficient communication. But also like other dialects, black English can hinder communication when the listener isn't as comfortable with the dialect as the speaker is. Black English is not the "common currency" for spoken communication in the United States, and so it is not

appropriate unless you know that it is the preferred dialect of everyone in your audience. It is not appropriate for speaking to large, diverse groups or for use in job interviews and general business situations. In these instances, Standard Spoken English is expected by the listener, and the use of black English brands the speaker as never having been taught or not being able to understand the standard dialect of English.

People who can speak only the Urban Black dialect simply cannot communicate their beliefs, goals, dreams, and other ideas to the general public of the United States. Instead of having listeners concentrate on *what* is being said, the dialect causes listeners to be more aware of *how* it is being said. Whenever this happens—whether the speaker is using Urban Black or any other dialect—when the form impedes rather than enhances communication, the form is inappropriate for that situation.

It is not surprising, then, that people who speak black English use Standard Written English for their writing. Like any other dialect, the Urban Black dialect is difficult to render in a written form. There is no standard for spelling many of the words and phrases used in this dialect, and some of the sentence structures would be quite impossible to punctuate. This fact brings up again the need to be able to communicate in Standard Written English. For all the many dialects that exist in spoken English, there is only one form—one set of universally understood and accepted rules—for writing, and that is Standard Written English. If any person wants to express his ideas in writing and wants other prople to be affected, persuaded, or entertained by what he has written, he must be able to com-

22

municate in Standard Written English. By failing to understand and use this form, a person condemns himself to a life of impotency—to never being able to tell anyone exactly what he thinks or feels in writing, to always being insecure and afraid of each attempt, to forever justifying his inability by telling others, and himself, that the skill is unnecessary and overly praised.

Many of the nonstandard forms that are most common in both speaking and in writing are not part of any particular dialect, but, instead, have their foundation in a very casual approach to language. These usages do not come from conscious decisions that involve conveying what the user actually means, but from a lackadaisical, careless disregard for effective communication. Some nonstandard forms are simply illogical, such as the use of the word *irregardless*. While the prefix *ir-* does mean "not" when added to words like *regular* or *responsible* (*ir*regular, *ir*responsible), it is illogical to add it to a word like *regardless* because this word already suggests "not" and already conveys exactly what the user of the nonstandard form wants to say. A speaker or writer who uses *irregardless* tells others that he has not thought about what he is saying, and he brands himself as careless or even sloppy. Misspellings create a similar impression because they tell the reader that the writer has very little concern for accuracy. A careless or sloppy attitude toward logic and accuracy in the way one expresses his ideas is frequently taken as an indication that the ideas themselves may have been founded on similarly shaky ground.

Carelessness in the way we speak and write is an all-too-easy habit to form. It is so much easier simply not to think or care about exactly what we are saying, and to associate with others who feel the same way. We select as friends the people with whom we feel most comfortable, and if we have the skill to communicate on only one, very casual, level, then our circle of friends is likely to be quite small and extremely uniform in its attitudes and beliefs.

Language habits and customs are not really very different from the other habits and customs we have all grown to accept. There is a definite similarity, for instance, between the purpose of language standards and the purpose of table manners. Why, for example, do we use a soupspoon instead of drinking directly out of the soup bowl? Why do we use utensils at all when our hands can accomplish the tasks so well? Why do we change the fork from our left hand to our right before placing a freshly cut morsel in our mouth? (I have never been able to figure out the sense of this one, and I hope that, like certain useless customs of language, it, too, will pass away.) Table manners are, in fact, just another set of customs or conventions. Like the customs and conventions that apply to language use, table manners developed over a long period of time, change slightly with each generation, and become more or less rigid depending upon the situation. The manners we demand of ourselves and our children are much more relaxed for a family meal at home than they are for a meal at a restaurant, or at a neighbor's, or when we entertain guests. Certain customs for eating can be appropriate in one setting and definitely inappropriate in another. Casual eating habits can become so thoughtlessly comfortable that we are unable to adopt more appropriate standards in more formal situations.

This analogy is rather good, and I think you can use it quite profitably in reasoning out the *why?*'s of language with your children. However, my favorite analogy for showing the similarities between language use and other accepted traditions has to do with the customs that surround clothes and appropriate dress. This analogy may be used in conjunction with the previous one as further evidence that language does not run counter to the rest of your child's experience. (You will discover that, as a general principle of teaching, having multiple examples for explaining and demonstrating the same point is a practice that not only increases the chances for reinforcement, but also decreases the chances of being stumped by a wholly unexpected question.)

Your children are probably not only aware that there are different standards of dress for different situations, but have also probably asked why this should be so. In response, you have probably told them that certain clothes have become customary at certain functions, and that it is wrong to judge people by the clothes they wear. But children should also be told that a person's clothes do make a statement about that person, a statement that identifies and characterizes that person until more useful and factual information can be obtained. The people who know you very well—and they are few—do not change their opinion of you when they see you in formal or casual attire. They know the "real" you, and your manner of dress at any particular time will not alter this impression. But the many people who don't know you, or who don't know you intimately, are eager for any information you might give them about who you are and what you believe. The way you choose to dress (just like the way you choose to eat) tells these people about you and about your attitudes. You may be able to change this impression later, but the impression has been made just the same, and it would certainly be to your benefit to have that impression be the one you wanted to convey.

We alter our manner of dress because different standards are expected at different occasions. That is, a certain style is appropriate in one situation and quite inappropriate in another. Wearing a tuxedo to a backyard barbeque is just as "wrong" as wearing bluejeans to a formal dinner party. Both cover the body and provide the necessary warmth, but each makes a statement about the wearer when it is worn in an inappropriate situation. Reverse the scenes, however, and notice that the statement made by appropriate attire causes others to concentrate on the person—not on what he is wearing.

We have always been told that "proper" attire is that which does not stand out from the crowd—either because it is too formal or too casual. We also know, however, that when we are in doubt about what is appropriate for an occasion, we should always dress a little "better" than we think will be necessary. This bit of wisdom can save us in two ways. First, we can quite easily make our attire seem less formal when we discover that others are more casually attired. Making casual clothes appear more formal, on the other hand, is quite difficult and, many times, impossible. Second, if we can't alter our dress to blend in with the surroundings, we know that we will feel much less ashamed of our error in judgment if we are a bit too well dressed than if we had been dressed not well enough.

Everything that I have said about apparel

24

applies to language, too. Your language does make a statement about you to strangers, and it can create a positive or a negative impression. Certain usages and dialects are appropriate or inappropriate depending upon the situation, and no set of usages is appropriate all the time. The language standards that are "proper" for the occasion are those that do not make the user stand out from those with whom he is communicating. There is wisdom, too, in adopting a little more formal level of usage than you think will be required in a given situation. Not only can your speech easily become more casual if you find that to be appropriate, but it is embarrassingly difficult (and sometimes impossible) to recover from the impressions you make by initially adopting a too-casual, too-familiar level of speech.

I have said that many nonstandard usages are simply careless, unthinking, rather sloppy forms that would be changed if the user had much regard for the logic or precision of what he was saying. All of us, however, had to be taught that regard; at some point we had to be instilled with the notion that accuracy and precision actually did make a difference and were worth working to obtain. How true this is of our attire as well. We don't have to teach our children how to dress in a slovenly manner. In some almost-mystical way they are born with a highly developed knowledge about casual attire and with a pronounced desire to be constantly disheveled. Our duty is to see that they learn how to dress according to other standards; how to avoid making negative impressions in situations they have not as yet experienced, but situations we know they will experience just the same.

Many children cannot imagine a situation that will demand a well-written letter or require anything more than casual speech. Parents know that this perception will change in time, but they worry that there won't be time enough for their children's language habits to change with it.

Let me add one final similarity between language and clothes. Understanding and mastering the standard forms of spoken and written English requires both time and effort. But once you reach the point where standard usage is second nature to you, where you use nonstandard forms only by design, you will discover that language can be comfortable to use. Just as a perfectly tailored suit of clothes "feels right" and allows so much freedom of movement that the wearer almost forgets that he is attired at all, so it is with language. When you are able to freely correspond and converse in the most diverse situations by perfectly tailoring your use of language to each occasion, your language will not bind or restrict you in any way. It will allow you to convey your ideas smoothly, gracefully, and unimpeded. Your language will not stand out, it will not be obvious to you or to anyone else, but it will speak for you and present you in the way you want to be seen.

You may very well accept the idea that there is a standard form for writing, a standard form for speaking, and that any deviation from these forms is nonstandard. But you may, quite properly, wonder what happened to the notions of "right," "wrong," "correct," and "incorrect" that were so much a part of your previous language study. Is there no "right" and "wrong" after all?

As I said earlier, I prefer to think of a usage as being appropriate or inappropriate for a particular occasion. The labels "right" and "wrong" seem to imply that there is a fixed and rigid standard that should be adhered to on all occasions. Unfortunately, perhaps, language does not have the natural precision of mathematics, and so it is difficult to locate usages that even a majority of language scholars would agree are "errors" and would brand as "wrong" or "improper" for all occasions. Although the phrase "*between you and I" violates a standard and enduring rule of grammar, it is frequently used by speakers of English, and it conveys a consistently clear meaning that an incorrect mathematical phrase like 2 + 5 = 9 simply cannot. Many language usages that were branded as errors in the past have come to be accepted and now are even taught as standards simply because they are *used* so frequently by so many people. To continue the comparison with mathematics, all of us realize that no matter how long we persist in making errors in simple arithmetic when we balance our checkbooks, these errors will never be accepted as "correct" by our bank or by anyone else.

Within the study of written and spoken English, there is, however, one area that has more precision—that is, more universally accepted rules and standards—than any other. This is the area commonly called "mechanics": spelling, punctuation, and capitalization. It is true that certain words may be spelled in two (or more) ways, and either variation is considered "acceptable." Still, most people would agree that labels like "correct" and "incorrect" can and should be applied to spelling, punctuation, and capitalization. It is in these areas that established standards have a clear and accepted dominance over "general use."

The area that includes word definitions and pronunciations has a good deal less precision to it and is less likely to withstand judgments such as "right" and "wrong." Not only can words have different meanings and pronunciations in different regions, but many of these variations are not listed in any dictionary. The phrase "to champ at the bit" is pronounced (and even spelled) "*to *chomp at the bit*" by the majority of people in several regions of the United States, in spite of the fact that it is hard to find a dictionary that even acknowledges the existence of the word *chomp.*

The area of English that has the least precision of all is the general area of usage. Although there are rules that govern the case, tense, and position of words in a sentence, these rules do not have the "force of law" that a dictionary gives to the spelling of words. If a certain usage violates a rule but is common to a certain group or region, it makes more sense to label that usage "nonstandard" and judge it by its appropriateness in specific situations. By now, if my describing a certain usage as "nonstandard" still means to you that the usage is "wrong," then either I have been less than persuasive or we are using different words to convey exactly the same idea.

Usage rules are by no means fixed: They are undergoing subtle changes all the time. Trying to keep them rigid and pure is like trying to carry a cat home by the tail: Not only is it practically impossible to do, but it isn't a particularly good idea, anyway. Still, there are certain usage rules that I think should be observed and retained in spite of the fact that they seem to be vanishing rather quickly. There are other rules that are simply not worth preserving, and to these I gladly bid a fond farewell.

Earlier I said that some usages—the word *irregardless,* for example—are nonstandard because they are illogical. The usage rules that keep us from employing illogical words and phrases, then, are the most worthy of preservation. Many double negatives, improper comparisons, and misplaced participles are illogical constructions, and I will not argue with anyone who wishes to brand these usages as "errors" because they are, indeed, errors in logic.

Another set of usages that I think are well worth observing and preserving includes those that contribute to differences in meaning. The distinction between *that* and *which*, for example, is crucial in the sentence: Jerry has one briar pipe (*that/which*) he smokes every day. When *which* is used, we know that Jerry has one and only one briar pipe. But when *that* is used instead, we don't know how many briar pipes Jerry has; we know only that he smokes a certain one every day. Similar distinctions, such as the one between *disinterested* and uninterested, are meaningful because they contribute to the precision of the language; they deserve to be preserved.

There are, on the other hand, distinctions that do not deserve preservation at all. The difference between *shall* and *will,* for instance, is so artificial and so difficult to understand that I am glad to see it disappearing as quickly as it is. Shakespeare, Chaucer, and Milton didn't observe all the rules concerning *shall* and *will* simply because these rules are rather recent additions to our language. They were not created by observing what happens in the language, but rather by decreeing what should happen. Grammarians in the not-so-distant past wanted to impose on all future speakers and writers an obligation to:

Use *shall* for predictions of simple futurity in the first person, and for statements of conviction or determination in the second and third person. Use *will* for predictions of simple futurity in the second and third person, and for statements of conviction or determination in the first person.

Now, if all of us would have—or even could have—followed this rule, the distinction between the words might have had a practical impact on meaning and been worth preservation. But when General MacArthur left Corregidor and stated "I *shall* return," clearly implying a powerful determination, the game was up. The distinction between *shall* and *will* is now (for the most part) dead, and I know of no modern textbook that has attempted to resurrect it. I will not long mourn its passing.

Finally, there are a great many distinctions between standard and nonstandard forms that don't pertain to logic or to differences in meaning. Many of these distinctions go unobserved solely out of ignorance—that is, out of a failure to realize that a standard form does, in fact, exist. People who are not aware of these forms assume that forms customary to them are the standard ones, and, consequently, they unwittingly portray themselves to others as being careless. Only by knowing the difference between standard and nonstandard forms is the user able to choose the forms that will cast him in the light he desires. If he is not aware of what the standard forms are, he cannot choose whether to accept or reject these forms for his own use. The person who doesn't know that "*between you and I*" is nonstandard suffers the same consequences that he would had he known the standard form and erred in employing it.

Each of us has it within his power to make language work for us—both to convey our thoughts and to convey the ideas about ourselves that we want others to know. If we fail to understand this power or to use this power for our own benefit, we have only ourselves to blame. If, however, we fail to convince our children that this power is within their reach and is worth their effort to obtain, then we must suffer the blame for their becoming unwitting victims of others who would use this power against them.

4. UNDERSTANDING THE PARTS OF SPEECH

Ah, yes, here we are again, those eight parts of speech that were drummed into you year after year but somehow always got confused or forgotten. Are they really that important after all? Probably not, but they provide a standard set of terms so that we can discuss words and sentences using a common vocabulary. The parts of speech are merely labels for groups of words that function in the same way. By just using the proper label—such as *noun*, for example—we can refer to all the thousands of words that belong to that class and function in that particular way.

Once words have been grouped according to their function, it really doesn't matter what labels you use for each group, as long as everyone understands what each label means. The labels that I have used throughout this book are very traditional, and, although I fully understand the arguments offered by the structural and transformational grammarians in favor of their groupings and labels, I have opted for the more traditional terms because they are much more widely understood and accepted by people throughout the country.

This chapter is not designed to be a complete and thorough study of everything involving the parts of speech. Rather, its purpose is to provide a "refresher course" in the ways that words function and in the terms that are used to describe those functions.

Understanding these terms and functions won't, by itself, make you a better speaker or writer, but it will help you understand why certain usages are standard while others are considered nonstandard; it will help you understand the terminology used in your children's language texts; and it will help you discuss language improvement with your children and with their teachers.

Each of the eight parts of speech is discussed separately; each section begins by defining a part of speech and showing how it functions in a sentence. These textbook-like reviews of the various forms and functions of each part of speech may be studied in depth or glossed over now and referred to when needed. These sections are set in a slightly smaller type size. Each is followed by a section that deals with the common difficulties that adults have in using a particular part of speech. These sections should be studied so that you can avoid the errors they describe. If you do not understand why these errors (or the errors that are given in a checklist at the end of the chapter) are considered errors, you can go back to the more complete discussions of the individual parts of speech and find the answers.

At the end of each part of speech, there is a section that deals with teaching that part of speech to your children. Some of the suggestions and methods given in these sections are more suitable to teaching children who are in elementary school; others are better suited for children in the secondary grades. No matter what the age of a child, however, it is helpful for him to learn to understand and recognize a part of speech so that he may later be taught its finer points of usage. Therefore, you must decide whether your child needs help in understanding, recognizing, or using a particular part of speech. Don't be afraid to begin at a very basic level; it will not help you or your child to assume that he knows (or should know) any concept by this point in his education. Home education is not designed to provide you a chance to berate the schools, teachers, or your own children for their various failures. Remember, too, that many sources besides this book can be used as tools for language improvement. Use exercise sentences from your child's textbooks and workbooks, and adapt these exercises by changing a few words in each sentence or by having your child write a similar exercise as a test for you.

Nouns

Understanding Nouns

A noun is usually defined as a word that names a person, place, or thing.

name of person:
   Alice, F. Lee Bailey, friend, sister
name of place:
   home, Chicago, school, State Street
name of thing:
   book, air, wall, Fido

With these words we can talk about the things that exist around us because we can give everything a name. Even things that we can't explain and that we don't fully understand can be given a name, and, therefore, nouns like *gravity, life, death, God,* and *cancer* can be discussed intelligently even though not a single person actually understands what these words mean. Most nouns name things that can be seen or touched; these nouns are called *concrete nouns.* But ideas and feelings have names, too, and these concepts cannot be seen or touched. Words like *hate, ambition, courage,* and *happiness,* then, are called *abstract nouns.*

COMMON NOUNS AND PROPER NOUNS

Many nouns name an entire class of things and are called *common nouns.* The noun *woman,* for example, names a group and may refer to any of the billions of people in that group. Some nouns, however, name a particular person, place, or thing. These nouns are called *proper nouns* and are always capitalized.

Common Noun	Proper Noun
woman	Susan B. Anthony
school	G. E. Thompson High School
street	Prairie Street
bank	First National Savings Bank
sister	Carolyn

IDENTIFYING NOUNS

One thing you *must* remember in identifying parts of speech is that no word can be classified as being a particular part of speech until it has been used in a sentence. A word that appears to be a name of something can be used in a way that makes it no longer a noun. The word *round,* for example, can be any of five different parts of speech simply by changing its use in a sentence.

There are, however, certain things that can be said about nouns that help distinguish them from other parts of speech and help you locate and identify them in a sentence. For instance, a noun frequently follows a word like *a, an, the, some, their, many, my, your, Tom's,* etc., (such words are called *determiners* or *noun markers*) in a sentence. Nouns do not always occupy this position, but almost all nouns *can* follow one of these words, and seeing a determiner or a noun marker is a good indication that a noun will follow.

Another characteristic of nouns that will help you in identifying them is that common nouns can be singular or plural. The singular form of a noun indicates that the noun is referring to only one person, place, thing, or idea (including one group); the plural form of a noun refers to more than one.

The plural form of most nouns is just the singular form plus *-s*.

Singular	Plural
one *paper*	two *papers*
one *window*	ten *windows*
one *collection*	several *collections*

But singular nouns that end in *s, x, ch, sh,* or *z* usually add *-es* to create their plural form.

Singular	Plural
one *tax*	two *taxes*
one *match*	ten *matches*
one *loss*	several *losses*

Nouns whose singular form ends in *y* preceded by a consonant create their plural form by changing *y* to *i* and adding *-es*. If the singular form ends in *y* preceded by a vowel, the *y* is kept and only an *s* is added.

Singular	Plural
one *fly*	two *flies*
one *country*	ten *countries*
one *berry*	several *berries*
one *valley*	two *valleys*
one *boy*	some *boys*

Most nouns whose singular form ends in *o* preceded by a consonant create their plural form by adding *-es*, but some add only *-s*.

Singular	Plural
one *hero*	two *heroes*
one *potato*	ten *potatoes*
one *banjo*	several *banjos*
one *piano*	some *pianos*

Some nouns have much more pronounced differences between their singular and plural forms. A few of these *irregular nouns* are shown below.

Singular	Plural
f or *fe* changes to *ves*	
one *wife*	several *wives*
one *thief*	two *thieves*
vowel changes	
one *man*	two *men*
one *foot*	two *feet*
one *mouse*	some *mice*

A few nouns have identical singular and plural forms.

Singular	Plural
one *deer*	two *deer*
one *sheep*	several *sheep*

The fact that nouns have both singular and plural forms may not be surprising to you at all. But there are only two other parts of speech for which "singular" and "plural" have any meaning at all, and so understanding this characteristic might very well help you distinguish nouns from other parts of speech.

Earlier I said that common nouns can be singular or plural. What about proper nouns? Most proper nouns cannot be made plural because, as proper nouns, they refer to a specific person, place, thing, or idea. There may be several *monuments* (common noun) that honor George Washington, but there is only one *Washington Monument* (proper noun). Proper names of people, however, both first and last names, can be made plural. For example, there may be two *Karens* in a classroom and, perhaps, several *Smiths*. These plurals are formed by following one simple rule: If the name ends in *s, x, ch, sh,* or *z,* add *-es;* if the name ends in any other letter, add only *-s.*

Still another characteristic of nouns is that they can show possession or relationship. By changing to its *possessive form,* a noun can show that it "owns" or "possesses" the item or quality named by a following noun. [1]

The possessive form of most singular nouns is created by adding *-'s.*

Singular Noun	Possessive Form
Joe	*Joe's* apartment
James	*James's* toys
a *day*	a *day's* wages
a *dollar*	a *dollar's* worth

(Notice that none of the examples above shows direct "ownership" of the following noun, as does "*Kay's* purse." The possessive form can indicate connections and relationships of various kinds including ownership.)

The possessive form of plural nouns that do not end in *s* is also created by adding *-'s.*

Plural Noun	Possessive Form
women	*women's* clubs
children	*children's* toys

The possessive form of plural nouns that end in *s* is created by adding only an apostrophe.

Plural Noun	Possessive Form
boys	the *boys'* team
birds	the *birds'* migration
officers	the *officers'* club

So, in deciding whether to use *-'s* or just an apostrophe to form a possessive noun, first determine whether the noun is singular or plural. If it is singular, your worries are over—always add *-'s.* If it is plural—and only if it is plural—you must determine whether the plural form ends in *s.* If it does, just add an apostrophe; if it doesn't, add *-'s.* (By all means, throw out the notion that you should consider adding *s':* You shouldn't. Just decide upon the correct singular or plural form first, and then add *-'* or *'s* as described above.)

TEACHING YOUR CHILDREN ABOUT NOUNS

It isn't necessary (or good) to have children classify nouns according to whether they name a person, a place, a thing, or an idea because there is so much overlapping in these labels. Is the noun *room,* for example, a "thing" or a "place"? Besides, the word *thing* is so broad that it applies to all nouns.

Getting the "feeling" for what nouns are is the best way for children to be able to locate and identify nouns in a sentence. One method for creating this awareness is to have a young child orally supply nouns of his choosing in sentences of your design. For example, you might start a sentence with a determiner; the child would then supply a noun; you might add an action verb, a preposition, and a determiner; the child would supply another noun.

---

1. The possessive form of a noun may be thought of as modifying or limiting the meaning of the noun that follows it. The possessive noun *Eleanor's,* for example, is used to modify the noun *cake* in the following sentence.

Eleanor's cake won first prize at the fair.

For this reason, possessive nouns are sometimes referred to as adjectives. But possessive nouns can also stand alone, without another noun following them.

The cake that won first prize at the fair was *Eleanor's.*

It is best to classify all possessive nouns as nouns, but to realize that they can, and frequently do, function just like adjectives in a sentence.

Parent: ⸝This . . .
Child: dog . . .
Parent: jumped over the . . .
Child: chair.

These sentences can get more complex, and they don't have to make sense. The idea is to give the child the feeling for where nouns fall in any given sentence.

You might make this exercise a bit more demanding by having the child write down in a column each noun that he supplies. When a column is completed (perhaps ten nouns), ask the child whether each noun is singular or plural. If the noun is singular, have him write its plural form in another column; if it is plural, he should write its singular form. (This will undoubtedly bring up some spelling problems, and troublesome words should be kept on a separate spelling list.)

When the child actually has the "feeling" for nouns, he will be able to change roles with you in the conversation. The child will begin each sentence and pause when he thinks you should supply a noun. This is not an easy task, and so you should build up to this role-reversal gradually.

If your child has an understanding of the function of nouns, he might enjoy playing "Alphabet Nouns" with you. The first player announces a noun that begins with the letter *a* (*anchor,* for example), and the next player must come up with a noun that begins with *b* (*bathtub*), and so on. Several players can participate (on family automobile trips, for instance), and many variations are possible. My favorite variation is to require each player to supply a noun that begins with the letter that *ended* the previous player's noun (an-cho*r*, rak*e*, ech*o*, orang*e*, etc.). You may decide that each player must correctly spell

the noun he supplies, or that he must use the noun correctly in a sentence. Use your imagination and gear the rules to the ability and the interest of the players.

Older children can look for specific types of nouns such as proper nouns, possessive nouns, or plural nouns in newspaper and magazine articles. You might tell them that you found eighteen plural nouns in a specific article, for example, and see if they can locate and circle all eighteen. On another day they might look for words that have the endings *-ance, -ence, -hood, -ism, -ist, -ity, -ment, -ness, -tion,* and *-ure.* These suffixes are common to nouns (ignor*ance,* differ*ence,* brother*hood,* alcoho*lism,* femin*ist,* pur*ity,* state*ment,* tender*ness,* reduc*tion,* fail*ure*) and are rather uncommon at the end of words that cannot be nouns. (The suffixes themselves, however, are not worth memorizing.)

You and your children might find it interesting to keep an eye out for "curious" nouns. For example, are the following nouns singular or plural?

athletics, billiards, oats, riches, shears, tweezers, spectacles

If they are plural, what is their singular form?

What about the following nouns, are they singular or plural?

news, measles, mumps, economics, physics, politics, mathematics

If they are singular, what is their plural form?

If the noun *pants* is plural (and doesn't have a singular form), why wouldn't a "pair of pants" mean "trousers for two"? How about a "pair of scissors," a "pair of pliers," or a "pair of glasses"?

33

What would you do if you had to refer in writing to more than one *3* or more than one *and*? How do you spell the plural of *3* and *and*? Solution: Plurals of symbols, letters used as letters, and words used as words are the only cases in which an apostrophe is used in forming the plural. (Plurals of numbers, however, may be written without an apostrophe.)

Do your figure *8*'s (or *8*s) again without any *if*'s, *and*'s, or *but*'s.

(See Chapter 14, page 200.)

IMPROVING YOUR OWN USE OF NOUNS

The most common of all the noun problems continues to be the difficulty people have in forming plurals and possessives. For all practical purposes, **an apostrophe does not belong in the plural form of a noun.** Plural forms of common nouns and people's names are created by adding *-s* or *-es* to the singular form, depending upon the last letter in the singular form.

Many people who put a family name on their house or mailbox think that they must use an apostrophe in spelling the plural form. The apostrophe indicates possession or ownership, and if that is what the family wants to indicate, the apostrophe should be placed at the end *of the plural form of the name.* A house that has "The Joneses" painted on it says that this is the house in which several people named "Jones" reside. A label stating "The Joneses'" means that several people named "Jones" own or occupy this house. Other forms such as "The Jones'" or "The Jones's" tell passersby that if a family named "Jones" resides here, accurate spelling is not its dominant family trait.

PRONOUNS

UNDERSTANDING PRONOUNS

A pronoun is usually defined as a word that takes the place of a noun. By using pronouns a speaker or writer can refer to a person, place, thing, or idea without restating its specific name.

Mary left school because *she* didn't feel well.

In the sentence above, the pronoun *she* takes the place of the noun *Mary.*

A pronoun may take the place of a noun that appears in another sentence.

Jamie just arrived back home.
He had just spent two months in San Diego.

The pronoun *he* in the second sentence refers to, takes the place of, and means the same as the noun *Jamie,* which was mentioned in the first sentence.

Sometimes a pronoun will take the place of several nouns, or it may replace not only a noun, but all the words around that noun as well. Occasionally one pronoun will take the place of another pronoun.

Curly, Moe, and Larry were so famous that almost the whole world knew of *them.* (The pronoun *them* takes the place of three nouns: *Curly, Moe,* and *Larry.*)

The tall, well-dressed bandit was nabbed as soon as *he* left the bank. (The pronoun *he* cannot be replaced by just the noun *bandit;* it stands for the entire group of words *the tall, well-dressed bandit.*)

Some wondered whether *they* would ever get out alive. (The pronoun *they* takes the place of the pronoun *some.*)

ANTECEDENTS

No matter whether a pronoun replaces one noun, several nouns, or entire noun groups, it must stand for or refer to something for its meaning. A pronoun simply has no meaning all by itself. The noun or noun group that the pronoun refers to for its meaning is called the pronoun's *antecedent,* which means "something that comes before."

Scientists believe that *they* will soon discover the secret.

In the sentence above, the antecedent of the pronoun *they* is the noun *scientists.* Notice that *they* is plural; it implies "more than one." This

plural pronoun is proper because its antecedent (*scientists*) is also plural. A singular antecedent requires that a singular pronoun be used to refer to it.

PERSONAL PRONOUNS

All the pronouns I have used as examples so far belong to a group known as *personal pronouns.* While most of the pronouns in this group do refer to people, the name for the group comes from the titles that have been given to the three ways speakers or writers have of making statements: first person, second person, and third person.

	Singular	*Plural*
First Person	I, me, my, mine	we, us, our, ours
Second Person	you, your, yours	you, your, yours
Third Person	he, him, his she, her, hers it, its	they, them their, theirs

The pronouns in the *first person* are used when a speaker or writer says something about himself or about others including himself. Those in the *second person* refer to the person spoken or written to. The pronouns in the *third person* refer to the people or things that are being spoken about or written about.

Now, in two of these three categories there are some forms that are singular and different forms that are plural. Singular pronouns are used to refer only to singular antecedents, and plural pronouns are used to refer only to plural antecedents.

The pronouns in the second person are identical in their singular and plural forms.

One major difference between most personal pronouns and the nouns they can replace is that personal pronouns that are used as subjects have different forms from those that are used as objects.[2] The *subject form* of a personal pronoun is used when the pronoun is the subject of a verb or is a subject complement. (See Chapter 6, pages 86, 89-91.) Generally speaking, if a pronoun performs an action, or if it immediately follows a form of the verb *be,* (is, are, was, were, am, be, or

---

2. In classical Latin and Greek, all words that acted as subjects or objects had different forms or endings depending upon how the words were used in a sentence. Each form or ending represented a different *case.* Many years ago the English language, too, made use of endings to distinguish the case of its nouns and pronouns. In modern English, however, only three case-forms have been retained, and they appear only in some pronouns and in the possessive form of nouns. Modern English uses word order and various prepositions to indicate ideas that were expressed by the "dative," "ablative," "locative," and other case-endings in Latin and Greek.

In the traditional terminology used to discuss case-forms in English, words that function as subjects were said to be in the *nominative case* (sometimes called the *subjective case*); words that functioned as objects were said to be in the *accusative case* (sometimes called the *objective case*); and words that showed possession were said to be in the *genitive case* (sometimes called the *possessive case*). I prefer to concentrate on the function itself rather than on classifications by case, especially since the differences in the various forms are few, and even these are gradually disappearing. Consequently, I have used *subject form* instead of *nominative* or *subjective case, object form* instead of *accusative* or *objective case,* and *possessive form* instead of *genitive* or *possessive case* throughout this book. You may choose to retain the more traditional terminology, and it is perfectly all right to do so. I just wanted you to know that there is a simpler and, I think, more effective alternative.

been), it must be in its subject form. The subject forms of the personal pronouns shown in the table on page 35 are reprinted below.

Subject Forms	Singular	Plural
First Person	I	we
Second Person	you	you
Third Person	he, she, it	they

The *object form* of a personal pronoun is used when the pronoun is a direct object, an indirect object, or the object of a preposition (see Chapter 6, pages 88-89 and Chapter 8, pages 103-104). If a personal pronoun receives the action of a verb or closely follows a word like *to, of, from, on, by, after, for, with,* etc., it must be in its object form. The object forms of the personal pronouns shown in the table on page 35 have been reprinted below.

Object Forms	Singular	Plural
First Person	me	us
Second Person	you	you
Third Person	him, her, it	them

A major reason that people have more difficulty in using personal pronouns than they do in using nouns is that nouns keep exactly the same form whether they are used as subjects or as objects, but the subject form of most personal pronouns is different from their object form. You will become much more familiar with the problems involved in using personal pronouns correctly (and the solutions to those problems) when you read Chapters 6 through 9, but for now,

concentrate on tuning your ear to the forms that are used correctly in the example sentences below. You may find that it will help if you read these sentences aloud. Your ear is a very precise language instrument, and you should not only train it to alert you to nonstandard usages, but you should learn to trust it in times of indecision as well.

I work very hard. (not **Me* work . . .)[3]
You and *he* both did well. (not *You and *him* . . .)
Janet left *them* in the store. (not *Janet left *they* . . .)
The Snyders received a letter from *her.* (not *. . . a letter from *she.*)
If somebody must win, I hope it will be *he.* (not *. . . it will be *him.*)

I realize that this last sentence may sound strange, but the subject form *he* is absolutely correct. When a personal pronoun immediately follows a form of the verb *be*, the chances are very great that it should be in its subject form. When you hear people answer a telephone question about their identity by saying, "This is *he*," "I am *she*," or "It is *I*," you might think that they are putting on airs or adopting a British dialect. The use of these pronouns in these situations, however, is quite standard and, in my opinion, preferable to "*This is *him*," "*I am *her*," and "*It's *me.*"

Like the nouns that they replace, personal pronouns have *possessive forms* that show ownership, possession, or other relationships.[4] The pos-

---

3. An asterisk (*) is used throughout this book to identify words, phrases, and sentences that do not conform to the principles of standard usage.
4. The possessive forms *my, our, your, his, her, its,* and *their* are sometimes referred to as "possessive adjectives" because they modify or limit the meaning of the noun they precede. In the sentence "*Your* coat is in the hall closet," for example, *your* functions as an adjective to describe the noun *coat.* but, because these words take the place of nouns and must refer to those nouns for their meaning, it is best to classify them as pronouns and realize that they also function just like adjectives in a sentence.

sessive forms of the personal pronouns shown in the table on page 35 are reprinted below.

Possessive Forms	Singular	Plural
First Person	my, mine	our, ours
Second Person	your, yours	your, yours
Third Person	his	their, theirs
	her, hers	
	its	

The pronoun *I*, for example, is a subject form; its object form is *me;* its possessive form can be either *my* or *mine. My* is used when the noun it "owns" or "possesses" follows the pronoun in the sentence.

The first thing he sees in the morning is *my* face.

Mine is used when it stands alone—that is, the noun it "owns" or "possesses" does not follow the pronoun in the sentence.

The first face he sees in the morning is *mine.*

Notice that *his* and *its* are the only possessive forms for the subject forms *he* and *it.* Each of these pronouns can be used alone or preceding the noun they "own" or "possess." The other personal pronouns have two possessive forms; however, *your* and *yours* can be either singular or plural.

REFLEXIVE PRONOUNS

By adding the suffix *-self* or *-selves* to certain personal pronouns, you can create forms that are called *reflexive pronouns.* Reflexive pronouns are used to refer to a noun or a pronoun that was previously stated in the sentence. The forms that are considered standard for reflexive pronouns are the following:

Reflexive Pronouns	Singular	Plural
First Person	myself	ourselves
Second Person	yourself	yourselves

Third Person	himself	themselves
	herself	
	itself	

The suffixes *-self* and *-selves* cannot be added to all personal pronouns. Nonstandard forms such as **hisself, *themself,* and **theirselves* can easily be replaced by the standard forms *himself,* and *themselves.*

The reflexive pronouns can also be used to intensify a noun by restating it.

You, *yourself,* must decide what is right.

When used in this way, these forms are sometimes called *intensive pronouns,* and they are generally set off by commas. Notice the difference between the intensive use of *yourself* in the sentence above and its reflexive use in the sentence that follows.

You have only *yourself* to blame.

No matter whether these pronouns are used reflexively or intensively, only the standard forms should be used, and they should be used only when they refer to a noun or a pronoun that has been previously stated in the sentence.

DEMONSTRATIVE PRONOUNS

The pronouns *this, that, these,* and *those* are known as *demonstrative pronouns* and are used to point to a specific person, place, thing, or idea. *This* and *that* are singular and refer only to singular nouns; *these* and *those* are plural and refer only to plural nouns.

Put *these* plates in *that* cabinet against the wall.

Keep in mind that the pronoun *them* is a perfectly acceptable personal pronoun, but it should not be used as a demonstrative pronoun—that is, it should not precede the noun it refers to in a sentence.

*Let me help you with *them* boxes. (non-standard)

But: Let me help you with *them*. (personal pronoun, standard usage)

Let me help you with *those* boxes.

Let me help you with *these* boxes.

Other frequent nonstandard usages occur in connection with the phrases *kind(s) of* and *sort(s) of.*[5] When these phrases are used to mean "of a particular type or types," they are frequently preceded by a demonstrative pronoun.

I don't like *that sort of* entertainment.

You must avoid eating *these kinds of* mushrooms.

Remember that the nouns *kind* and *sort* are singular and must be referred to by the singular demonstrative pronouns *this* and *that. Kinds* and *sorts*, on the other hand, are plural, and the plural pronouns *these* and *those* are the only demonstrative forms that can refer to plural nouns.

*I won't tolerate *those kind of* ideas.

I won't tolerate *those kinds of* ideas.

INTERROGATIVE PRONOUNS

A few pronouns are commonly used in asking questions. These *interrogative pronouns* are *who, whom, whose, which,* and *what.* They frequently appear as the first word in a question, although they may be preceded by a preposition such as *to, by, for, from, on,* etc. Sometimes the pronoun will modify the noun that immediately follows it, and sometimes the pronoun will stand alone.

Which will you choose? (pronoun stands alone)

Which road is under construction? (pronoun modifies *road*)

Who left that door open?

To *whom* am I speaking?

Whose turn is it to dry?

What was the author's name?

RELATIVE PRONOUNS

The pronouns *who, whom, whose, which,* and *that* are called *relative pronouns* because they can be used to relate or connect two sentences into one.[6] For example, here are two simple sentences:

I met the woman.

The woman lives next door.

By using the relative pronoun *who,* the two sentences can be combined into one:

I met the woman *who* lives next door.

The relative pronoun *who* has two functions in the sentence above: It replaces its antecedent (*the woman*), and it acts as a subject within its own word group or clause. *Who* acts just like the subjects *the woman* or *Mary* in the sentences:

The woman lives next door.

Mary lives next door.

(*who* lives next door)

It replaces a noun (that makes it a pronoun) and it relates one idea to another (that makes it a relative pronoun).

Notice how the italicized relative pronouns in the following sentences not only connect word groups, but each acts as a subject, object, or a modifier within its own word group as well.

The person to *whom* I spoke was Mrs. Samolinski. (object of *to*)

---

5. For the nonstandard use of *kind of* and *sort of* to mean "somewhat" or "rather," see Chapter 10, page 133-134.

6. Because they introduce dependent clauses, relative pronouns are also discussed in Chapter 8, (see pages 105-107).

This is the man *who* saved my life. (subject of *saved*)

I returned the book *that* I borrowed. (object of *borrowed*)

Our plant, *which* was built in 1920, will close next month. (subject of *was built*)

The poet *whose* works I most admire is T. S. Eliot. (modifies *works*)

You will frequently have to rearrange the word order of the group introduced by the relative pronoun in order to see clearly how the pronoun functions within its group. (The third sentence above, for example, can be rearranged as follows: I returned the book. I borrowed *that*.)

The pronouns *who, whom, whose,* and *which* were previously called interrogative pronouns, and *that* was called a demonstrative pronoun. Classifying and labeling pronouns, just like classifying and labeling parts of speech in general, is done according to the way that a word functions in a sentence. Just as the same word can act as a noun in one sentence and as a verb in another, a pronoun can act as a relative pronoun in one sentence and as a different type of pronoun in another sentence.

INDEFINITE PRONOUNS

One final group of pronouns, the largest group of all, is composed of pronouns that refer to unknown or indefinite persons or things. These *indefinite pronouns* function just like nouns in a sentence, and they can be used in all the places nouns can be used. They are pronouns, however, because they have no meaning by themselves; instead, they must refer to unknown nouns or indefinite ideas. The three groups that follow contain the most common indefinite pronouns.

Group 1: another, anybody, anyone, anything, each, either, everybody, everyone, everything, neither, nobody, no one, nothing, one, somebody, someone, something

Group 2: all, any, both, few, many, more, most, much, none, others, several, some

Group 3: whatever, whichever, whoever, whomever, whosever

Each of the pronouns in the first group is singular, and so a singular verb must be used when one of these pronouns functions as a subject (see "Subject-Verb Agreement," pages 95-99). Not all of the pronouns in the three groups have possessive forms, but those that do, spell their possessive form by adding -'s. The five pronouns in the third group also function as relative pronouns and are frequently called *indefinite relative pronouns.*

Notice how the italicized indefinite pronouns in the sentences below could be replaced by nouns if the nouns they referred to were known or could be known.

Someone drove over our lawn.
Whoever it was should be punished.
I put *some* in your lunchbox.
He opened the door, but *no one* was there.
Is this *anyone's* notebook?
She had left *everything* to her cats.

TEACHING YOUR CHILDREN ABOUT PRONOUNS

Children should be aware of the many similarities between nouns and pronouns (they are used to name things, they occupy the same positions in a sentence, they have singular, plural, and possessive forms). What many children don't realize, however, is that while there are thousands upon thousands of nouns in the English language (and more are being created every day), pronouns are a very limited and fixed group: There are fewer than 100 pronouns in the entire language. Two important observations can be made from this fact. First, these relatively few pronouns are among the most frequently used words of all because they can stand in place of any of the much-more-numerous nouns. Second, because there are so few pronouns, a person can quite easily know and use *all* the members of this one part of speech.

Indeed, even elementary-school children can be expected to use every pronoun correctly in a sentence. The personal pronouns should be concentrated on first, and the relative and indefinite pronouns last. Make a chart of the personal pronouns (like the one on page 35), and direct your child to use each one in a sentence of his own design. When he has done this successfully, ask him to use two of the pronouns in the same sentence. He might then choose two for you to use, and so on. Gradually introduce the reflexives, demonstratives, and interrogatives (even without their labels) to the list, and be sure to watch for the correct use of subject and object forms as the sentences become more complex. This exercise may be done orally, but having the child also write each sentence (with the list of pronouns in front of him) will help cement in his mind the standard forms of the frequently misspelled possessives.

Children should also be made aware of the concept of antecedents—that is, the idea that each pronoun must refer to another word (or words) for its meaning. Newspaper and magazine articles that are written on the child's reading level, or the child's school books (in any subject) can be used to show the connection between pronouns and the words they refer to. Have the child circle each personal pronoun (lightly in pencil if he is using a school text), and have him draw an arrow to the word or words each pronoun refers to for its meaning. Go over the sentences with him and occasionally ask him how a particular sentence would have to be written if there were no pronouns at all. The necessary repetition of nouns will demonstrate not only the use of pronouns, but the concept of antecedents as well.

You must be constantly vigilant about nonstandard pronoun usage in your child's speech. The common nonstandard demonstratives *this here* and *that there* should not be allowed to slip by without correction. Similarly, any use of *them* to mean *these* or *those* (*Give me one of *them* apples) should demand an immediate interruption that stresses the proper form.

The nonstandard personal pronouns that result from compound subjects and objects demand some explanation as well as interruption. When a sentence has two or more connected subjects and one of them is a personal pronoun, the pronoun must be in its subject form. Children who correctly use *I* when it is the only subject in a sentence frequently use *me* in a compound subject.

*Chris and *me* had to stay after school.

These forms are also confused when a sentence has two or more connected objects.

*Dad brought my friends and *I* back home.

In these cases you must ask the child to break the sentence down into separate sentences using each subject or object independently. The standard pronoun forms will be obvious. Now you must have the child build the sentences back into one, keeping the standard pronoun forms. If you do not have the child attempt to rebuild his original sentence, the lesson will be completely without value.

*Chris and *me* had to stay after school.
Chris had to stay after school.
I (not **Me*) had to stay after school.
Therefore: Chris and *I* had to stay after school.

*Dad brought my friends and *I* back home.
Dad brought my friends back home.
Dad brought *me* (not **I*) back home.
Therefore: Dad brought my friends and *me* back home.

Another problem that children have using pronouns in compound subjects and objects is actually a matter of politeness and courtesy. Whenever a personal pronoun that refers to the speaker is used in a compound subject or object, this pronoun should be stated last.

*The coach asked *me, Frank, and Willy* about the game.
The coach asked *Frank, Willy, and me* about the game.

**Me and Sandi* couldn't wait any longer.
**I and Sandi* couldn't wait any longer.
Sandi and I couldn't wait any longer.

This is a problem that is more easily corrected through constantly hearing the polite forms than through practicing these forms in exercises. Once a child understands that naming himself last is considered polite, you must tune his ear by having him recast his errors using the polite form, and by employing only the polite usages yourself.

IMPROVING YOUR OWN USE OF PRONOUNS

Adults seem to have more difficulty with pronouns than they do with any other part of speech. Much of this can be attributed to the fact that many pronouns have distinctly different singular, plural, subject, object, and possessive forms. The resulting problems of pronoun-verb agreement and of personal pronouns as subjects and objects will be discussed in chapters 7 and 9. The pronoun problems I will deal with now are the nonstandard uses of reflexive pronouns and the nonstandard possessive forms of personal pronouns.

The reflexive pronouns (those that end in *-self* or *-selves*) should be used only to refer to a noun or pronoun *that was previously stated in the sentence.* That is, the reflexive pronoun must *restate* a noun or pronoun; it should not name the person, place, thing, or idea for the first time in a sentence.

Tony decided to buy a present for *himself.*

In the sentence above, the reflexive pronoun *himself* refers to the noun *Tony,* which was previously stated in the sentence. But what does the pronoun *myself* refer to in the following sentence?

*The boss invited my wife and *myself* to dinner.

Although we understand that *myself* refers to the writer, it is nonstandard because it does not *restate* that idea. It is, instead, the *only* mention of that person in the sentence. The writer could have very easily used the personal pronoun *me,* and the resulting sentence would have been quite standard and proper.

The boss invited my wife and *me* to dinner.

Some writers (and many speakers) think that using reflexive pronouns makes them appear more learned or important. Using these pronouns improperly, however, has just the opposite effect.

The reason for the frequency of adult errors in spelling the possessive forms of personal pronouns is that these forms are unlike their noun counterparts. The possessive forms of nouns are spelled using an apostrophe, but **an apostrophe is not used in spelling the possesive forms of personal pronouns.** The pronouns *yours, hers, its, ours,* and *theirs* are already possessive and cannot be anything but possessive. There is no need to add an apostrophe, and doing so is definitely nonstandard.

The possessive pronoun *its* is the trickiest one of this group, by far. When an apostrophe is added to this pronoun, a new word is created. *It's* is a contraction meaning "it is." *It's* is a perfectly standard form, but not as a possessive pronoun.

> *It's* a great day for a ballgame. (meaning: *It is* a great . . .)
> *Its* leg was caught in a trap. (possessive pronoun)

A similar problem occurs with the possessive form *whose,* which is commonly used in asking questions.

Whose turn is it to bat?

Unless you realize that *whose* already shows possession, you might mistakenly use a form that has an apostrophe.

**Who's* turn is it to bat?

But *who's* does not show possession at all; it is a contraction that means "who is."

> *Who's* in charge here? (meaning: *Who is* in charge here?)

The best way to remember the standard possessive forms of personal pronouns is to think about the pronoun *his*. You know that this form is possessive, and you would never spell it with an apostrophe. Therefore, *hers* should not be spelled with an apostrophe, and neither should the other possessive forms *yours, its, ours,* and *theirs*.

VERBS

UNDERSTANDING VERBS

A verb is usually defined as a word that expresses an action or a state of being. The verb is the driving force behind every English sentence, and no sentence can be truly complete without at least one verb. The verb tells what the subject of the sentence is doing or what is being done to the subject. Generally speaking, verbs can be separated into groups: action verbs and linking verbs.

ACTION VERBS

As the name implies, *action verbs* tell what someone or something does—that is, the action that someone or something performs.

My brother *runs* five miles each day.
The wind *blew* fiercely all night.

Not all action verbs, however, convey the idea of physical motion. Some action verbs show no motion at all; many describe a mental action.

We *listened* to him for an hour.
I *believe* in that motto.
All of us *thought* about our situation.

LINKING VERBS

Many verbs, instead of expressing a physical or mental action, merely provide a link between the subject and a word that identifies or describes that subject. These *linking verbs* act like an equal sign (=) in a sentence.

Carolyn *is* a wizard with numbers.

In the sentence above, the linking verb *is* connects the subject, *Carolyn,* with the noun *wizard,* which identifies the subject: *Carolyn = wizard.* In the following sentence the linking verb *are* connects the subject, *trees,* with a word that describes the subject.

The trees *are* beautiful at this time of year.

The word *beautiful* follows the linking verb and describes the subject: *trees = beautiful* or *beautiful trees.*

All of the forms of the verb *be* (*is, am, are, was, were, be, being, been*) can be used as linking verbs in a sentence. While the forms of *be* are the most frequently used linking verbs, the verbs in the following list often function in the same way.

taste, feel, sound, smell, look,
grow, appear, remain, stay, seem, become

The verbs in the first row all deal directly with the senses, but all the verbs in this list can be replaced by a form of *be* without altering the general meaning of the sentence.

Geri *felt* ill throughout her vacation. (*Geri = ill, Geri was ill*)

In the sentence above, *felt* is not an action verb because *Geri* is not "feeling," that is, she is not "touching" anything. However, *felt* (and many of the other linking verbs in the previous list) *can be* used as an action verb, as the following sentence demonstrates.

Geri *felt* the rough surface with her fingers.

In this sentence Geri *is* performing an action, and the verb *felt* tells what that action is. It does not connect *Geri* to any other word that identifies or describes *Geri* (**Geri = rough?* or **Geri = surface?* or **rough Geri?*)

Notice how the verbs in the following sentences can be linking verbs when used in one way and action verbs when used in another.

The food *tasted* terrible. (linking: *food = terrible* or *terrible food*)
We *tasted* the chicken first. (action)
The corn *grew* tall and straight. (linking: *corn = tall, straight* or *tall, straight corn*)
We *grew* corn and beans last summer. (action)

VERB PHRASES

One verb alone frequently cannot express exactly what the subject does or is. In order to convey precise ideas of time and mood, you may have to use one or more additional verbs along with the original verb in a sentence. These additional verbs are called *helping verbs* (or *auxiliary verbs*), and they join with the original verb—that is, with the *main verb*—to form a *verb phrase*. **A verb phrase is a group of two or more verbs that act together as a single verb.** Each verb phrase consists of a main verb and one or more helping verbs.

While there are thousands of verbs that can be used as main verbs, there are only a few helping verbs in the entire language. All verb phrases, then, must include one or more of the helping verbs shown below.

is	do	have
are	does	has
was	did	had
were	can	may
am	could	might
be	shall	must
been	should	
	will	
	would	

Notice how these helping verbs can combine with a main verb to form verb phrases of two, three, or four words in length.

		(Main Verb)	
Harley		*walks*	to work.

	(Helping Verb)	(Main Verb)	
Harley	*will*	*walk*	to work.

	(Helping Verbs)	(Main Verb)	
Harley	*could have*	*walked*	to work.

	(Helping Verbs)	(Main Verb)	
Harley	*must have been*	*walking*	to work.

Just like one-word verbs, verb phrases can be classified as "action" or "linking" depending upon how their main verb is used in the sentence.

You *should have stayed* in the car. (action)

Your clothes *might have stayed* dry that way. (linking: *clothes = dry* or *dry clothes*)

Sometimes the verbs in a verb phrase will be interrupted by a word that is not a verb.

I *must* not *think* about that now. (verb phrase: *must think*)
You *could have* easily *tripped* on that rug. (verb phrase: *could have tripped*)

Even the contraction *n't* that is added to a helping verb is not part of the verb phrase.

Buffy *did*n't *know* any better. (verb phrase: *did know*)

TENSE

Unlike any other part of speech, verbs can place an event in time. Merely by changing their form or by joining a helping verb in a verb phrase, verbs can show whether something happened or existed in the present, in the past, or in the future. Verbs can place events in any of six *tenses* or times. Within each of these tenses there are also various forms that verbs can adopt to convey a variety of feelings and conditions.

Present Tense

When a verb tells that the subject is performing an action or existing *now*—that is, at the present time or habitually—that verb is said to be in the *present tense*.

Let's use the verb *paint* as an example. When this verb is used without any helping verbs, it shows present action or habitual action: "What do you do for a living?" "I *paint*." If the subject is changed to a plural noun, a plural pronoun, or to the singular pronoun *you,* a verb in the present tense keeps this same form: The boys *paint*. We *paint*. You *paint*. But when the subject is a singular noun or the pronouns *he, she,* or *it*, a verb in the present tense changes its form by adding a final -*s*: Kristy *paints*. She *paints*. Thus, all verbs in the present tense use one form (called the *base form*) for all subjects except those in the third person singular. When the subject is a singular noun or *he, she,* or *it,* these verbs add -*s* to their base form. (They add -*es* if their base form ends in *s, x, z, ch,* or *sh.*)

Present Tense	Singular	Plural
First Person	(I) paint	(We) paint
Second Person	(You) paint	(You) paint
Third Person	{He She It} paints	(They) paint

The base form of the verb (sometimes called the *infinitive* or the *infinitive stem*) is the form that you will find listed as an entry in a dictionary.

Past Tense

When a verb shows an action or a condition that existed in the past, the verb is said to be in the *past tense:* Yesterday I *painted* that barn. The past tense form of a verb is the base form plus the ending -*ed* or -*d*. (The final letter of the base form may have to be doubled before adding -*ed*.) Unlike the present tense, this same form is used for all subjects, even for the third person singular.

Present Tense	Singular	Plural
First Person	(I) painted	(We) painted
Second Person	(You) painted	(You) painted
Third Person	{He She It} painted	(They) painted

Many dictionaries list the past tense form of a verb next to its base form. Some dictionaries, however, show only the -*d* or -*ed* ending, and others show only those past tense forms that are created in unusual or irregular ways.

Future Tense

The present tense and the past tense are the only tenses that can be formed without the use of a helping verb. A main verb all by itself cannot show actions or conditions that will occur or exist in the future. To do this, the helping verb *will* (or *shall*) must accompany the main verb in a verb phrase. The *future tense,* then, is expressed by the helping verb *will* (or *shall*) and the base form of the main verb: I *will paint* that barn tomorrow. (The difference in meaning between *will* and *shall* is so complex that very few speakers or writers use the helping verb *shall* at all today, except in asking questions such as "Shall we go now?" or "Shall I answer the phone?" For a further look at *will* and *shall,* see Chapter 3, page 27.) The main verb remains in its base form for all subjects in the future tense.

Present Tense	Singular	Plural
First Person	(I) will paint	(We) will paint
Second Person	(You) will paint	(You) will paint
Third Person	{He She It} will paint	(They) will paint

Principal Parts of Verbs

Every verb has four variations that are called its *principal parts*. These principal parts, with the addition of the proper helping verbs, are used to create all the tenses and forms that verbs use to change their meaning. The base form of a verb, for example, is one of its principal parts. A verb's base form is not only its present tense form (for most subjects), it is also the form that always appears in the verb's future tense, too: *will* (or *shall*) + base form = future tense.

The second principal part of any verb is its past tense form. This form is, of course, used in forming the past tense.

The two remaining principal parts are called

participles (pronounced *par'•ti•sip•uls*): the *present participle* and the *past participle*. The present participle of a verb is simply that verb's base form plus the ending *ing*. The present participle of the verb *paint* is *painting*; the present participle of the verb *go* is *going*. By placing different helping verbs in front of the present participle, you can create *progressive forms* for all the verb tenses. The present tense statement *I paint,* for instance, can become *I am painting* and can show an action that is occurring at precisely this instant. The progressive form in the past tense, *I was painting,* uses a different helping verb, as does the progressive form in the future tense, *I will be painting.* Other helping verbs such as *can, should, would, may, might,* and *must* can also be added to these verb phrases, and the meaning of the phrase changes dramatically with each addition. Throughout all these changes, however, the present participle keeps its same form and position within the verb phrase.

While the present participle is *always* formed by adding *-ing* to a verb's base form, the formation of the *past participle* is accomplished in one of several ways depending upon the verb.

The past participle for most verbs is exactly the same as the verb's past tense form. For instance, *painted* is both the past tense and the past participle form of the verb *paint.* The past participle combines with a form of the verb *have* to create the *perfect tenses* (see pages 46-47). The following sentences all use a form of *have* and the past participle *painted* to express actions that took place over a period of time.

Tony *has painted* twelve portraits.
He *had painted* only one before last year.
He *will have painted* more than fifty by this
    time next year.

Other helping verbs can be added to these verb phrases, but a form of *have* must always be in a verb phrase that includes a past participle.

So, the four principal parts of every verb are its base form, its present participle, its past tense, and its past participle. (The principal parts of verbs are traditionally given in this order, although sometimes the present participle is omitted.) These are the building blocks for all the verb tenses.

The Perfect Tenses

The names "present tense," "past tense," "future tense," even "progressive form" give us a good idea of the time period a verb is expressing. The "perfect tenses," however, give us no clue at all. It is best, I think, just to remember that the three perfect tenses require (1) a form of the verb *have* and (2) a past participle.

The *present perfect tense* uses the helping verb *have* (*has* in the third person singular) and the past participle of a main verb to describe an action that began in the past, continued for a time, and is now completed.

I *have painted* many houses.
Joe *has painted* only a few.

The *past perfect tense* uses the helping verb *had* and the past participle of a main verb to describe an action that began in the past and was completed before a stated time or before another action took place.

By noon, they *had painted* the entire north side.
He *had painted* several portraits before he was
    ten years old.

The *future perfect tense* uses the helping verbs *will* and *have* along with the past participle of a main verb to describe an action that will be completed before a certain moment in the future.

She *will have painted* a dozen storm windows by tomorrow.

REGULAR AND IRREGULAR VERBS

The verb that I have used for all the previous examples, *paint,* is known as a *regular verb.* **Regular verbs are those whose principal parts are formed in regular ways.** That is, regular verbs form their past tense by adding *-d* or *-ed* to their base form. Regular verbs also use the same form for both their past tense and their past participle.

base form	*present participle*
paint	painting

past tense	*past participle*
painted	painted

Most of the verbs in the English language are regular verbs, but some of the most frequently used verbs of all are highly irregular.

Irregular verbs either don't form their past tense by adding *-d* or *-ed* to their base form, or they don't use the same form for both their past tense and past participle, or both. Some irregular verbs merely change a letter or two from their base form in creating their past tense: *become* (base form), *became* (past tense). Others use completely different words for their base form and their past tense: *go* (base form), *went* (past tense). Some have exactly the same base form as their tense: *burst* (base form), *burst* (past tense). Others spell the two forms alike, but their pronunciations are different: *read* (base form—pronounced *reed*) *read* (past tense—pronounced *red*). There are even more variations in the ways that irregular verbs form their past participles. The principal parts of irregular verbs must be studied, memorized, and put into practice in order to fix their proper forms in your mind.

I have listed the principal parts of the most common irregular verbs below. The principal parts of other irregular verbs can be found in your dictionary; some dictionaries may not show the present participle, but it is always the verb's base form plus *-ing.* Most dictionaries do not show the principal parts (other than the base form) of regular verbs; they depend upon you to know how to form principal parts in regular ways.

Common Irregular Verbs			
base form	*present participle*	*past tense*	*past participle*
beat	beating	beat	beaten
become	becoming	became	become
begin	beginning	began	begun
bite	biting	bit	bitten
blow	blowing	blew	blown
break	breaking	broke	broken
burst	bursting	burst	burst
buy	buying	bought	bought
choose	choosing	chose	chosen
come	coming	came	come
draw	drawing	drew	drawn
drink	drinking	drank	drunk
drive	driving	drove	driven
eat	eating	ate	eaten

(continued)

base form	present participle	past tense	past participle
fall	falling	fell	fallen
feel	feeling	felt	felt
find	finding	found	found
fly	flying	flew	flown
forget	forgetting	forgot	forgotten
freeze	freezing	froze	frozen
go	going	went	gone
grow	growing	grew	grown
hide	hiding	hid	hidden
hit	hitting	hit	hit
know	knowing	knew	known
lay	laying	laid	laid
lie (recline)	lying	lay	lain
make	making	made	made
read	reading	read	read
ride	riding	rode	ridden
ring	ringing	rang	rung
rise	rising	rose	risen
see	seeing	saw	seen
set	setting	set	set
shake	shaking	shook	shaken
show	showing	showed	shown
sing	singing	sang	sung
sink	sinking	sank	sunk
sit	sitting	sat	sat
speak	speaking	spoke	spoken
steal	stealing	stole	stolen
swear	swearing	swore	sworn
swim	swimming	swam	swum
think	thinking	thought	thought
teach	teaching	taught	taught
tear	tearing	tore	torn
throw	throwing	threw	thrown
wear	wearing	wore	worn
weave	weaving	wove	woven
write	writing	wrote	written

The Most Irregular Verb: *be*

The most frequently used verb of all in English is also the most irregular. The principal parts of the verb *be* are:

base form	present participle
be	being

past tense	past participle
was	been

These principal parts alone, however, do not show how truly irregular the verb *be* actually is. Unlike any other verb in the language, this verb has eight different forms: *is, are, was, were, am, be, been,* and *being.* While all other verbs have only two present tense forms (one for the third person singular and one for everything else), *be* has three.

Present Tense	Singular	Plural
First Person	(I) am	(We) are
Second Person	(You) are	(You) are
Third Person	{He She It} is	(They) are

While other verbs use the same past tense form for all subjects, either of two forms is used in the past tense of the verb *be.*

Present Tense	Singular	Plural
First Person	(I) was	(We) were
Second Person	(You) were	(You) were
Third Person	{He She It} was	(They) were

In standard spoken and written English, the base form itself, *be,* is seldom used alone. It is almost always preceded by a helping verb in a verb phrase (*might be, should be,* etc.)

TRANSITIVE AND INTRANSITIVE VERBS

Action verbs are sometimes described as being either *transitive* or *intransitive.* Many dictionaries indicate this distinction by placing the abbreviation *vt.* or *trans.* next to listed action verbs that are transitive, and *vi.* or *intrans* next to listed verbs that are intransitive. The meaning of these two labels is quite easy to understand: **Transitive verbs have a direct object, and intransitive verbs do not.**

Compare the following sentences:

Grandma is baking bread.
The baby is sleeping soundly.

In the first sentence the verb phrase, *is baking,* has a direct object: the noun *bread.* Bread is a direct object because it follows the verb and answers the question "What?" or "Whom?" about the subject and the verb.

Grandma is baking *what*?
Grandma is baking *bread.* (Direct Object)

Bread receives the action expressed by the verb phrase and is the direct object of that verb phrase. Therefore, in this sentence, the verb phrase *is baking* is transitive.

In the second example sentence the verb phrase, *is sleeping,* is followed by the word *soundly,* but this word does not answer the question "What?" or "Whom?" about the subject and the verb. *Soundly,* then, does not receive the action of the verb, and, therefore, *soundly* is not a direct object. Because the verb phrase *is sleeping* does not have a direct object, this verb phrase is intransitive.

While some verbs, such as *sleep,* are always intransitive, and others, such as *read,* are always transitive, most verbs cannot be classified as transitive or intransitive until they are used in a sentence. The verb *fly,* for example, can be intransitive in one sentence and transitive in another.

Birds *fly* even on windy days. (intransitive: no direct object)
Children *fly* kites on windy days. (transitive: direct object = *kites*)

ACTIVE AND PASSIVE VOICE

In all of the example sentences used so far, the subject of the sentence performed the action of the verb. Sentences in which the subject is the doer of the action described by the verb are said to be in the *active voice:*

(Sub.)   (Verb)
Jamie   painted that house.

In some sentences, however, the subject does not

act, but rather, *the subject is acted upon.* These sentences are said to be in the *passive voice:*

(Sub.)   (Verb)
That house   was painted by Jamie.

Notice that the subject (*house*) is not performing the action—it is not doing any painting. Instead, it is being acted upon.

Each of the following sentences has been changed from active to passive voice:

Active
(Sub.)   (D.O.)
Ford makes many fine cars.

(Sub.)   (D.O.)
JoAnne delivered the graduation address.

(Sub.)   (D.O.)
The crew had deserted the ship.

Passive
(Sub.)
Many fine cars are made by Ford.

(Sub.)
The graduation address was delivered by JoAnne.

(Sub.)
The ship had been deserted by the crew.

The passive voice is useful for those occasions on which you may not want to show the direct cause of an action or when that cause is unknown. The doer of the action can be left out of a passive sentence, but the subject cannot be removed from an active sentence.

Active: The President approved the illegal plan.
Passive: The illegal plan was approved by the President.
Passive (without showing responsibility): The illegal plan was approved.

Active: Someone in this room has stolen my watch.
Passive: My watch has been stolen by someone in this room.
Passive (responsibility unknown): My watch has been stolen.

TEACHING YOUR CHILDREN ABOUT VERBS

"ALPHABET VERBS"

Younger children can get a feeling for verbs and tenses by playing "Alphabet Verbs" with you. Create a base sentence in which a variety of verbs can be used. For example, "Last year on our vacation we _____." Now the players supply verbs that fit in the blank, but each verb must be in alphabetical order according to its first letter.

Player #1: "Last year on our vacation we *argued.*"
Player #2: "Last year on our vacation we *bathed.*"
Player #3: "Last year on our vacation we *canoed.*"

Players may also supply an additional word or phrase after the verb.

Player #4: "Last year on our vacation we *drilled* for oil."

When the players have gone as far through the alphabet as they can, change the base sentence, and change the tense of the verb.

Player #1: "By noon all of us had *arrived.*"
Player #2: "By noon all of us had *begun.*"

This will produce chances for nonstandard forms of irregular verbs, so watch out. Alert the child who uses a nonstandard form to what the standard form is, and have the child use that standard form *in a complete sentence*—not by itself.

NONSTANDARD VERB FORMS

Even students in high school have difficulty in using standard verb forms consistently. These difficulties not only involve using forms that are always nonstandard, but they also include using standard forms in nonstandard ways.

Many children simply do not know the standard past tense forms for some common irregular verbs, and so they, quite naturally, just add *-ed* or *-d* to the base form of the verb. If your child uses one of the nonstandard forms shown below, don't just shout out the standard form to him. Make sure that he understands the form's pronunciation (and, perhaps, its spelling), *and have him use the form in a complete sentence of his own design.* (Anytime you can have a child correct a usage error by using the standard form in a complete sentence, don't pass up the opportunity to do so.) Be particularly vigilant for these nonstandard usages:

*axed	to mean	*asked*
*buyed	to mean	*bought*
*drug	to mean	*dragged*
*gived	to mean	*gave*
*seed	to mean	*saw*
*sticked	to mean	*stuck*
*throwed	to mean	*threw*
*taked	to mean	*took*

Remember, also, that many of the uses of the verb *be* that are customary in the Urban Black Dialect are considered nonstandard in other dialects. If you want your child to speak standard English, you must call to his attention any nonstandard uses of *be*, especially the use of *be* all by itself, without the necessary helping verbs:

* He *be* home by Tuesday. (He *will be* home by Tuesday.)

Children also frequently use perfectly standard verbs in nonstandard ways. The use of the verb *can* instead of *may,* for example, is particularly irritating to many parents. Some parents, however, fear that they are being overly rigid and pedantic in this regard; they think that the distinction between these verbs may have been important only in the past. But *can* and *may* do have different meanings, and they are not interchangeable. Precision in the use of language is such a worthwhile goal for your children that you should never fear being overly conscientious in helping them pursue it. Precision in usage demands knowledge first of all. Because of your vigilance and constant repetition, your child will come to see that *can* refers to "ability" while *may* refers to "permission." Teach your child always to associate the word please with the verb *may:* If *please* should be used in a sentence, then the verb should be *may*—not *can.*

Child: Mom, can Bobby and I ride our bikes to the park?
Parent: Didn't you forget to say *please*? And what word do you use with *please*?
Child: *MAY* Bobby and I ride our bikes to the park, *PLEASE*?
Parent: That was much better, and yes, you *may.*

51

Some of the other nonstandard uses may require more complete explanations. The difference between the verbs *learn* and *teach*, for example, depends upon whether a person is receiving or giving information. Similarly, because *let* means "to permit" and *leave* means "to go away," the phrases "*Leave* go of me" and "*Leave* that go" are nonstandard and should be avoided. Having the child become accustomed to hearing and using "*Let* go of me" and "*Let* that go" will help him until he is able to understand the precise meaning of these verbs.

There is one other common childhood verb error that should not go unchallenged. Children frequently use the past tense contraction *don't* instead of *doesn't* for the subjects *he, she, it,* and singular nouns. Phrases such as *he don't, *she don't,* or **it don't* should be caught immediately, and the child should always be instructed to use the standard form *doesn't* in a complete sentence or two before continuing.

CROAKERS

Older children (and adults) can have a good deal of fun looking for and creating Croakers. Croakers are sentences in which the last verb is punningly related to what is said in the rest of the sentence. Croakers are just like Tom Swifties (see page 63) except that the humor is supplied by the verb instead of the adverb (and "Tom" is replaced by "he" or "she."). A few examples.

"I had to run back to change my trousers," he *panted.*
"The gas must be leaking," she *fumed.*
"I'll never learn to play this guitar," he *fretted.*

Croakers were named by Roy Bongartz,

whose examples in the *Saturday Review* demonstrate how witty and complex Croakers can be.

"That's my gold mine," he *claimed.*
"But it used to be mine," she *exclaimed.*
"The fire is going out," he *bellowed.*
"I spent all day sewing and gardening," she *hemmed* and *hawed.*

Inventing Croakers is not an easy task, and children should not be expected to come up with many—or any—of their own. They should, however, see how the verb provides the humor in the sentence, and most children will try to create their own Croakers right away (generally with limited success). You can help their creative efforts by keeping a list of verbs that have good "Croaker potential," such as *muttered, uttered, clamored, crowed,* etc.

IMPROVING YOUR OWN USE OF VERBS

THE SUBJUNCTIVE MOOD

Throughout this rather lengthy discussion of verbs, I have made no mention of the fact that verbs can be classified according to their *mood.* Few people have any problems at all with the *indicative mood* (used for making statements and asking questions) or the *imperative mood* (used for making requests or giving commands and directions). But the *subjunctive mood* of verbs has been a source of irritation to grammar students for decades, and this has resulted in a general inability on the part of adults today to use standard subjunctive forms in very common speaking and writing situations.

Many of the situations that required the

subjunctive mood years ago rarely occur in modern speech and writing. In fact, 95 percent of the errors that are made (and recognized) involving the subjunctive mood today occur in just two situations, and all of these involve the misuse of the same verb.

If you simply remember that the subjunctive form of the verb *was* is *were,* and that **this subjunctive form is proper for (1) wishes and desires, and (2) statements contrary to fact,** you will never have to think about the subjunctive mood again.

The following sentence is nonstandard because it requires the subjunctive form *were.*

   *I wish I *was* a cop in this town.

Even though the pronoun *I* and the verb *was* are both singular, the subjunctive form *were* should be used in sentences showing wishes or desires no matter whether the subject is singular or plural.

   I wish I *were* a cop in this town.

   *I wish he *was* here now.
   I wish he *were* here now.

   *She wishes she *was* old enough to drive.
   She wishes she *were* old enough to drive.

The following sentence is also nonstandard because it requires the subjunctive form *were* instead of *was*:

   *I'd take it right back, if I *was* you.

The statement *if I was you* is contrary to fact because, obviously, *I* am not, and cannot be, *you.* The subjunctive form should be used in all statements that are contrary to fact.

   I'd take it back, if I *were* you.

   *If this *was* my house, I'd paint it red.
   If this *were* my house, I'd paint it red.

   *If he *was* alive today, we wouldn't be in this mess.
   If he *were* alive today, we wouldn't be in this mess.

As a way of helping you recall the correct use of the subjunctive *were,* think about the lyrics "If I *were* a rich man..." (from *Fiddler on the Roof*) and "If you *were* the only girl in the world, and I *were* the only boy."

THE PROBLEM OF LIE AND LAY

I know of no two verbs that give adults more trouble than *lie* and *lay.* One of the reasons they are so troublesome is that both are highly irregular verbs. *Lie* even has, for one of its principal parts, the form *lay.* Another reason, though far less frequently admitted, is that the verb *lay* has a widely understood, rather coarse meaning that pertains to the act of making love. Unwitting misuses of these verbs, then, are both easy to commit and potentially embarrassing. Each of these verbs has several different meanings, but the two that are most often confused are *to lie,* meaning "to rest in a horizontal position" and *to lay,* meaning "to put or place something down." The traditional method of teaching the difference between these two verbs is to have the student memorize their principal parts.

base form	present participle
lie	lying
lay	laying

past tense	past participle
lay	(have) lain
laid	(have) laid

Knowing these principal parts is important, but merely memorizing them without being able to use them properly does little, if any, good at all.

When you are confronted by the problem of *lie* or *lay,* you actually have two separate difficulties:

1. Which verb expresses the meaning you want to convey? and
2. Which form of that verb should you use?

In solving the first problem remember that *lay* is a transitive verb—that is, it always has an object. In order "to put or place *something* down," there must always be a *something* to put or place. Therefore, a noun or pronoun will always answer the question "What?" or "Whom?" about the subject and a form of the verb *lay.*

> Notice how he *lays* his hand on her forehead. (He lays *what*? He lays his *hand*.)
> We *laid* a trap for them and waited. (We laid *what*? We laid a *trap*.)

The verb *lie,* on the other hand, is intransitive and never has an object. The questions "What?" or "Whom?" will not make sense when asked about the subject and the verb that means "to recline."

> We *lie* in the sun almost every afternoon. (*We lie *what*?)
> She had been *lying* down for well over an hour. (*She had been lying *what*?)

Remember, too, that objects as well as people can "rest in a horizontal position."

> The car was *lying* on its side and spilling gasoline.

Our little sailboat now *lies* on the bottom of the pond.

Once you have solved the problem of which verb to use, the matter of choosing the proper form of that verb remains. Once again, take a look at the principal parts of *lie* and *lay* that are shown on page 53. The principal parts that cause most of the difficulty adults experience in using these verbs are the present participle and the past tense. The present participle should actually pose no problem once you have selected the proper verb; it is merely the *-ing* form of the verb you want to use. If your verb means "to *lie* down," then *lying* is the present participle to use.

> I could be *lying* on the beach right now.
> He has been *lying* in that same position since early this morning.

If, on the other hand, the verb means "to put or place (something)," then the present participle is *lay* + *-ing* = *laying.*

> The workers will be *laying* our new carpet this morning.

The problem of using the past tense forms of these verbs correctly is a much more difficult one to solve. Because the past tense form of *lie* (meaning "recline") is pronounced and spelled in exactly the same way as the base form of the verb *lay,* its correct use in a sentence appears and sounds to be incorrect. The only way to become comfortable and confident in your use of this form is to train your ear by orally practicing sentences in which this form is used correctly. Here are a few examples; I urge you to create several more of your own and to practice saying them until the past tense form *lay* begins to sound correct to you.

> Yesterday we *lay* in the sun until three o'clock.
> He just *lay* there, unable to move.
> The papers *lay* on the porch throughout our vacation.

Few people have difficulty in using the past participles of these verbs because there are relatively few opportunities that call for these forms. In fact, if you will just let the forms *laying* and *laid* act as alarms or signal flares— alerting you to the possibility that error may be near—you will stand a good chance of avoiding the most common misuses of the two verbs that are most commonly misused. *Laying* and *laid* do have uses that are entirely proper, but these forms are so frequently used in places where *lying* and *lay* should be used that it is best to treat them with caution and question their use every time.

ADJECTIVES

UNDERSTANDING ADJECTIVES

An adjective is usually defined as a word that modifies a noun or a pronoun. The most important word in this definition is *modify,* and its meaning is a bit different from what we normally intend when we "modify our behavior" or "modify our automobile." As it is used in language study, *modify* means "to limit the meaning of" another word or phrase. The noun *office,* for instance, can bring to mind examples of various types of offices, each quite different from every other, but each still capable of being labeled an "office." When an adjective such as *large* precedes the noun *office,* the noun's meaning is limited or modified. A *large office* reduces the number of offices conjured up

by just the noun *office* alone because it eliminates all offices that are not large. When other adjectives are applied to this noun, the meaning that is conveyed becomes more and more precise—that is, the meaning of the noun becomes more and more limited: a *large, modern, sunlit, oval* office.

You may wish to think of adjectives as *describing,* rather than *limiting* the nouns and pronouns they modify. Most of the adjectives in the previous example do describe a particular office, and, even though there are adjectives (such as *a, an, the, which, some,* etc.) that are hard to call "descriptive," the important point is that you see how adjectives can affect the meaning of a noun or a pronoun. Whether you call this effect "limiting," "describing," "restricting," or "qualifying" is up to you—"modifying" encompasses them all.

Adjectives answer the questions "What kind?" "Which one?" "How much?" and "How many?" about the nouns and pronouns they modify.

Adjective	Noun	
ripe	apples	(What kind?)
this	hotel	(Which one?)
more	weight	(How much?)
several	attempts	(How many?)

POSITION OF ADJECTIVES

Several adjectives can all modify the same noun in a sentence. When two or more adjectives precede the noun they modify, a comma is generally placed between the adjectives if the word *and* would make sense in place of the comma.

Long, dark tunnels connected the rooms.

A comma is used between the adjectives *long* and *dark* because *and* makes sense in its place: Long *and* dark tunnels connected the rooms.

Three reserve officers were called up for duty.

No comma is used between the adjectives *three* and *reserve,* however, because *and* does not make sense in its place: *Three *and* reserve officers were called up for duty.

Adjectives do not always precede the nouns or pronouns they modify in a sentence. When they appear immediately after this noun or pronoun, they are usually set off by commas.

> The sky, *dark* and *eerie,* was perfect for Halloween.

The adjectives *dark* and *eerie* describe the noun *sky* just as surely as if they had preceded the noun in the sentence: The *dark* and *eerie* sky was perfect for Halloween.

Adjectives frequently follow linking verbs such as *be (is, are, was, were, being, been), become,* and *seem* in a sentence. The verb provides a link between the noun or pronoun that is the subject and an adjective that describes that noun or pronoun.

> Paul is *thrifty.* (*thrifty* Paul)
> The dance had been *successful.* (*successful* dance)
> The winner will become *rich* and *famous.* (*rich* and *famous* winner)
> Her face seemed *familiar.* (*familiar* face)

Other linking verbs that frequently connect adjectives with nouns or pronouns are those that involve the senses: *look, smell, taste, sound, feel.*

> The entire meal tasted *delicious.* (*delicious* meal)
> The fish, however, smelled *terrible.* (*terrible* fish)

ARTICLES

The most frequently used adjectives of all are the words *a, an,* and *the.* While these words do not provide a very vivid description of nouns, they do limit or modify nouns, and so they are considered adjectives. Because these words are so similar and are used so frequently, they have been given a special group label: *articles.* Just remember that there are only three articles (*a, an,* and *the*) and that they are always used as adjectives to modify nouns or pronouns. (The proper use of the articles *a* and *an* is discussed on page 59-60.)

PROPER ADJECTIVES

Many adjectives are formed from nouns. The adjective *heroic,* for example, is formed from the noun *hero.* When an adjective is formed from a proper noun—that is, from a capitalized noun that refers to a particular person, place, thing, or idea—it is called a *proper adjective,* and it is also capitalized.

Proper Noun	Proper Adjective
Egypt	*Egyptian* art
Shakespeare	*Shakespearean* sonnets
Christ	*Christian* ethics

Occasionally, a proper noun will be used as an adjective without any change in form: *Panama* hat, *Iowa* corn, etc. When used in this way, the proper noun becomes a proper adjective and is, of course, capitalized.

COMPARISON

Adjectives have different forms that are used to compare a quality that is shared by two or more words. For example, the adjective *large* can describe a quality or a characteristic of one house: This is a *large* house. But in order to show how large this house is in comparison to one other house, another form of the adjective must be used: This house is *larger* than the house next door. A third form of the adjective is required for showing how large a house is in comparison to two or more other houses: This is the *largest* house on the block.

These three forms of an adjective are called its *degrees of comparison.* The basic adjective form is called its *positive degree.* It has no special ending, and it merely describes a quality without suggesting any comparison: John is *tall.* The *comparative degree* compares the same quality in exactly two nouns or pronouns: John is *taller* than Jim. The *superlative degree* shows that a quality exists in its highest form; it compares the same quality in three or more items: John is the *tallest* of the three boys in the family.

Most adjectives form their degree of comparison in one of two regular or customary ways. In one of these methods, the comparative degree is formed by adding the suffix *-er* to the positive degree, and the superlative degree is formed by adding the suffix *-est* to the positive degree: *thick, thicker, thickest.* If the basic adjective (the positive degree) ends in a silent *e*, the silent *e* is dropped before adding *-er* or *-est: wise, wiser, wisest.* If the positive degree ends in *y,* the *y* is changed to *i* before adding *-er* or *-est: heavy, heavier, heaviest.* If the adjective ends in a single consonant preceded by a single vowel, the final consonant is doubled before adding *-er,* or *-est: thin, thinner, thinnest* (see pages 147-151).

The second method of *regular comparison* applies to many adjectives of two syllables and almost all adjectives of more than two syllables. These adjectives form their comparative degree by using the word *more* along with their positive degree. They form their superlative degree by using the word *most* along with their positive degree: *recent, more recent, most recent.*

Many adjectives can also show lesser amounts of a quality by using the word *less* in the comparative degree, and the word *least* in the superlative degree.

a *painful* injury (positive)
a *less painful* injury than Tom's (comparative)
the *least painful* injury of all (superlative)

Most adjectives, however, have opposites or antonyms whose degrees of comparison indicate lesser amounts.

This house is *less large* than the one next door.
This house is *smaller* than the one next door.

PRONOUNS USED AS ADJECTIVES

Once again, it should be noted that no word should be labeled as a certain part of speech until it has been used in a sentence. Words that you previously learned were pronouns, for example, can be *used* as adjectives in a sentence. When a word is *used* in place of a noun, it is a pronoun; when that same word is *used* to modify a noun, it is an adjective.

This is the one I want. (pronoun)
This table is the one I want. (adjective modifying *table*)

Possessive pronouns and relative pronouns can modify nouns in a sentence, yet are still considered pronouns because they also replace nouns as well.

His coat and *her* scarf lay on the table. (possessive pronouns)
This is the author *whose* book became a movie. (relative pronoun)

NOUNS USED AS ADJECTIVES

Possessive nouns are always used as adjectives because they describe or modify the noun they are related to: *Sharon's* baby. They frequently follow a form of the verb *be* and modify the subject of the sentence: That award should have been *Ken's.*

Many words that would appear to be nouns can also be used as adjectives. Each of the underlined words below is frequently used as a noun, but here functions as an adjective.

our *basement* stairs
that *house* trailer
a *dog* kennel
my *desk* lamp
two *newspaper* publishers

VERBS USED AS ADJECTIVES

The present participle and the past participle of a verb can also be used to modify nouns in a sentence. When used in this way, these words are considered adjectives.

Tom is *shooting* freethrows. (present participle)

That was a *shooting* star. (adjective modifying *star*)

They have *published* a book of poems. (past participle)

Published reports contradict her story. (adjective modifying *reports*)

TEACHING YOUR CHILDREN ABOUT ADJECTIVES

"ALPHABET ADJECTIVES"

The game of "Alphabet Adjectives" is designed to give your child a feeling for what adjectives do and where they appear in a sentence. There are two basic versions of this game, and each version has several variations.

In the first version you prepare a list of nouns in alphabetical sequence. You then take turns with your child supplying adjectives that describe each noun and that begin with that noun's initial letter.

Ants . . . Boys . . . Cake . . . Dog . . . (etc.)

If you supplied "*active* ants," your child might say "*big* boys." If you followed with "a *chocolate* cake," your child might say, "a *dirty* dog," and so on. Or, you might take turns supplying adjectives that begin with *a* to modify "ants" until someone becomes stumped. Then take turns modifying the *b* noun on your list with adjectives that all begin with *b*.

The second version of this game gives children the feeling for using adjectives after linking verbs. Start with a base sentence that uses one of the sense verbs:

That house looks _____.

Now the players take turns adding adjectives whose initial letters are in alphabetical sequence. After each player supplies an adjective, he must turn the sentence around so that the adjective precedes the noun. For example, "That house looks *awful*. That is an *awful* house." "That house looks *beautiful*. My, what a *beautiful* house that is." After each miss, change the entire sentence, including the linking verb. (Remember: Base sentences that use a form of *be* are more difficult to turn around and require additional changes. A sentence like "My best friend is _____" can generate many adjectives, but some children might have difficulty changing it into "I have a (or an) _____ friend.")

MODIFYING

The most important concept that you can impart to your children concerning adjectives is that of *modifying*. Once they grasp how adjectives can "change" or "limit" the meaning of nouns, it will be much easier for them to understand adverbs, prepositions, verbals, phrases, and clauses in the future. The adjective is the key to understanding these other ideas because it most clearly and easily demonstrates the effect of modifying.

Have your child think about a simple noun, *bird,* for instance. Write the word down, and ask the child to concentrate upon what that word means to him. Now write an adjective in front of the noun, "*yellow* bird," for example, and ask him if that is what he was picturing. Then, "Did you see how just by adding one word like *yellow,* an adjective, the meaning of *bird* has changed? The meaning of *yellow bird* is more definite, and you can picture it more clearly in your mind." Now add another adjective, such as "*huge,* yellow bird," and ask, "Is this the 'yellow bird' you were imagining?" You can keep adding adjectives as long as logic permits.

Now let your child supply the adjectives. Find a color picture that clearly shows some familiar object—a picture of a house in a magazine advertisement, for example. Have your child try to describe that house to you by using only one-word descriptions or "modifiers." Underneath the word *house,* you or your child should list each adjective that he thinks describes that house.

House
red
brick
large
new
ranch

Now let him build all these adjectives into a sentence of his own design. He will probably use prepositional phrases and clauses as well as the one-word adjectives on the list, and you should not discourage him from doing so. The point that you are trying to have him see (and that you should return to when he has finished his sentence) is that the noun *house* has a very general meaning that must be *modified* by adjectives in order to clearly describe one particular house.

IMPROVING YOUR OWN USE OF ADJECTIVES

CHOOSING BETWEEN A AND AN

There is occasionally some confusion about whether to use the article *a* or *an* before certain nouns. (Did you win *an* honorable mention or *a* honorable mention?) Much of this confusion stems from our being taught that *a* is proper before words that begin with a consonant, and *an* is proper before words that begin with a vowel. Like many all-too-memorable rules from our school days, this one comes close to being accurate, but not quite close enough, I'm afraid. Actually, the point at issue here is not the initial *letter* of the word following *a* or *an,* but rather, the *sound* that begins that word. The word *union,* for example, begins with a vowel (*u*), but it *sounds* as though it begins with a consonant (*you*). The word *honor,* on the other hand, begins with a consonant (*h*), but this letter is silent, and so the word *sounds* as though it begins with a vowel (*on*).

The article *a* should precede words that begin with a consonant sound (*a* union, *a* one-in-a-million chance, *a* ewe, etc.). **The article *an* should precede words that begin with a vowel sound** (*an* h our, *an* honorable mention, etc.).

ABSOLUTE ADJECTIVES

A few adjectives have no comparative or superlative forms at all. These adjectives describe an absolute condition to which the ideas of "more" or "less" simply don't apply. The adjective *priceless,* for example, means that an item is so valuable that no price can possibly be applied to it. Another item cannot be "*more priceless" than the first, nor can anything be the "*most priceless" item of all. The adjective *dead* is also absolute and cannot be compared. Something is either *dead* or it is *not dead*—there simply is no middle ground and no meaning for the terms "*more dead" or "*most dead." Other adjectives that fall into this category are *perfect, unique,* *true, matchless, infinite, universal, circular, square, parallel,* and *pregnant.*

ADVERBS

UNDERSTANDING ADVERBS

An adverb is usually defined as a word that modifies a verb, an adjective, or another adverb. Because this definition violates the rule of logic that cautions against using a word as part of its own definition, some texts define an adverb as "a part of speech that is used to modify a word other than a noun or a pronoun." Neither of these definitions will do you any good, however, unless you understand the meaning of the word *modify.*

Just as adjectives "describe" or "limit the meaning of" the nouns and pronouns they modify, so adverbs have the same effect on verbs, adjectives, and other adverbs. Adverbs usually answer the questions "How?" "When?" "Where?" or "To what extent?" about the words they modify.

> Diana removed the pin *carefully.* (*How* did Diana remove the pin?)
> I took my chemistry test *yesterday.* (*When* did I take my chemistry test?)
> A police car brought us *home.* (*Where* did a police car bring us?)
> We had to admit that we were *hopelessly* lost. (*To what extent* were we lost?)

ADVERBS AS MODIFIERS

Adverbs most frequently act as modifiers of verbs or verb phrases. By describing or limiting the meaning of a verb, an adverb answers the questions "How?" "When?" or "Where?" about the verb it modifies.

> Marjorie answered *timidly.* (Modifies *answered* and tells "how?")
> Alvin was promoted *recently.* (Modifies *was promoted* and tells "when?")

Bring the newspaper *here.* (Modifies *bring* and tells "where?")

The words *not* and *never* are adverbs that are used to modify verbs. They are called "negative adverbs" because they change a sentence that has a positive meaning to one that conveys an opposite idea.

> I told you that.
> I *never* told you that. (Modifies the verb *told*)
>
> She could have committed the crime.
> She could *not* have committed the crime. (Modifies the verb phrase *could have committed*)

The adverb *not* is frequently written as the contraction *n't* and added to the first helping verb in a verb phrase.

> The medicine did*n't* help me at all. (*n't* modifies the verb phrase *did help*)

When *n't* is added to the helping verb *will,* however, the verb changes to the form *won't.* Other adverbs such as *hardly, barely,* and *scarcely* also convey a negative meaning and are frequently part of nonstandard constructions called *double negatives* (see pages 64-65).

Adverbs differ from adjectives in that, while adjectives are usually positioned immediately next to the word they modify (or separated from that word by a linking verb), adverbs are much more "moveable" within a sentence. Notice the position of the italicized adverb in the sentences below.

> *Suddenly* the defendant sprang to his feet.
> The defendant *suddenly* sprang to his feet.
> The defendant sprang *suddenly* to his feet.
> The defendant sprang to his feet *suddenly.*

The sentences above all have the same meaning. Even though the position of the adverb *suddenly* changes, this adverb still modifies the verb *sprang* in each sentence.

Not all adverbs, however, can be moved so freely without altering the meaning of the sentence. The adverbs *just* and *only* deserve special attention in this regard. These adverbs should always be placed as close as possible to the word you intend them to modify. Notice the slightly different meanings conveyed by each of the following sentences.

Only our teacher thought she needed a vacation.

Our teacher *only* thought she needed a vacation.

Our teacher thought *only* she needed a vacation.

Our teacher thought she *only* needed a vacation.

Our teacher thought she needed *only* a vacation.

To avoid confusing the people to whom you speak or write, place the word that is modified by *just* or *only* immediately after these words in the sentence.

Adverbs can also be used to modify or limit the meaning of adjectives. The adverbs *too* and *very* are frequently used in this way, but many other adverbs can modify adjectives as well.

This wine is *fairly* expensive.
This wine is *surprisingly* expensive.
This wine is *outrageously* expensive.

The italicized adverbs in the sentences above all modify the adjective *expensive,* which modifies the noun *wine.*

When an adverb is used to modify an adjective in a sentence, the adverb always immediately precedes the adjective it modifies. Adverbs that modify adjectives cannot be moved from place to place as most adverbs that modify verbs can.

An adverb can also be used to limit the meaning of another adverb.

I arrived at the office *unusually* early that day.

The adverb *early,* in the sentence above, modifies the verb *arrived* and answers the question "When?" The adverb *unusually* modifies the adverb *early* by giving it a more precise meaning. Other adverbs such as *too, very, extremely, rather, quite,* and *somewhat,* for example, could replace *unusually* in this sentence and change the meaning of the adverb *early.* An adverb that modifies another adverb will always immediately precede the word it modifies in a sentence.

You may have noticed that many adverbs end in *-ly,* and this ending is a good indication that the word is an adverb. But not all adverbs end in *-ly,* and not all words that do end in *-ly* are adverbs. In fact, some of the most commonly used adverbs (*too, very, not, here, there, well,* etc.) do not have this *-ly* ending.

Some adverbs have exactly the same form as adjectives.

The pitch was thrown *low.* (adverb telling "where?")

It was definitely a *low* pitch. (adjective telling "what kind?")

I'll try to be home *early.* (adverb telling "when?")

I'll take the *early* train. (adjective telling "which one?")

As with all other parts of speech, adverbs are identified by their function, not by their form. In order for a word to be called an adverb, it must be *used* to modify a verb, an adjective, or another adverb.

COMPARISON OF ADVERBS

Like adjectives, adverbs have *degrees of comparison* that show the degree to which a certain quality is present. The *positive degree* is the basic adverb itself; it shows no comparison at all. The *comparative degree* is used to compare exactly two things. The *superlative degree* is used to compare three or more things.

Most adverbs form their comparative and superlative degrees by using the words *more* and *most*.

> Richard sang *beautifully*. (positive degree)
> Thomas sang *more beautifully* than Richard. (comparative degree)
> Robert sang *most beautifully* of the three. (superlative degree)

A few adverbs, however, use the suffixes *-er* and *-est* to form their comparative and superlative degrees.

Positive	Comparative	Superlative
near	nearer	nearest
early	earlier	earliest
soon	sooner	soonest
late	later	latest
long	longer	longest
high	higher	highest

The adverbs *badly* and *well* are irregular and use wholly different words to form their comparative and superlative degrees.

Positive	Comparative	Superlative
badly	worse	worst
well	better	best

> Chris played *badly* in the tournament. (positive)
> Pat played *worse* than Chris did. (comparative)
> Dale played the *worst* of all. (superlative)

Several adverbs cannot be compared at all. The ideas of "more," "most," "less," and "least" have no meaning at all when applied to adverbs like those in the following list.

here	quite	too	not
lately	there	now	somewhat
down	once	very	somewhere
never	always		

Other adverbs such as *singly, only, uniquely,* etc. express an absolute meaning that cannot be made "more" or "less" because it is complete or perfect as it is.

CONJUNCTIVE ADVERBS

A few adverbs are more important for the punctuation they require than for their function in a sentence. The *conjunctive adverbs* in the following list can all be used to join two sentences into one. When used in this way, a conjunctive adverb is always preceded by a semicolon (;) and followed by a comma.

also	for example	moreover
accordingly	furthermore	nevertheless
as a result	however	on the other hand
consequently	meanwhile	therefore

> We all purchased snow-throwers this winter; *however,* our area had only three inches of snow.

When these words are not used to join sentences, but rather, to introduce a single sentence, they are always followed by a comma. When they merely interrupt a single sentence, they generally have commas on either side. Notice that some of these conjunctive adverbs are composed of more than one word.

> *Consequently,* I propose that we adjourn.
> We could, *for example,* give up our lunches for a week.

SENTENCE ADVERBS

Some adverbs do not clearly modify one verb, adjective, or adverb in a sentence. Rather, they qualify or limit the meaning of the entire sentence in which they appear. These adverbs are sometimes called *sentence adverbs.* Notice how the underlined sentence adverbs that follow do not actually modify any single word.

Unfortunately, no one could find it.
Not *surprisingly,* I soon received a letter from the bank.
The thieves, *obviously,* used disguises.

Sentence adverbs usually appear at or near the beginning of a sentence, and they are generally set off by commas. (For *hopefully* as a sentence adverb, see Chapter 10, pages 136-137.)

TEACHING YOUR CHILDREN ABOUT ADVERBS

MODIFYING

As with the teaching of adjectives, the most important point you can convey to your child about adverbs is the meaning of the word *modify.* If the child already has an understanding of the way in which adjectives modify nouns and pronouns, use this knowledge to show that adverbs have the same effect upon verbs, adjectives, and other adverbs.

The modifying function of adverbs is most easily seen in the ways they change or limit the meaning of action verbs. Start out with a simple base sentence that has an action verb your child can perform: "Paul is walking," for example. While your child is demonstrating this action, add an adverb to the end of the sentence, and have the child show how the action has changed: "Paul is walking *quickly.*" Follow this with as many adverbs as you wish (*slowly, loudly, softly, carefully*), and let your child see if he can come up with any more. Now ask your child whether these

adverbs have changed the meaning of "Paul" or the meaning of "is walking." Then try another action verb and another set of adverbs for your child to act out. Gradually your child will come to see that adverbs limit, restrict, or modify the meaning of verbs just as adjectives modify nouns and pronouns.

The concept of modifying can also be taught through the game of "Alphabet Adverbs," which is played just like the other alphabet games discussed earlier in this chapter. Start out with a base sentence that contains an action verb ("The cowboy rode his horse into town _____"), and have the players take turns adding adverbs in alphabetical sequence (*artfully, backwards, carelessly,* etc.)

TOM SWIFTIES

Older children and adults have, for decades now, enjoyed hearing and creating puns that are commonly called "Tom Swifties." In a Tom Swiftie, the message that is said by "Tom" is humorously connected to the adverb that tells how the message was said. The pun in a Tom Swiftie is created by the final adverb, where the pun in a Croaker (see page 52) is created by the verb. Here are a few examples of Tom Swifties. I urge you to try creating some of your own and to encourage your children to do the same.

"This is the maid's night off," Tom said *helplessly.*
"This steak doesn't taste like beef," Tom yelled *hoarsely.*
"I knew I shouldn't have bid four hearts," Tom said *passively.*
"But, Your Honor, I shouldn't be the defendant in this case," Tom said *plaintively.*

"It rained throughout our entire camping trip," Tom said *intently*.

IMPROVING YOUR OWN USE OF ADVERBS

FORMING ADVERBS FROM ADJECTIVES

Many adjectives can be changed into adverbs by adding the suffix *-ly*.

> a *recent* (adjective) event that happened *recently* (adverb)
> Her *quick* (adjective) wits allowed her to act *quickly* (adverb).

You must be careful, however, to add the *-ly* ending only to the adjective form. For example, the word *accident* is a noun; its adjective form is *accidental*. Some people who want to form the adverb meaning "not planned" add the *-ly* ending to the noun *accident* and write or say **accidently* (four syllables). If they had remembered that this adverb is formed by adding *-ly* to the adjective *accidental*, they would have written or pronounced the adverb correctly as *accidentally* (five syllables).

> I *accidentally* bumped into your car.

Other adverbs such as *incidentally* and *originally* are commonly misspelled and mispronounced for this same reason.

> noun: *incident*
> adjective: *incidental*
> adverb: *incidentally* (not **incidently*)
> noun: *origin*
> adjective: *original*
> adverb: *originally* (not **originly*)

DOUBLE NEGATIVES

The adverbs *never* and *not* (and the contraction *n't*) are negative words; they modify a verb by giving it a negative meaning. But our language has many other negative words as well, including *no, none, nothing, no one, nowhere*, and several prefixes such as *un-, ir-, dis-, non-, and in-*. A good general rule to follow is to **avoid using more than one negative word or prefix to express a single idea.** For example, the sentence below is nonstandard because it contains a *double negative* —that is, it employs two negative words when only one would have been enough.

> **I can't do *nothing* right today.

Both the contraction *n't* and the word *nothing* have a negative meaning, and each can convey that meaning all by itself.

> I can't do anything right today.
> I can do *nothing* right today.

Double negatives are frequently created by using the negative words *hardly, barely,* or *scarcely* with the contraction *n't*.

> **You can't *hardly* tell the difference.
> **I couldn't *barely* keep my eyes open.
> **There wasn't *scarcely* enough time left.

These usages can be easily corrected by removing the contraction from the end of the helping verb. Sometimes additional changes must be made.

> **He didn't *hardly* know what hit him.
> He hardly knew what hit him.

Sometimes a negative prefix can combine

with another negative word in a sentence without causing a double negative. In the examples below, both negative expressions are necessary because the meaning of the sentences would change if one of their negative expressions was removed.

>She *never dis*approved of my actions before now.
>Some usages should be avoided even though they are *not in*correct.
>The plan is*n't* exactly *ir*responsible.

These sentences demonstrate that the notion of "two negatives canceling out each other and making a positive" is rooted in mathematics, not in language. Saying that someone is "not unattractive" or "not dishonest" puts the matter in a vague, middle-ground and is wholly different from saying that the person is "attractive" or "honest."

CONJUNCTIONS

UNDERSTANDING CONJUNCTIONS

A conjunction is usually defined as a word that joins other words or word groups. There are only a relatively few conjunctions in English, but these conjunctions are among the most frequently used words in the language. Whenever a sentence has two or more subjects, shows two or more actions, or conveys two or more ideas, a conjunction will generally be needed to join the different elements into one sentence.

The most common conjunctions of all are *and, but, or, nor, for, yet,* and *so.* These words are called *coordinating conjunctions,* and they are used to connect words or groups of words that are of the same general type. For example, the con-

junction *and* is used to join two similar words in the following sentence.

>*Books* **and** *papers* were piled high on the shelves. (joins two nouns)

The conjunction *but* joins two similar groups of words in the sentence below.

>The soldiers departed *in the right direction* **but** *on the wrong road.* (joins two prepositional phrases)

In the next example, the conjunction *or* joins two complete sentences into one.

>*We must leave now,* **or** *we will never escape alive.*

These coordinating conjunctions—*and, but, or, nor, for, yet,* and *so*—should be memorized as a group because they are the keys to a common problem of punctuation. **When *and, but, or, nor, for, yet,* or *so* are used to connect two complete sentences into one, a comma should always precede the conjunction.**

>Most of us were tired, *so* we went to bed early.

The sentence above would be considered nonstandard if the comma was removed. For very brief sentences, some texts say that the comma is unnecessary. But you will always be safe by keeping the comma before the conjunction, even for cases in which two short sentences are joined.

>They couldn't use it, *so* they didn't want it.

Remember: The comma is used only when the word groups that are joined could stand by themselves as complete sentences.

>Most of us went to bed early *and* fell asleep quickly. (no comma)

Another set of coordinating conjunctions is made up of conjunctions that always are used in pairs. These conjunctions (sometimes called *correlative conjunctions*) are still used to join similar words or word groups. The most common conjunctions of this type include the following:

both . . . and
either . . . or
neither . . . nor
not only . . . but also
whether . . . or
if . . . then

Both hydrogen *and* oxygen must be present. (joins two nouns)
Either you stop that immediately *or* I must leave. (joins two sentences)

A completely different type of conjunction is used to join word groups that are *not* similar or equal. *Subordinating conjunctions* always appear at the beginning of a group of words that has a subject and a verb, but the entire word group—including the conjunction—cannot stand alone as a sentence. (This construction is called a *dependent clause* and is discussed in Chapter 8, pages 104-107.)

We were terribly sick *when* we left for Spain.

In the sentence above, the subordinating conjunction *when* introduces a group of words that cannot stand alone as a sentence: *when we left for Spain*. Notice how different the sentence is when a coordinating conjunction—that is, one that joins words or groups of equal rank—is substituted for the subordinating conjunction.

We were terribly sick, *but* we left for Spain.

The most common subordinating conjunctions are the following:

after	if	whenever
although	since	where
as	than	wherever
as if (though)	though	while
because	unless	why
before	until	
how	when	

If the group of words introduced by these conjunctions appears at the beginning of a sentence, it is always followed by a comma.

While you were out enjoying yourself, I was slaving over a hot stove.

If the subordinating conjunction appears later in the sentence, it is not preceded by a comma.

If you take care of them, they will last forever. (comma necessary)
They will last forever *if* you take care of them. (no comma)

The important thing to remember about subordinating conjunctions is that the word groups they connect are *unequal*. The group introduced by the conjunction *depends* upon the other group for its meaning.

TEACHING YOUR CHILDREN ABOUT CONJUNCTIONS

USING COORDINATING CONJUNCTIONS

The most frequently used conjunctions of all are the coordinating conjunctions *and*, *but*, *or*, *nor*, *for*, *yet*, and *so*. To give your child a feeling for how these conjunctions are used to join two complete sentences, write the conjunctions down and take turns creating the sentences they join. You might begin by stating a simple, but complete, idea: "I went to the drugstore," for example. Your child now picks out a conjunction from the list and completes your sentence by using the conjunction to introduce a sentence of his own: "*but* it was closed." Now your child starts out the next sentence, and you must complete it by using a different conjunction. Try to channel your child into using *nor, for, yet,* and *so* by beginning your sentences with constructions that can make use of these conjunctions. "I didn't bring any money," for instance, can accommodate the conjunction *nor*: "*nor* did I bring any credit cards."

It is a good idea always to say the word *comma* at the end of the first clause. This drills into your child the idea that a comma belongs before a coordinating conjunction that connects two complete sentences.

"You may go to the movie *comma* . . . "
"*but* you must come right home."

Avoiding Run-on Sentences

One of the most important lessons you can give your children about conjunctions involves helping them avoid using too many conjunctions. Many children fall into the habit of using *and, but,* and *so* to string together several unrelated ideas into one long sentence. Such a sentence, called a "run-on sentence," frequently occurs in both speech and writing, and results from the user's failure to know when and how to stop.

Making a decision to end one thought with a period and begin another with a capital letter is quite difficult for some writers—even some adult writers. Their main problem is that they do not see their thoughts as separate, distinct ideas; rather, they see all their thoughts as contributing to one general idea. People who speak in run-on sentences use

conjunctions as "fillers"—that is, as sounds to fill in the silences they find so uncomfortable between sentences. The problem of run-on sentences in writing can be eliminated or greatly diminished by attacking spoken run-ons.

After your child has just read a story, seen a television program, or returned from a movie, have him tell the story to you in his own words. If he has difficulty separating his thoughts into complete sentences and resorts to connecting them with conjunctions instead, tell him to say each period, question mark, or exclamation point he would use if he were writing the story. You may interject an appropriate mark from time to time, but your child should repeat that mark when you do.

Because your concern is the elimination of run-on sentences, concentrate your attention only on the use of end marks for the time being. Let the child throw in other punctuation marks if he chooses, but don't worry about the accuracy of their use.

IMPROVING YOUR OWN USE OF CONJUNCTIONS

BEGINNING A SENTENCE WITH A CONJUNCTION

One of the immutable laws of grammar that teachers preached not long ago was "A sentence should never begin with a coordinating conjunction." This "law" was frequently violated because *and, but, or, nor, for, yet,* and *so* just seemed to "sound right" at the beginning of some sentences.

I am happy to report that this "law" is now rarely taught and even more rarely observed. I am glad to see it pass away because there was simply no good reason for it in the first place. Conjunctions have begun the sentences of great writers for centuries, and removing the conjunction from the start of many common sentences creates a stilted, broken uncomfortable style.

Two of the sentences below begin with conjunctions, and each is perfectly standard, proper, and acceptable.

The pressure inside the volcano kept building as the movement below it forced gasses to compress. *But* no one in town had any idea of what was happening below the surface. They had felt the tremors and had written them off as the "shivers" that always occurred around May. *And* the scientists at the university hadn't issued any warnings, had they?

Of course, you must also avoid becoming too fond of this construction. When successive sentences begin with a conjunction, or when this construction is too frequently used in a piece of writing, the effect can be a negative one.

So don't be afraid to begin a sentence with a coordinating conjunction, but also don't fall into the habit of using this device so often that it is noticeable and irritating to the reader.

COMMA PRECEDING CONJUNCTION IN A SERIES

Conjunctions are part of a conflict that is occurring today—a struggle between two styles of usage. The battle is over the proper way to punctuate three or more items in a series when the last two items are connected by the conjunction *and, or,* or *nor.* Should a comma precede the conjunction (as in X, Y, and Z), or should the last two items be connected by the conjunction alone (as in X, Y and Z)?

The New York Times, Time magazine, and some textbooks have decided that this final comma is unnecessary. They follow the rule that *either* a comma *or* a conjunction should separate items in a series.

This item can be made of wood, iron **or** copper.
There were several dishes to choose from each morning: pancakes, waffles, ham **and** eggs.

Notice that the second sentence above is slightly ambiguous. Were there four dishes on the menu each morning (1. pancakes, 2, waffles, 3. ham, 4. eggs) or just three (1. pancakes, 2. waffles, 3. ham and eggs)?

Because adequate punctuation can avoid even some far-fetched misreadings, most textbooks, style manuals, and authorities today recommend using *a comma and a conjunction* between the last two items in a series. There is very little advantage to dropping this comma (except, perhaps. a saving of ink), and retaining it can contribute to clarity. Therefore, using the comma with the conjunction is a good habit to form, and I hope that this style will ultimately prevail.

I have never seen a movie that was more forceful, more beautiful, **or** more technically perfect than this one.

PREPOSITIONS

UNDERSTANDING PREPOSITIONS

A preposition is usually defined as a word that shows the relationship between a noun or pronoun and another word in the sentence. Notice how the underlined preposition in each of the following sentences indicates a different relationship between the noun *house* and the verb *built.*

A bird built its nest *on* our house.
A bird built its nest *in* our house.
A bird built its nest *near* our house.
A bird built its nest *under* our house.
A bird built its nest *behind* our house.

There are a limited number of prepositions in the English language, but these words are used very frequently. The list that follows includes the most common prepositions, and these words should be studied so that you can recognize them in a sentence.

aboard	from
about	in
above	into
across	like
after	near
against	of
along	off
amid	on
among	over
around	past
at	since
before	through
behind	throughout
below	to
beneath	toward
beside	under
between	underneath
beyond	until
but (=except)	unto
by	up
down	upon
during	with
except	within
for	without

A preposition almost always precedes the noun or pronoun that it relates to another word in the sentence. This noun or pronoun is called the *object of the preposition.*

The characters *in* this *play* are fictitious.

In the sentence above, the preposition *in* relates the noun *play* to the noun *characters. Play,* then, is the object of the preposition *in.*

The group of words that begins with a preposition and ends with its object is called a *prepositional phrase* (see Chapter 8, pages 103-104). The entire prepositional phrase acts as a modifier and functions either as an adjective or as an adverb. In the previous example sentence the prepositional phrase *in this play* functions as an adjective to modify the noun *characters* by answering the question "Which characters?" In the following example, the preposition *before* relates its object, *audience,* to the verb phrase *was filmed.*

This program was filmed *before a studio audience.*

The prepositional phrase *before a studio audience* functions as an adverb to modify the verb phrase and answer the question "Where?"

A single preposition can have more than one object.

We were now *between the devil and the deep blue sea.*

In the sentence above, the preposition *between* has two objects: the noun *devil* and the noun *sea.* (For a look at the problems involving compound objects and pronouns used as objects of prepositions, see Chapter 9, pages 119-120.)

The group of words in the following list are called *compound prepositions.* Each includes more than one word, but each acts just like a one-word preposition in a sentence.

according to	in spite of
because of	instead of
in back of	out of
in front of	together with

TEACHING YOUR CHILDREN ABOUT PREPOSITIONS

DEMONSTRATING RELATIONSHIPS

One way to have younger children see how different prepositions show different relationships is to give them an object—a mixing bowl, for example—and have them act out the meaning of a sentence that can use many different prepositions. With the list of prepositions (page 69) in front of you, have your child act out "Sarah's hand is *above* the bowl." Then, "Sarah's hand is *against* the bowl," and so on. Later, give the child another object and a different base sentence. Now have the child follow along the list of prepositions until she finds one that she can act out using the base sentence.

REBUSES

Older children can use the list of prepositions to create a rebus: a puzzle or riddle that uses drawings to represent words or sounds. The preposition *over,* for example, is part of the solution to the following rebus:

MIND   (answer: mind over matter)
MATTER

The preposition *between* is the clue to:

R|E|A|D|I|N|G (answer: reading between the lines)

Some rebuses describe prepositions even though the actual words represented are not prepositions at all. For example, the preposition *under* clues the following rebus but doesn't appear as a preposition in the answer:

WEAR   (answer: long underwear)
LONG

Here are some other rebuses that can be clued by prepositions:

1. MAN
   BOARD

2. STAND
   I

3. T
   O
   W
   N

4. T
   O
   U
   C
   H

5. GROUND
   FEET
   FEET
   FEET
   FEET
   FEET
   FEET

6. HE'S / HIMSELF

7. DEATH LIFE

8. YOU   J U S T   ME

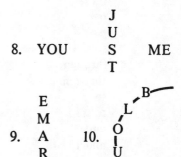

9. E
   M
   A
   R
   F

10.

(Answers: 1. man overboard 2. I understand 3. downtown 4. touchdown 5. six feet underground 6. he's beside himself 7. life after death 8. just between you and me 9. frame-up 10. see-through blouse)

Not all rebuses, of course, involve prepositions. Some can be very complicated, indeed, and are not likely to be understood by children. However, if your child enjoys creating or deciphering rebuses, let him go beyond the limits of rebuses that involve prepositions. Curiosity about language use, and creativity with language, are far too important to be confined to a single part of speech.

IMPROVING YOUR OWN USE OF PREPOSITIONS

USE AT THE END OF A SENTENCE

Of all the "laws" we were taught about grammar and usage in school, the most memorable one surely must be "Never end a sentence with a preposition." (One popular version of this maxim demonstrates how easy it is to violate: "Never use a preposition to end a sentence *with*.") Not only has this rule been dropped from most textbooks today, but it was always more frequently taught than observed. Many (if not most) of the greatest British and American writers have chosen to construct occasional sentences ending in prepositions simply because that arrangement produced a more natural and less stilted style. Winston Churchill's famous retort to an accusation that he ended a sentence with a preposition illustrates how strict observance of the "rule" can produce impossibly artificial constructions: "That is just the type of nonsense up with which I will not put!"

A brief story will demonstrate how a preposition at the end of a sentence can actually contribute to communication, and how natural this construction sounds to the listener.

There once was a boy whose father read to him each evening at bedtime. When the child had tucked himself in, the father would come upstairs with a book from which that night's story would be taken.

One evening the father came upstairs with a book that a child did not particularly like. The child then asked a wholly understandable question, but one that *ended in five prepositions:*

"What did you bring that book that I didn't want to be read *to out of up for?*"[7]

Suffice it to say that prepositions have been, can be, and even should be used at the end of certain sentences and clauses. If, however, by placing a preposition in this position, the sentence doesn't sound right or look right to you, then recast the sentence. For example, if "What do I owe this pleasure *to?*" doesn't seem as natural in a certain situation as "*To* what do I owe this pleasure?" then choose the latter construction. But if your listener or reader finds "These are the rules we will play *under*" less noticeable than "These are the rules *under* which we will play," then don't be afraid to use the sentence that suits your audience, even though that sentence happens to end in a preposition. As long as you have the ability to recast your sentences into the form that will most contribute to communication, use that ability and don't let a "false rule" sway your judgment.

PARTICLES

One reason that some prepositions seem so natural at the end of sentences and clauses is

---

7. Two of these prepositions are actually part of a compound preposition, and another is actually a particle (see pages 71-72). Still, the point should be obvious.

that they are not actually prepositions at all. Words such as *out, in, up, down, off, on,* and others are prepositions when they show the relationship between their object and another word in the sentence. But these words can also be *particles*—that is, they can act as part of a verb instead of as prepositions.

For example, in the following sentence the word *out* is a preposition showing the relationship between the verb *looked* and the noun *window.*

He looked *out* the window.

The prepositional phrase *out the window* tells where he looked. In the next example, however, the word *out* does not show any relationship at all.

He took *out* the garbage.

The word *out* doesn't connect the verb *took* with the noun *garbage.* Instead, *out* is actually part of the two-word verb *took out.* You could substitute a one-word synonym such as *removed* and retain the sentence's meaning. In this example, then, *out* is a particle, not a preposition.

While all this may sound quite complicated and academic, there is one distinction between prepositions and particles that you might find interesting. A word that is a true preposition cannot be moved from its position in the sentence, but a particle can be moved without changing the meaning of the sentence. In the following example the word *off* is a particle—that is, it is part of the verb *turned off.*

I turned *off* the light.

Because it is a particle, it can be moved to another position in the sentence.

I turned the light *off.*

Now consider the word *off* as it is used in the following sentence.

I jumped *off* the bridge.

Here it is a true preposition, and it begins the prepositional phrase *off the bridge.* Because it is a preposition, it cannot be moved to another position as a particle can.

*I jumped the bridge *off.*

Although knowing the difference between true prepositions and particles will not, by itself, make you a better speaker or writer, understanding that some ideas are movable within a sentence while other ideas are not can increase your awareness of, and interest in, language and usage.

INTERJECTIONS

UNDERSTANDING INTERJECTIONS

An interjection is usually defined as a word or group of words that is used to express a strong or sudden feeling. Interjections are not related grammatically to any other word in the sentence; they are completely independent in meaning. The underlined words in the sentences below are all interjections:

Well, here she comes now.
Good grief! You can't be serious.
Why, you never told me that before.

When the feeling expressed by an interjection is a mild one, the interjection is separated from the rest of the sentence by a comma. When the interjection expresses a strong emotion, it is followed by an exclamation point. These strong interjections can also appear as separate structures, not connected to another sentence at all.

My God! Well, I should have guessed it would happen.

Some words (such as *oh, alas, yippee, hurrah, ouch*) can be used only as interjections, while others (such as *well, my, why, goodness*) can function as other parts of speech as well.

TEACHING YOUR CHILDREN ABOUT INTERJECTIONS

OVERUSED INTERJECTIONS

Perhaps the most important idea that you can teach your children about interjections is that they are generally overused and almost always inappropriate. All parents discourage the use of vulgarisms and obscenities by their children, but few take the time to drive home the point that these interjections make a negative statement about their user. Not only can profanity be embarrassing, but when the same expressions are used over and over in many different situations, they lose all of their meaning and most of their force.

Mark Twain believed that there was a release that came from swearing that was unmatched even by prayer. But even he reserved his swearing for only the most trying of times and for those occasions on which it would have its greatest effect. Twain's attitude toward swearing can be applied to interjections in general. Interjections should always be used intentionally—not automatically. Speakers who rely on one pet word or phrase to function in a wide variety of circumstances discover that their interjection has become a "filler" and is being unknowingly included in simple statements and questions—often with embarrassing results.

Yet there are certain occasions on which we cannot always use our best language. When we feel sudden pain or extreme surprise, we acknowledge these emotions orally. But all of us have been in situations where our sudden verbal release shocked those who happened to be within earshot. It would benefit every one of us, adults and children alike, to have a forceful but inoffensive interjection waiting in the wings that can be summoned up in times of extreme surprise or pain. Each of us should keep an expression of our choice (such as W. C. Fields's immortal "Godfrey Daniels!") in readiness for just these occasions, and not employ the usage at any other time. The expression can be anything at all, but it cannot be one that is, itself, so shocking that it will cause embarrassment long after the shock of the situation has passed.

Vulgarities and obscenities should be purged from your children's language whenever possible, but these words and phrases are more likely to stay out of their speaking vocabularies if the children have a reasonable alternative to use in their place.

IMPROVING YOUR OWN USE OF INTERJECTIONS

EXPLETIVES

Certain verbs and nouns that make up the bulk of common English obscenities and vulgarities are frequently called *expletives,* a term that achieved great popularity when President Nixon's Watergate tapes were transcribed using the phrase "expletive deleted" to show that a vulgar interjection had been removed. While the word *expletive* does, indeed, have this meaning, it also has another meaning that is quite different.

To grammarians, an expletive is an introductory word that has no connection to the rest of the sentence, but is just used to "get the sentence started." Notice how the words *it* and *there* have no real meaning at all within the sentences below; they are expletives that allow these sentences to be written as they are.

It was certainly cold this morning.
It might as well be winter.
There is no excuse for your actions.
There will be thunderstorms tonight.

It and *there,* when used in this way, are not obscenities, but they are expletives just the same.

5. COMMON PROBLEMS WITH PARTS OF SPEECH

The usage problems that are discussed in this chapter are problems that are faced by many adults, both in speaking and in writing. In discussing these problems and their solutions, it is necessary to use terms and concepts that were defined and explained in Chapter 4. If you are unsure about the exact meaning of some of the more technical words used in this chapter, consult the index at the back of the book to see where in Chapter 4 these terms are discussed.

AGREEMENT BETWEEN PRONOUN AND ANTECEDENT

A pronoun has no meaning at all by itself; it must get its meaning from the antecedent to which it refers. The pronoun and its antecedent may appear in the same sentence or in separate sentences, but no matter where they appear, the pronoun and antecedent must be *in agreement*. The rule that is generally taught is that **a pronoun must agree (or match) its antecedent in number, gender, and person.** This last condition—agreement in person—can be discarded from the discussion at hand because it rarely causes any problem at all. But agreement in number and agreement in gender do cause problems, even for very learned speakers and writers.

A pronoun agrees with its antecedent in number when both refer to the same number of people or things. That is, a singular antecedent must be referred to by a singular pronoun; a plural antecedent requires a plural pronoun.

> A *contract* is binding only after *it* has been signed.
>
> These *checks* have no value until *they* are signed.

In the first example sentence above, the pronoun *it* agrees with its antecedent, *contract,* because both are singular—that is, both refer to only one item. In the second example sentence the plural pronoun *they* agrees with the plural noun *checks:* They both refer to more than one item.

The following example sentence is nonstandard because it contains a pronoun and an antecedent that do not agree in number. The antedecent (*employee*) is singular, but the pronoun that refers to it (*they*) is plural.

> *When an *employee* is late, *they* are docked an hour's pay.[1]

---

1. An asterisk (*) has been used throughout this book to identify words, phrases, and sentences that do not conform to the principles of standard usage.

Frequently, agreement problems result from two or more antecedents that are joined by a conjunction. When two (or more) singular antecedents are joined by *and,* a plural pronoun must be used to refer to them.

> *Nancy and Karen* play handball in *their* bare feet.

The two singular antecedents (*Nancy* and *Karen*) must be referred to by a plural pronoun (*their*) because they are joined by *and,* and they act as a unit consisting of more then one person. Naturally, when *and* joins two plural antecedents, or a singular and a plural antecedent, a plural pronoun must also be used: All antecedents joined by *and* create a plural unit.

When two (or more) singular antecedents are joined by *or* or *nor,* however, a singular pronoun must be used to refer to them.

> *Nancy or Karen* will take *her* handball lesson tomorrow. (not: **their*)

In the sentence above, the singular pronoun *her* agrees with its antecedent: *Nancy or Karen.* Because the singular antecedents are joined by *or,* each must be thought of separately—not as combining into a unit. Either *Nancy* will take her lesson *or Karen* will take her lesson.

When two or more plural antecedents are joined by *or* or *nor,* each is thought of separately, but, because each is plural, a plural antecedent is proper.

Although the case does not arise frequently, the question of what to do when *or* or *nor* joins a singular antecedent with a plural antecedent does tend to bother people.

When *or* or *nor* joins a singular and a plural antecedent, the meaning intended is almost always plural, and so a plural pronoun is called for. When a singular pronoun is used instead, a slightly different meaning is conveyed.

> Neither *Professor Moews* nor his *students* want *their* relationship to end. (Compare: *Neither *Professor Moews* nor his *students* want *his* relationship to end.)

The most frequent problem in agreement between pronouns and antecedents involves both agreement in number and agreement in gender. The problem originates, however, in the failure of many people to realize that some pronouns are always singular, some are always plural, and some can be either singular or plural. The following pronouns are *always* singular: *everyone, everybody, anyone, anybody, someone, somebody, no one, nobody, each, one, either,* and *neither.* Commit this list to memory, and always group these pronouns together in your mind. When one of these pronouns acts as an antecedent, only singular pronouns (*he, him, his, she, her, hers, it, its*) can be used to refer to it.

> *Each* of the boys has *his* own car. (not: **their* own car)

The antecedent of the pronoun *his* in the sentence above is the singular pronoun *each,* not the plural noun *boys.* Think of it this way: *Boys* could have been stated in a previous sentence, and the example sentence written *Each has his own car.* Now it is more obvious that *his* refers to *each,* not to *boys. Each* is one of those pronouns that are always singular, and so a pronoun that refers to *each* must also be singular: *his,* not **their.*

> *Someone* on the girls' basketball team left *her* uniform at home. (not: **their* uniform)

In the sentence above, the singular pronoun *her* refers to its antecedent, *someone,* which is also singular. The pronoun *someone* is always singular and can be thought of as meaning "some individual one." Similarly, *somebody* can be thought of as meaning "some individual body," *everyone* as "every individual one," *everybody* as "every individual body," and so on.

The following pronouns are always plural and, when they act as antecedents, must be referred to by another plural pronoun: *both, many, few,* and *several.* These pronouns pose little difficulty because it seems natural to refer to them with plural pronouns such as *they, them, their,* and *theirs.*

> The two criminals were brought to trial.
> *Both* were sentenced to jail for *their* crimes.

The following pronouns can be singular in some uses and plural in others: *some, any, most, all,* and *none.* Of this group, the pronoun *none* seems to offer the most usage problems. When *none* means "not a single one," it is generally considered singular and is referred to by a singular pronoun.

> *None* of the trees has lost *its* leaves.

However, some grammarians suggest *none* should be considered singular when it answers the question "How much?" and plural when it answers the question "How many?"

According to this rule, the previous example sentence should have been written: *None* of the trees have lost *their* leaves.

I prefer always to treat *none* as a singular pronoun unless doing so creates such a stilted and awkward sentence that the construction is more noticeable than the meaning I want to convey. When singular verbs and singular pronouns don't produce a natural agreement with *none,* I replace them with plural forms, and I feel no remorse whatsoever about doing so. Neither should you.

Earlier I said that the most common pronoun problem involves both agreement in number and agreement *in gender.* When a pronoun agrees with its antecedent in gender, they both refer to the same sex: The masculine pronouns *he, him,* and *his* refer to masculine antecedents, and the feminine pronouns *she, her,* and *hers* refer to feminine antecedents.

> *Uncle Chuck* played *his* harmonica while *Aunt Ethel* sang *her* favorite song.

When the antecedent is plural, no matter whether it refers to just one sex or both, the plural pronouns *they, them, their,* and *theirs* will agree in both number and gender.

> The *students* lined up early for *their* tickets.

A problem arises, however, when a singular pronoun that is used as an antecedent has a meaning that includes both males and females.

> Everybody should bring (*his, her, their*) plate into the kitchen.

Which pronoun should you use, *his, her,* or *their?* If you knew that *everybody* in attendance was a male, or that *everybody* was a female, the choice would be easy. But what if the group in question was composed of both males and females?

The easiest solution, of course, is to use *their* instead of *his* or *her*. But *their* is a plural pronoun, and the antecedent in question, *everybody,* belongs to that group of pronouns that are always singular. Using the plural pronoun *their* to refer to the singular antecedent *everybody* would mean that the pronoun and its antecedent would not agree in number and that the resulting sentence would be nonstandard.

> **Everybody* should bring *their* plate into the kitchen.

The traditional method for solving this problem is to use a masculine pronoun (*he, him,* or *his*) to refer to singular antecedents like *everybody, someone, anybody, no one,* etc.

> *Everybody* should bring *his* plate into the kitchen.
> If *anyone* calls, tell *him* I'll be back shortly.

This convention has stood for many years in spite of its seemingly sexist nature. English, you see, simply does not have a singular, neuter, personal pronoun that can be used in situations like these. There have been a few recent attempts to create such a word, but, like all efforts to "force" new words into a language rather than have them grow naturally, these attempts have failed miserably.

Some people argue that agreement in number is not as important as the damage caused by giving dominance to masculine forms. They suggest that the plural forms *they, them, their,* and theirs should be considered "correct" when used to refer to antecedents like *everybody* and *someone.* Indeed, there is sense in this view, and I believe that during the next few decades the "rules" of agreement will take into account the fact that some singular pronouns (*everybody,* for example) do convey a plural idea (*all people*), and that some plural pronouns (such as *their*) also convey a singular notion in certain constructions. This would not differ drastically from the dual nature accorded the pronouns *none, some, all, any,* and *most.*

However, the fact remains that, for now, the principle of agreement in number is considered rather fixed in standard usage: If you use a singular pronoun as an antecedent, you must refer to it with a singular pronoun. It is common today to hear (and read) the phrases "him or her," "he or she," and "his or her" used in place of *him, he,* and *his* to agree with a singular antecedent.

> *Everybody* should bring *his or her* plate into the kitchen.

While this substitution does solve the problem of gender, it also creates awkward and obvious repetitions that destroy the flow of the sentence.

> *No one* in *his* or *her* right mind would force *his or her* child to follow the same path *he or she* did in life.

Ugh! This is just awful! You may be able to use *he or she, his or her, him or her,* or *his or hers* once in a while, but repeated use of these phrases detracts from the idea you are trying to convey. I cannot recommend this solution to you any more than I can recommend your using the nonstandard plural pronouns for this use.

The answer lies, I think, in our ability to recast a sentence so that this problem of number and gender simply does not occur. For instance, by replacing the singular pronoun that is used as an antecedent with a plural noun, plural pronouns can be used later in the sentence.

> *Anyone* who wants to exchange *his* token can do so tomorrow.
> Recast: *All commuters* who want to exchange *their* tokens can do so tomorrow.

Or the entire sentence can be restructured.

> Tomorrow *you* will be able to exchange *your* tokens.
> *You* should *all* bring *your* plates into the kitchen.

In speaking, when you find yourself beginning a sentence with one of those singular pronoun antecedents, don't be afraid to refer to it with a masculine pronoun: That is a much better choice than using a nonstandard, plural form. You don't want to break up your conversation by recasting in mid-sentence, and you should be aware of the fact that once you start using phrases such as *his or her*, you may be trapped into using them over and over again in the same sentence. In writing, or when you have more time to structure what you are saying, avoid the situation entirely by using the ability you have to convey your idea in a form that is best suited to your audience.

PRONOUN REFERENCE

In order for the meaning of a pronoun to be clearly conveyed, the listener or reader must understand precisely which word or idea acts as the pronoun's antecedent. A common error, called *faulty pronoun reference*, occurs when a pronoun does not clearly refer to its intended antecedent.

The most common type of faulty reference stems from the fact that pronouns always *seem* to refer to the noun nearest them, even though their actual antecedents may be further back in the sentence or even in a previous sentence.

> *When I stumbled over the toys again, I glared at the children and threw *them* into the garbage pail.

The example sentence above *seems* to say that the *children* were thrown into the garbage pail. The actual antecedent of the pronoun *them,* of course, is the noun *toys.*

The ambiguity caused by faulty reference is not always humorous or far-fetched. The following example can convey two quite logical, but quite different, ideas.

> *The members of the city council met last night to discuss the city's laws concerning teenage drinking. More than half of *them* are sixty years old.

Are most of the *laws* sixty years old, or are most of the *council members* sixty years old?

Correcting this type of faulty reference requires placing the pronoun as close as possible to its intended antecedent or removing the pronoun and repeating the previous noun.

When I stumbled over the toys again, I threw *them* into the garbage pail and glared at the children.

The members of the city council met last night to discuss the city's laws concerning teenage drinking. More than half these laws are sixty years old.

Another type of faulty reference occurs when a sentence has no stated antecedent at all and depends upon the reader to supply one. The pronouns *it, they, this, that,* and *which* are frequently misused in this way.

*In Europe *they* pay twice as much for gasoline.

*Whenever the subject of inefficiency comes up, most people think of government. *This* is not true.

The italicized pronouns in the sentences above have no antecedents. The intended meaning of the first sentence is rather clear, but does the second sentence mean that most people do *not* think of government as being inefficient, or that government is *not* inefficient no matter what most people think? By replacing the pronoun in question with a meaningful noun or by recasting the sentence so that it includes all the information required by the reader, these examples of weak, vague, faulty reference can be eliminated.

In Europe motorists pay twice as much for gasoline.

Whenever the subject of inefficiency comes up, most people think of government. But government is no more inefficient than any other sector of society.

CHOOSING BETWEEN ADJECTIVES AND ADVERBS

The problem of choosing between *good* and *well, bad* and *badly, real* and *really,* or *slow* and *slowly* is the problem of choosing between adjectives and adverbs. It is one of the most widespread usage problems in the United States today, and it frequently causes many of the nonstandard usages that characterize the speech of sportscasters, game-show hosts, and weather reporters. The problem can be cured quite easily by following three simple steps:

1. Understand how the functions of adjectives and adverbs differ.
2. Decide whether the word in question functions as an adjective or as an adverb in the sentence at hand.
3. Know the difference between adjective and adverb forms.

The first two steps involve knowing how adjectives and adverbs change or limit the meaning of the words they modify. This topic is thoroughly discussed in Chapter 4, and you should read the sections titled "Understanding Adjectives" and "Understanding Adverbs" if you have any doubt about how these parts of speech function in a sentence.

That play wasn't *nearly* (not: *near*) as good as the last one.
You take yourself too *seriously*. (not: *serious*)
I have always wanted a *really* (not: *real*) fine pair of shoes.

The problem of incorrectly using an adverb when an adjective is called for occurs, primarily, after linking verbs. Remember: Linking verbs do not express an action; they merely link a noun or pronoun with an adjective that describes that noun or pronoun. Few errors result from linking verbs that are forms of the verb *be,* but when the linking verb is one of the "sense verbs" (*feel, taste, smell, look, sound*), adverbs frequently appear where adjectives should be.

> The food tasted *delicious.* (not: *deliciously)
> The explosion made the entire lab smell *terrible.* (not: *terribly)

The linking verb and adjective that cause the most difficulty for most people are *feel* and *bad.* When *feel* is a linking verb, that is, when it does not convey the idea of touching, it combines with the adjective *bad* to mean "upset" or "unhappy." In this context the adverb *badly* should not be used, and the expression *feel badly* is nonstandard.

> We all *feel bad* (not: *feel badly) about your accident.
> After I failed the test, I *felt bad* (not: *felt badly) for a week.

The adverb *badly,* however, is perfectly proper when it modifies a verb or an adjective.

> She was hurt *badly* (not: *bad) in the accident. (modifies the verb phrase *was hurt*)

Just remember that the phrase *feel bad* should sound as proper to you as *feel glad* or *feel sad* does. You wouldn't say "*I feel gladly*" or "*I feel sadly*," would you? Train your ear so that the phrase "*I feel badly*" sounds just as improper.

The most frequently misused adjective/ad-verb pair of all is *good/well.* Radio and television personalities continually bombard us with their misguided notion that these words are interchangeable.

> *You have done *good* up to this point.
> *He has been throwing *good* and running *good* throughout the first half.
> *Friends, if you aren't seeing so *good* these days, come to Ben's lenses.

Remember: *Good* is an adjective, and it can modify only nouns and pronouns; it cannot answer the question "How?" about a verb. The word you want in this case is the adverb *well.*

> You have done *well* up to this point.
> He has been throwing *well* and running *well* throughout the first half.
> Friends, if you aren't seeing so *well* these days, come to Ben's lenses.

Because it is an adjective, *good* can modify a noun or pronoun separated from it by a linking verb.

> Church bells sound *good* in the morning. (modifies *bells: good bells*)

When the linking verb describes someone's appearance or attitude, either *good* or *well* can be used as an adjective.

> Kay looks *good* in a bathing suit.
> Kay looks *well* in a bathing suit.

There is one case, however, in which *well* should be used as an adjective in place of *good.* When the linking verbs *look* or *feel* are used to express the idea of "illness" or "health," choose *well* instead of *good*. Train your ear so that *well* sounds correct in sentences like the following:

> Terry stayed home yesterday because he didn't feel *well*. (not: *good*)
> I feel *well* enough now to run five miles. (not: *good*)
> The nurse didn't think I looked *well*, and so she called the doctor. (not: *good*)

PROBLEMS IN MAKING COMPARISONS

A very common set of nonstandard usages springs from a general lack of understanding about the ways that adjectives can be compared. If you are unfamiliar with the meanings of the terms *positive degree, comparative degree, superlative degree, regular comparison,* and *irregular comparison,* read the material concerning "degrees of comparison" in the "Understanding Adjectives" section of Chapter 4.

DOUBLE COMPARISONS

Occasionally speakers and writers will create nonstandard adjective forms by changing an adjective's form twice when only one change is necessary. For example, a person who doesn't understand that the superlative form of the adjective *fast* is *fastest*, might use both methods of regular comparison and create a nonstandard *double comparison:*

> *Suzanne was the *most fastest* sprinter on the track team.

Double comparison also frequently results from a failure to understand the form of irregular adjectives. The adjective *worse,* for instance, is already in its comparative form, and so adding the suffix *-er* (*worser) creates a double comparison and a nonstandard adjective. Other forms to avoid are *bestest, *more better, *worstest, *more worse, *more farther,* and *most farthest.*

ILLOGICAL COMPARISON

Another nonstandard usage that comes from a failure to understand comparison of adjectives is called *illogical comparison.* This occurs when a speaker or writer compares one item with a group that includes that item.

> *My grandmother is *older* than anyone in our family.

The example sentence above attempts to compare the age of *my grandmother* with the age of all the members of *our family.* But the grandmother is also a member of that family, and she simply cannot be older than herself. This illogical comparison can be corrected by changing the sentence so that it can use the superlative degree, or by adding the word *other* or *else.*

> My grandmother is the *oldest* member of our family.
> My grandmother is older than any *other* member of our family.
> My grandmother is older than anyone *else* in our family.

FAULTY PUNCTUATION IN COMPARISONS

There is one other very common error that involves comparison of both adjectives and adverbs, and that is the use of a hyphen in forms that use the words *more, most, less* and *least.* Comparative and superlative forms that begin with these words do not require a hyphen. They are simply different forms of an adjective or adverb—just as a noun has a plural form or a personal pronoun has a possessive form. Do not fall into the trap of thinking that the first word in these comparative and superlative forms is like a prefix (such as *self-, ex-,* and *all-,* which are followed by a hyphen), or that the forms are compound adjectives (such as *well-planned* programs or *rose-colored* glasses).

*She was the *most-ambitious* person I had ever met.

She was the most ambitious person I had ever met.

*He seemed *less-confident* in front of an audience.

He seemed less confident in front of an audience.

USAGE CHECKLIST

The sentences in the following checklist contain usage problems that are discussed in Chapter 4 and Chapter 5. Some of the sentences contain usage errors, some contain two usages (only one of which is standard), and some are perfectly standard, requiring no changes at all. The answer key at the end identifies the change that each nonstandard sentence requires (shown in italic type), identifies the proper choice of the two usages given, or identifies (with the letter *C*) the sentences that are correct. The page numbers refer to the pages on which each particular usage problem is discussed.

1. The Jones' car is parked in our driveway.
2. At the end of the first round, we knew that the winner would be (he, him).
3. I don't particularly enjoy those (kind, kinds) of movies.
4. The inspector gave my partner and myself a small fine and a stern warning.
5. The plane was grounded because it's engines had not been properly inspected.
6. Whose the stranger over there in the corner?
7. The superintendent gave Fred and (I, me) a tour of the plant.
8. I wish I (was, were) as young as you are.
9. If my wife (was, were) here now, she would tell you the same thing.
10. I enjoy (laying, lying) out on a freshly cut lawn.
11. Yesterday we (laid, lay) out in the sun all afternoon.

12. Tell Larry that he (can, may) go to the game, but he must come right home.
13. Too much salt had made the food taste terribly.
14. I don't know which tasted worse: the steak, the salad, or the dessert.
15. We arrived (a, an) hour before the play began.
16. I (accidentally, accidently) dropped the hammer on my foot.
17. It was a difficult decision; however, it was one that had to be made.
18. Either Jake or Floyd will have to give (his, their) speech on Friday.
19. Someone in the soprano section is not singing (her, their) part correctly.
20. Babe Ruth is more famous than any player in baseball.
21. Everybody should be concerned about the education (his, their) children receive.
22. My opponent had a good net game and a real strong serve.
23. I felt bad about losing that match.
24. Johnny didn't feel (good, well) enough to come to school today.
25. This is the (most-wonderful, most wonderful) gift I have ever received.

Answers: 1. *Joneses'* (p. 34) 2. he (p. 35) 3. kinds (p. 38) 4. my partner and *me* (p. 41) 5. *its* (p. 42) 6. *Who's* (p. 42) 7. me (p. 36) 8. were (p. 53) 9. were (p. 53) 10. lying (p. 54) 11. lay (p. 54) 12. may (p. 51) 13. taste *terrible* (pp. 56, 80-82) 14. *worst* (p. 56) 15. an (p. 59) 16. accidentally (p. 64) 17. C (p. 62) 18. his (p. 76) 19. her (p. 77) 20. any *other* player (p. 82) 21. his (p. 77) 22. *really* (p. 80) 23. C (p. 81) 24. well (p. 81) 25. most wonderful (p. 82)

6. Understanding the Parts of a Sentence

Many students become confused (and many adults remain confused) about the terminology used in discussing language; because of this, they become disenchanted with the entire subject. A great deal of this confusion is, I believe, a direct result of the failure on the part of textbooks and teachers to effectively separate the *parts of speech* from the *parts of a sentence*. After reading this chapter you should be able to distinguish these sets of terms and understand how they are used in the chapters that follow.

The sentence is the basic unit of communication in the English language. A sentence is the only unit that can convey a complete thought. A sentence can also combine with other sentences to convey larger, more complex thoughts and single thoughts more precisely.

Every English sentence—that is, every complete thought—is a structure built of several parts. These sentence parts, although meaningless in themselves, can be easily identified and labeled according to how each contributes to the expression of a complete thought. The parts of a sentence are groups of words (sometimes only single words) that act in different ways to convey the idea expressed by the sentence. The parts of speech that were discussed in Chapter 4 can help you describe the words within each group, but a part-of-speech label tells you virtually nothing about the role a word plays in helping express a particular complete thought.

Keep the definitions and labels that apply to the parts of a sentence grouped together in your mind and separated from the parts of speech. If you view these two sets of terms as independent groups, you will be able to understand more easily how one group can be used to discuss the other.

The Sentence

A sentence is usually defined as a group of words that expresses a complete thought. Because this seems to be a rather vague definition for the basic unit of communication in our language, many linguists and textbooks have proposed other definitions, but none has proved more useful or more acceptable than the traditional one. Actually, the only problem with the traditional definition is that a "complete thought" is somewhat difficult to explain. It is rather like the penalty of "holding" in football, which a referee once described with "I can't explain exactly what it is, but I know it when I see it." Most of us can tell the difference between complete thoughts and incomplete thoughts when we see them side by side. Complete thoughts "say something about something," but incomplete thoughts do not. An incomplete thought that is punctuated as though it were a complete thought is called a *fragment*.[1]

We had a visit from Dr. Bower. (complete thought)

*The minister at our church. (fragment)[2]

---

1. For a complete look at sentence fragments, see Chapter 8, pages 110-111.
2. An asterisk (*) has been used throughout this book to identify words, phrases, and sentences that do not conform to the principles of standard usage.

Eleanor turned down the thermostat. (complete thought)
*Before leaving for the weekend. (fragment)

In order to express a complete thought, a sentence must have a *subject* and a *predicate*. These two elements—the subject and the predicate—are the most important sentence parts of all because they exist in every complete sentence.

THE SUBJECT

The subject of a sentence is the part about which something is being said. The subject can be found by asking "Who or what is doing the action?" or, if there is no action expressed in the sentence, "Who or what is the sentence talking about?"

The fiery meteor slammed into the mountain at tremendous speed.

Question: Who or what is doing the action? (That is, who or what *slammed into the mountain*?)
Answer: *the fiery meteor* The subject of this sentence is *the fiery meteor.*

Someone in this room is the murderer.

Question: Who or what is the sentence talking about?
Answer: *someone in this room* The subject of this sentence is *someone in this room.*

The subject of a sentence may consist of several words (as in the previous examples), or it may be just one word. Every subject, however, has a noun or a pronoun that is the most important word in that subject. This noun or pronoun is the main word in the subject because it names the person, place, thing, or idea that is talked about in the rest of the sentence. The noun or pronoun that is the main word in the subject is called the *simple subject*. The simple subject and all the words that modify it together form the *complete subject* of the sentence.

The questions that were asked about the previous example sentences helped reveal the complete subject of each sentence: *the fiery meteor* and *someone in this room.* The simple subject of the first sentence is the noun *meteor;* the simple subject of the second sentence is the pronoun *someone.* When there are no modifiers in the subject of a sentence, the simple subject and the complete subject are the same.

Harry Houdini was the first person to fly a plane over Australia.

Complete Subject: *Harry Houdini*
Simple Subject: *Harry Houdini*

Some sentences that give a command or make a request appear not to have a subject at all. Still they convey a complete thought.

Put that knife down!
Pass the catsup, please.

These sentences convey a complete thought (and, therefore, are complete sentences) because both the speaker and the listener understand whom the sentence is talking about. The unstated subject in sentences like these is always the pronoun *you* because the sentences are actually just shortened forms that have removed *you* and the helping verb *will.*

(You will) put that knife down!
(Will you) please pass the catsup?

The subject of commands and requests that refer to an unstated *you* is written as *you (understood).*

Come here this instant! [Subject: *you (understood)*]

THE PREDICATE

The predicate is the part of a sentence that says something about the subject. The predicate includes everything in the sentence that is not part of the subject. It answers the questions "What did the subject do?" or "What is being said about the subject?"

Three major companies announced record profits today.

Complete Subject: *three major companies*
Simple Subject: *companies*
Predicate: *announced record profits today*

The predicate usually follows the subject in a sentence, but it may precede it.

Under the bridge lived a haggard, old troll.

Complete Subject: *a haggard, old troll.*
Simple Subject: *troll*
Predicate: *under the bridge lived*

Just as subjects can be divided into complete subjects and simple subjects, so predicates can be divided, too. All the words that say something about the subject form the *complete predicate* of a sentence. Within that complete predicate there is always a verb (or verb phrase) that is the main word in the predicate. This verb or verb phrase is called the *simple predicate*. Because the simple predicate is always a verb, the term *verb* is sometimes used in place of the term *simple predicate*. (*Verb,* then, is the one term that can be either a part of speech or a sentence part.)

Huckleberry Finn is my favorite character in literature.

Complete Predicate: *is my favorite character in literature*
Simple Predicate: *is*

The Bickersons should have been here by now.

Complete Predicate: *should have been here by now*
Simple Predicate: *should have been*

COMPOUND SUBJECTS AND COMPOUND PREDICATES

Many sentences have more than one simple subject; many have more than one verb. A sentence that has two or more simple subjects—each using the same verb—is said to have a *compound subject*. The simple subjects within a compound subject are usually joined by commas or by the conjunctions *and* or *or.*

The *garage,* the *porch,* and the front *door* had been painted red.

In the example above, the three nouns *garage, porch,* and *door* are *compound subjects* because the verb in the sentence (*had been painted*) applies to each of them.

Either *Janet* or *Gail* will sing at the banquet.

Compound Subject: *Janet . . . Gail*

When a predicate includes two or more verbs that apply to the same subject, the sentence is said to have a *compound predicate.*

The candidate *spoke* for ten minutes and *left* immediately.

Simple Subject: *candidate*
Compound Predicate: *spoke . . . left*

In the sentence above, both verbs, *spoke* and *left,* say something about the same subject: *the candidate.* Therefore, this sentence has a compound predicate (or *compound verb*).

Occasionally a sentence will have both a compound subject and a compound predicate. In this case, all the verbs must apply equally to all the subjects.

The legislators and their aides studied the bill and worked for its passage.

Compound Subject: *legislators . . . aides*
Compound Predicate: *studied . . . worked*

COMPLEMENTS

Some complete sentences need only two words: a subject and a verb.

Birds fly.

Even some long sentences can be reduced to just a single subject and a verb, and still convey a complete thought.

Everyone in our group swam across the lake.

Simple Subject and Verb: *Everyone swam.*

Although some verbs need only a subject in order to express a complete thought, many verbs require more. When a subject is added to these verbs, their meaning is still incomplete. Notice how the following subject/verb pairs demand something that will complete their meaning.

Uncle Don raises _____. (*What* does he raise?)
Miss Munhall thanked _____. (*Whom* did she thank?)

Each of these groups is incomplete by itself, and, therefore, neither is a complete sentence. When the missing element is added, however, each expresses a complete thought.

Uncle Don raises *horses.*
Miss Munhall thanked *everyone.*

A complement is a word or a group of words that completes the meaning begun by the subject and the verb. The word *complement* means "something that completes," and is sometimes replaced by the term *completer.*[3] The complements in the following sentences are in italic type. Notice how each completes the meaning begun by the subject and the verb.

On weekends I mow *lawns.*
The leaves on the trees turned *red* and *gold.*
For Mother's Day I sent *her flowers.*
I always say *whatever comes into my head.*

There are five main types of complements: direct objects, indirect objects, predicate nouns, predicate pronouns, and predicate adjectives.[4]

Direct Objects

When a sentence contains an action verb, a complement called a *direct object* is necessary in order to show upon what or upon whom the subject performed the action of the verb. **A direct object is a noun or a pronoun that receives the action expressed by an action verb.** A direct object answers the question "What?" or "Whom?" about the subject and an action verb.

Jim broke his *wrist* yesterday.

Direct Object: *wrist* (Jim broke *what*?)

I must tell *her* before I go.

Direct Object: *her* (I must tell *whom*?)

Direct objects, like all nouns and pronouns, may be modified by adjectives and prepositional phrases. Only the noun or pronoun, however, is considered the direct object.

Direct objects may also be compound—that is,

---

3. *Complement,* like the word *complete,* begins with the letters *comple-.* Do not confuse *complement* with the word *compliment,* which means "a flattering remark."

4. Sentences that use verbs like *choose, call, name, make,* or *think* may have a direct object and an *object complement* (or *objective complement*). An object complement is a noun or an adjective that refers to the same person or thing as the direct object.

The court has appointed you the child's *guardian.* (Direct Object: *you,* Object Complement: *guardian*)
I call your idea ridiculous. (Direct Object: *idea,* Object Complement: *ridiculous*)

a single action verb may have two or more connected direct objects.

> I want two *hamburgers,* four *colas,* and some *napkins,* please.

> Direct Object: *hamburgers ... colas ... napkins*

Indirect Objects

Some sentences that have a direct object also require another complement to complete their meaning. **An indirect object is a noun or a pronoun that shows to whom or for whom an action was performed.**

> Dad gave *us* a stern lecture.

> Direct Object: *lecture*
> Indirect Object: *us*

> Dr. Potter lent *Tom* the money.

> Direct Object: *money*
> Indirect Object: *Tom*

Notice that each example sentence above also has a direct object. An indirect object always precedes a direct object in a sentence and answers the question "To whom?" or "For whom?" about the subject, the action verb, and the direct object.

To find an indirect object, first find the direct object by asking "What?" or "Whom?" about the subject and the action verb.

> We built Snoopy a new doghouse.

> Question: We built *what?*
> Direct Object: *doghouse*

Now ask "To whom?" or "For whom?" about the subject, the action verb, and the direct object.

>   (Sub.) (Verb)   (Dir. Obj.)
> Question: We built   a new doghouse *for whom?*

> Indirect Object: *Snoopy*

(Although indirect objects very often refer to people, they may also refer to inanimate objects. *We gave the boat a new coat of paint.* Indirect Object: *boat*)

If the preposition *to* or *for* actually appears in the sentence, the noun or pronoun that follows it is *not* an indirect object, but the object of that preposition.

> Yesterday the Congress sent that bill to the President.

> Direct Object: *bill*
> Indirect Object: (none)

> Yesterday the Congress sent the President that bill.

> Direct Object: *bill*
> Indirect Object: *President*

Subject Complements

Direct objects and indirect objects complement, or complete, the meaning of the verb in a sentence. Three other types of complements, however, complete the meaning of the subject in a sentence. For this reason, predicate nouns, predicate pronouns, and predicate adjectives are known as *subject complements.* **A subject complement is a noun, pronoun, or adjective that follows a linking verb and identifies or describes the subject.**

Subject complements can follow only linking verbs because, as the name "linking verb" implies, a linking verb provides the link or connection between the subject and the word that identifies or describes that subject. The most common linking verbs are the forms of *be,* including the verb phrases that end in *be, being,* and *been.*

> Physics is my favorite *subject.*
> She and I were *friends* long ago.
> The thief must be *someone* in this room.
> The winner should have been *he.*

The subject complements in the example sentences above are in italic. Notice that each follows a linking verb, and each identifies the subject of the sentence. If the subject complement is a noun (as in the first two example sentences), it is called a *predicate noun*. If the subject complement is a pronoun (as in the third and fourth example sentences), it is called a *predicate pronoun*.[5] The linking verb acts like an equal sign (=) because the predicate noun or predicate pronoun is just another name for the subject of the sentence.

Subject		Subject Complement
physics	=	subject
she and I	=	friends
thief	=	someone
winner	=	he

Notice that the subject form (*he*) was used as the predicate pronoun in the fourth example sentence. Because the subject complement refers to the subject of the sentence, the subject form should always be used when a personal pronoun functions as a subject complement. (See Chapter 7, page 100.)

When an adjective that follows a linking verb modifies and describes the subject of a sentence, that adjective is called a *predicate adjective*. Predicate adjectives are subject complements because they appear in the predicate and refer to the subject of the subject of the sentence.

Your complexion is *flawless.*
This exam will be *easy.*
This map should have been *larger.*

The predicate adjectives in the example sentences above are in italic. Notice that each follows a linking verb and that each modifies the subject of the sentence (*flawless* complexion, *easy* exam, *larger* map).

Predicate adjectives frequently follow other linking verbs as well as the various forms of *be*. The verbs *seem, taste, smell, sound, look, feel, appear, grow,* and *become* are commonly used as linking verbs to connect a subject with a predicate adjective that describes that subject.

His eyes looked *tired.* (*tired* eyes)
The child had grown *tall.* (*tall* child)
This fruit tastes *bitter* to me. (*bitter* fruit)

Subject complements, like direct objects and indirect objects, may be compound, as in the examples below.

Each entry must be *original, neat,* and *signed.*

Subject: *entry*
Predicate Adjective: *original . . . neat . . . signed* (*original* entry, *neat* entry, *signed* entry)

The victim could just as easily have been *you* or *I.*

Subject: *victim*
Predicate Pronoun: *you . . . I* (victim = *you,* victim = *I*)

Boston is the *capital* of Massachusetts and the largest *city* in the state.

Subject: *Boston*
Predicate Noun: *capital . . . city* (Boston = *capital,* Boston = *city*)

Although predicate nouns, predicate pronouns, and predicate adjectives appear in the predicate and seem to answer the question "What?" about the subject and the verb just as direct objects do, you must not confuse subject complements with direct objects. Keep in mind that subject complements differ from direct objects in two important ways. First, subject complements can follow only linking verbs, while direct objects can follow only action verbs. Second, subject complements always refer to, identify, or describe the subject of the sentence. Direct objects

---

5. Predicate nouns and predicate pronouns are often grouped together and called *predicate nominatives.*

(and indirect objects) almost never refer to the same person, place, or thing as the subject of the sentence.[6]

SENTENCE PATTERNS

By using abbreviations for the various sentence parts, you can reduce many English sentences to a series of a few letters, and you can classify these sentences according to the pattern of their parts.

subject = S
verb = V
direct object = DO
indirect object = IO
subject complement = SC

Simply place the abbreviations listed above over the sentence parts they apply to and then list the letters in the order they appear. The sequence of letters serves to classify the sentence according to its structure.

S   V
Walter walks. (Pattern: S–V)

S   V
Walter always walks to the store. (Pattern: S–V)

S   V IO   DO
Kathy gave us a report on sun spots. (Pattern: S—V—IO—DO)

       S   V SC
In 1961 John F. Kennedy became president of the United States. (Pattern: S–V–SC)

     S   V   SC
The edge of this knife has grown dull. (Pattern: S–V–SC)

DIAGRAMING

Another way that the structure of sentences can be shown is through a *sentence diagram*. While there are several different types of sentence diagrams, all use a series of lines to show how individual words function in a specific sentence. Keep in mind that sentence diagrams are only a means to an end—not an end in themselves. They are useful only to the extent that they help reveal the relationships between the various parts of a sentence. A person who has mastered the skill of drawing sentence diagrams correctly may not have any skill at all in creating standard English sentences. Properly used, however, sentence diagrams can be instructive and fun as well.

The most commonly used type of sentence diagram begins with the placement of the simple subject and the simple predicate (verb) on a horizontal line that represents the *sentence base*. A short vertical line is then drawn between the subject and the verb.

A complement is also part of the sentence base, and so any complement (except an indirect object) is also placed on this main horizontal line, to the right of the simple subject and the verb. A direct object is indicated by a short line extending straight up from (but not through) the main horizontal line. A subject complement (predicate noun, predicate pronoun, or predicate adjective) is indicated by a line extending up from the main horizontal line, but pointing back at an angle toward the subject.

All young jockeys soon learn an important lesson.

---

6. The only time a direct object can refer to the subject is when the direct object is a reflexive pronoun: Nancy injured *herself* during gym.

His extremely courageous act should be a symbol of the American spirit.

act | should be \ symbol

One way that sentence diagrams differ from the sentence patterns discussed earlier is that sentence diagrams show *all* the words that appear in a sentence, including all the modifiers. Adjectives and adverbs are written on diagonal lines that extend down from the words they modify.

All young jockeys soon learn an important lesson.

jockeys | learn | lesson.
All / young / soon / an / important

When possessive nouns and possessive pronouns function as adjectives in a sentence, they are placed on a diagonal line under the word they modify. When an adverb modifies an adjective or another adverb, its line is connected to that of the word it modifies.

Janet's day began almost too smoothly.

day | began
Janet's / smoothly / too / almost

Because prepositional phrases always function as adjectives or as adverbs, they, too, extend down from the words they modify. The preposition is written on a diagonal line, and the object of that preposition is written on a short, horizontal line extending to the right. Adjectives and other prepositional phrases that modify this object can then be written on diagonal lines below it.

Everyone in the audience laughed at the same line in the speech.

Everyone | laughed
in / audience / at / line / in / speech
the / the / same / the

Indirect objects are treated like prepositional phrases: The preposition that is implied but not stated (either *to* or *for*) is shown in parentheses beneath the verb, and the indirect object appears on a horizontal line to the right. (In some sentence diagrams the implied *to* or *for* is not shown at all.)

He gave me a black eye.

He | gave | eye
(to) / me / a / black

92

Conjunctions (and other connecting words) are written on a broken line that runs between the words they connect. Notice that the broken lines are sometimes horizontal and sometimes vertical.

A snide or careless remark can hurt the listener's feelings and can embarrass the speaker.

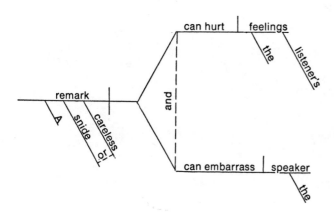

7. COMMON PROBLEMS WITH SENTENCE PARTS

In the last chapter I suggested that you keep the labels that apply to the parts of speech separate from those that apply to the parts of a sentence. It is important that you understand how each element differs from the others *in its group.* But if you now understand the various forms that nouns, pronouns, and verbs can adopt, and if you understand the relationship between subjects, predicates, and complements, you will be able to use both sets of terms to help you through the two usage areas that cause more errors than any others in the language: subject/verb agreement and personal pronouns as complements.

SUBJECT VERB AGREEMENT

The simple subject and the simple predicate (the verb) must agree in number. This hard and fast rule of English is easy to understand but sometimes difficult to observe. All it says is that if the noun or pronoun serving as the subject of a sentence is singular, the verb in that sentence must be in its singular form, too. If the subject refers to more than one person, place, thing, or idea, the verb must be in its plural form. The rule seems even simpler when you remember that, except for the verb *be,* it is only in the present

tense that main verbs even have different singular and plural forms. Then why is this rule so frequently violated?

One reason for the frequency of errors is that many sentences have two or more separate subjects that are joined by a conjunction. Do these compound subjects require a singular or a plural verb? If the subjects are joined by *and,* the answer is simple: *subjects joined by **and** take a plural verb.*

> *Toby **and** Fran are* on their way.
> Three *cookies **and** a sandwich were* left on the tray.

The one exception to this rule is the case in which the subjects joined by *and* are generally thought of as a unit. The phrase "ham and eggs," for example, means "one type of meal"; "Stein and Day" means "one publishing house." Although the nouns are joined by *and,* the nouns together form a single idea and require a singular verb.

> The *Stars and Stripes was* carried to the moon.

While the conjunction *and* tells you to lump the subjects together (thereby making their number "more than one"), the conjunctions *or* and *nor* tell you to view each individual subject separately. Therefore, *singular*

95

*subjects joined by **or** or **nor** take a singular verb.*

> Either the *coach* **or** the *general manager is* responsible.
> (Either the *coach is* responsible, *or* the *general manager is* responsible.)

Of course, when two or more plural subjects are joined by *or* or *nor,* a plural verb must be used. Each subject is considered separately, but each subject is plural.

> Neither the *paintings* **nor** the *sculptures were* damaged. (Neither the *paintings were* damaged nor the *sculptures were* damaged.)

But if *or* or *nor* indicate that the subjects should be considered separately, what do you do when one subject is singular and one is plural? *When a singular subject and a plural subject are joined by **or** or **nor**, the verb agrees with the subject that is nearer to the verb in the sentence.*

> Neither the *students* **nor** the *teacher was* on time.
> Neither the *teacher* **nor** the *students were* on time.

This construction, however, is often avoided because it appears rather awkward to many people. Usually the ideas can be easily recast into a more natural form.

> The students weren't on time; neither was the teacher.

Try to think of *and, or,* and *nor* as signal flares that warn you whenever you speak, write, hear, or read one of these constructions in a sentence. Their warning tells you to be careful about the form of the verb that follows in the sentence. If you remember that *and* tells you to lump the subjects together, while *or* and *nor* tell you to consider each subject separately, your problems will be few.

DETERMINING THE REAL SUBJUCT

While many errors in subject/verb agreement can be traced to difficulties with compound subjects, perhaps even more stem from an inability to properly identify the subject itself. The "real" subject of a sentence—the noun or pronoun that is the simple subject and actually determines the form of the verb—is sometimes hidden within the complete subject, and locating it requires some digging. Other nouns and pronouns that come between the real subject and its verb are often mistaken for that real subject.

> *A good set of tools are essential for this job.[1]

The example sentence above is nonstandard because the subject and verb do not agree in number. The verb *are* is plural and appears to agree with the plural noun *tools.* But the real subject of this sentence is the noun *set,* not tools.

> A good *set* of tools *is* required for this job.

The noun *tools* is the object of the preposition *of;* the prepositional phrase *of tools* modifies the subject, *set.* Because prepositional phrases always act as modifiers, the subject of

---

1. An asterisk (*) has been used throughout this book to identify words, phrases, and sentences that do not conform to the principles of standard usage.

a sentence is never part of a prepositional phrase.

A *team* of medics *was* sent to the scene. (singular subject and a singular verb)
The *boxes* on the deck of the ship *were* washed overboard. (plural subject and plural verb)

Expression such as "together with," "in addition to," and "as well as" frequently come between the real subject and the verb. A noun or pronoun that follows one of these expressions, then, cannot be the real subject and does not determine the form of the verb.

The *table,* as well as the chairs, *has* not been delivered.
The *book,* together with a bill of sale, *is* being shipped.
In an hour the *judge,* in addition to the twelve jurors, *is* due to return.

AGREEMENT WITH PRONOUN SUBJECTS

Errors in subject/verb agreement are very common when an indefinite pronoun serves as the subject of a sentence. These pronouns also pose problems in agreement between pronoun and antecedent (see Chapter 5, pages 75-79) because many people fail to understand which pronouns are singular, which are plural, and which can be either. However, they pose an additional problem in agreement between subject and verb because many people fail to identify them as the real subject of a sentence.

The pronouns *everyone, everybody, anyone, anybody, someone, somebody, no one, nobody, each, one, either,* and *neither* are always singular. When one of these pronouns functions as the subject of a sentence, subject/verb agreement demands that a singular verb also be used.

Everyone has a favorite hobby. (meaning: every single one *has* . . .)
Nobody was in the room. (meaning: no single body *was* . . .)

Indefinite pronouns that stand alone in the subject (as in the previous examples) pose little difficulty. But many times these pronouns will be followed by one or more prepositional phrases. Keep in mind that the subject of a sentence is never found in a prepositional phrase, and, therefore, the form of the verb is not determined by the nouns or pronouns within a prepositional phrase.

Everyone in both families *was* pleased.
Nobody in the stands *is* sitting.

Even though the nouns that separate the real subject from the verb in the sentences above are plural, the verbs are singular because the real subjects are singular pronouns.

The pronouns *both, many, few,* and *several* are always plural. When these pronouns function as the subject of a sentence, a plural verb must be used.

Several of the chores *were* left undone.
Many in the town *were* homeless.

The pronouns *some, any, most, all,* and *none,* can be either singular or plural depending upon how they are used in a sentence. Generally speaking, when these pronouns answer the question "How much?" they are singular; when they answer the question "How many?" they are plural.

Some of the cake *has* been eaten. (*How much* has been eaten?)
Some of the cakes *were* frosted. (*How many* were frosted?)

Most of the building *is* standing. (*How much* is standing?)

Most of the buildings *were* destroyed. *(How many* were destroyed?)

Of this group the pronoun *none* is by far the most troublesome. Some authorities argue that *none* should always be considered singular, while others contend that it can also have a plural meaning. I suggest that you use a singular verb to agree with the pronoun *none* unless doing so creates an obviously awkward construction. If your meaning clearly answers the question "How many?" you should not be afraid to use a plural verb when doing so conveys your idea more clearly to your audience.

None of the message *was* legible.
None of the passengers *was* injured.
or, *None* of the passengers *were* injured.

SPECIAL CASES

Nouns like *jury, crew, committee, team, family, class, band, flock,* etc., name a unit or group that is composed of several people or things. These *collective nouns* occasionally pose agreement problems because they can be used with a singular verb to refer to one group, or with a plural verb to refer to the several members of that group.

The school board *is* meeting at eight o'clock. (meaning: the board as a unit)
The school board *have* been arguing among themselves for hours. (meaning: the members of the board)

Using a plural verb to agree with a collective noun creates an awkward construction, and one that I suggest you avoid whenever possible. Use a singular verb whenever you can, and if you want to refer to the various members that are included in a collective noun, recast the sentence so that your meaning is clear to your audience.

The *members* of the school board *have* been arguing among themselves for hours.

Nouns that express amounts or measurements are considered singular.

Two *weeks is* too short for a European vacation.
Fifty *dollars was* taken in the robbery.

But when these nouns refer to several separate items or units, a plural verb must be used.

Only two *weeks are* remaining in the year.
Fifty *dollars are* printed every second.

The word *foot* can be used as part of an adjective describing height or distance: She landed a five-*foot* sailfish. But this form is nonstandard (and should be replaced with *feet*) in sentences like the following:

*The fish was more than five *foot* long.
*He stood six *foot* tall.

Fractions and other nouns referring to a part or portion are singular when they answer the question "How much?" and plural when they answer the question "How many?"

Half of a circle *is* a semicircle. (*How much* of a circle?)
Half of the eggs *were* broken. (*How many* of the eggs?)

Some singular nouns such as *mumps, measles, physics, checkers, news, economics,* etc., appear to be plural because they end in *-s*. All of these words, however, require singular verbs. Similarly, titles of books, movies, poems, plays, etc., may include plural nouns, but these titles refer to a single work and are, therefore, singular.

> The *news* from the front *is* good.
> "*Trees*" is my sister's favorite poem.

On the other hand, words like *eyeglasses, scissors* (be sure to spell it with a *c*), *pants, pliers,* and *trousers* refer to individual items, but they are still considered plural.

> *Scissors are* designed for right-handed people.

Sentences that include a predicate noun can cause an agreement problem when the subject and the predicate noun differ in number. Remember: The verb must agree with its subject; it does not have to agree with a predicate noun.

>   (Sub.)   (Verb) (P.N.)
> The best *part* of our trip *was* the *days* on the beach.

Two final cautions and then we'll move along. In all the sentences I have shown so far, the subject has preceded the verb. But many sentences that begin with the words *here* or *there* or with a prepositional phrase have a "delayed subject." That is, the subject follows the verb in the sentence. In these sentences, too, the subject must agree with its verb in number.

> *There *seems* to be a few *contradictions* in your story. (plural subject/singular verb)
> There *seem* to be a few contradictions in your story.

> *Around the edges *were* an intricate *design*. (singular subject/plural verb)
> Around the edges *was* an intricate design.

So many children (and adults, too) who correctly use the singular form *does* with singular subjects, and the plural form *do* with plural subjects, seem to forget that the contractions *doesn't* and *don't* also differ in number. *Doesn't* can be used with all singular nouns and pronouns (except *I*) while *don't* can be used only with plural subjects (and *I*). Errors such as the following should not be allowed to go unchallenged.

> *He *don't* know anything about it.
> He *doesn't* know anything about it.

> *It *don't* matter to me at all.
> It *doesn't* matter to me at all.

PERSONAL PRONOUNS AS COMPLEMENTS

Because personal pronouns are the only parts of speech that have different subject and object forms, you might expect that people would have difficulty in using personal pronouns as complements—and you would be right. These difficulties, however, can be overcome by knowing what the standard forms are and by training your ear to accept these standard forms as "natural."

The object form of a personal pronoun should be used when the pronoun acts as a direct object or as an indirect object. The pronouns *me, you, him, her, it, us,* and *them* can be used to receive the action of a verb (direct object) or to show for whom or to whom that action was performed (indirect object).

Miss Campbell sent *me* to the office. (direct object).

The bank lent *me* the money I needed. (indirect object)

The boss thanked *him* for helping. (direct object)

The fans gave *them* a standing ovation. (indirect object)

Very few people mistakenly use the subject forms for direct and indirect objects like those in the sentences above. But when there is more than one direct or indirect object in the sentence, mistakes become more common.

Miss Campbell sent *him* and *me* to the office. (not: *he* and *I*)

The bank lent Jim and *me* the money we needed. (not: *Jim and *I*)

The boss thanked Mary and *him* for helping. (not: *Mary and *he*)

The fans gave *them* and *us* a standing ovation. (not: *they* and *we*)

The subject form of a personal pronoun should be used when the pronoun follows a linking verb and acts as a predicate pronoun. The forms *I, we, you, he, she, it,* and *they* are the only personal pronouns that can be used as predicate pronouns. Predicate pronouns, you will recall, follow a linking verb (usually a form of *be*) and identify the subject of the sentence. Even when there is only one predicate pronoun in a sentence, mistakes are common, and so you must train your ear to accept the subject form as the "natural" form for a predicate pronoun.

It was *I* who called the other day. (not: *It was *me* . . .*)

It is *they* who are to blame. (not: *It is *them* . . .*)

It must have been *he* you saw. (not: *It must have been *him* . . .*)

When two personal pronouns act as predicate pronouns, both must be in their subject forms.

The first performers will be *she* and *I*. (not: *will be *her* and *me*)

The key to the standard usage of predicate pronouns lies in listening for a form of the verb *be*. When you hear *is, are, was, were, am,* or a verb phrase ending in *be* or *been*, it should set off an alarm telling you that if a personal pronoun is coming, it must be in its subject form. Keep in mind that *who* is a subject form and that *whom* is an object form. Standard usage of these pronouns and of pronouns that are used as objects of a preposition is discussed in Chapter 9, pages 119-123.

USAGE CHECKLIST

The sentences in the following checklist concern usage problems that are discussed in Chapter 6 and Chapter 7. Some of the sentences contain usage errors, some contain two usages—only one of which is standard, and some are perfectly standard, requiring no changes at all. The answer key at the bottom identifies the changes that each nonstandard sentence requires (shown in italic type), identifies the proper choice of the two usages given, or identifies (with the letter *C*) the sentences that are correct. The page numbers refer to the pages on which each particular usage problem is discussed.

1. Bell & Howell are developing a new movie projector.
2. Neither the sun nor the moon (was, were) visible through the dense smog.
3. A group of activists have blocked the entrance to the university.
4. My camera, together with all my lenses and accessories, (was, were) taken in the robbery.
5. Neither of the cars get very good gas mileage.
6. Only one of the apartments in the three buildings was vacant.
7. It used to be that fifty cents were all it took to see a movie.
8. Measles, on the other hand, (afflicts, afflict) children more than adults.
9. The best part of the series (was, were) the episodes near the end.
10. There (seems, seem) to be a couple areas of disagreement.
11. The police officer told him and I to be more careful.
12. The bank gave Jim and (I, me) two days to come up with the money.
13. A cab will take she and they to the meeting.
14. The real culprit in this matter was he.
15. It should have been (they, them), but it wasn't.

Answers: 1. *is* (p. 95) 2. was (p. 95) 3. *has* (p. 96) 4. was (p. 97) 5. *gets* (p. 97) 6. C (p. 96) 7. *was* (p. 98) 8. afflicts (p. 98) 9. was (p. 99) 10. seem (p. 99) 11. *me* (p. 99) 12. me (p. 99) 13. *her and them* (p. 100) 14. C (p. 100) 15. they (p. 100)

8. Understanding Phrases and Clauses

When introducing children to the functions of the eight parts of speech, it is best to use one-word examples for each. The simplicity of seeing how a single word can alter a sentence in a certain way improves the chances that the concept will be understood. Similarly, single-word examples of a subject or a direct object allow the child to see the position and function of these sentence parts. In this chapter we will depart from the one-word examples and show how several words can function together to act as a single part of speech or as a single part of a sentence.

THE PHRASE

In discussing the parts of speech in Chapter 4, I mentioned that a main verb could be coupled with helping verbs to form a *verb phrase*. The two or more words in a verb phrase all function together and act just like a one-word verb in a sentence. Similarly, all the words in the *complete* subject of the sentence below function together and act just like the one-word *simple* subject.

The long, dark night was over at last.

Complete Subject: *the long, dark night*
Simple Subject: *night*

The complete subject is actually a *noun phrase* because the noun *night* and all its modifiers function together and act as a single noun.

In Chapter 4 I also mentioned that a preposi-
tion, the object of that preposition, and all the words that modify that object form a unit called a *prepositional phrase*.

I fell *down the basement steps.*

Preposition: *down*
Object: *steps*
Modifiers: *the, basement*

In the sentence above, the entire prepositional phrase, *down the basement steps,* acts as an adverb to answer the question "Where?"

A prepositional phrase can also function as an adjective to modify a noun or a pronoun.

The face *in the crystal ball* was mine.

Preposition: *in*
Object: *ball*
Modifiers: *the, crystal*

All the words in the prepositional phrase *in the crystal ball* work together and act just like a one-word adjective to modify the noun *face* and answer the question "Which face?"

At this point you may be wondering about the fact that verb phrases act as verbs and noun phrases act as nouns, but prepositional phrases do not act as prepositions: They act as adjectives or adverbs. In order to remove some of this confusion, many texts refer to prepositional phrases as *adjective phrases* or *adverb phrases,* depending upon their function in a sentence. Whether you call them adjective phrases, adverb phrases, or prepositional phrases is up to you. Just remember that this type of phrase begins with a preposition, ends with a noun or a pronoun, and all the words in the phrase act together as an adjective or as an adverb.

The following definition, then, applies to verb phrases, noun phrases, and prepositional phrases as well: **A phrase is a group of related words that functions as a single part of speech but does not have a subject and a predicate.** The most important part of this definition is the last: "**. . . but does not have a subject and a predicate.**" In the section that follows, you will see why this distinction is so important.

THE CLAUSE

A clause is usually defined as a group of related words that has a subject and a predicate. That sounds rather like the definition of a sentence, doesn't it? And there is a good reason for this similarity: A clause can be a sentence, and a sentence can be a clause.

The example sentence that follows is a sentence because it has a subject and a predicate, and it expresses a complete thought.

The crowd cheered.

Because this sentence has a subject and a predicate, however, according to the previous definition it is also a clause. Now consider the following sentence.

The crowd cheered, and the band played.

This is obviously a sentence, too, because it expresses a thought; in fact, it expresses two complete thoughts.

1. the crowd cheered
2. the band played

Each of these complete thoughts has its own subject and its own predicate; therefore, each is a clause. Notice that each clause can stand by itself and can be written as a complete sentence.

The crowd cheered. The band played.

The original sentence, then,

The crowd cheered, and the band played.

is actually two separate clauses joined by a comma and the conjunction *and,* which is not part of either clause.

Now take a look at the following sentence.

This class will begin when the bell rings.

Can this sentence be broken down into two related groups of words, each with its own subject and predicate?

1. this class will begin
2. when the bell rings

The subject of the first word group is the noun phrase *this class,* and the predicate is the verb phrase *will begin.* The subject of the second word group is the noun phrase *the bell,* and its predicate is the verb *rings.* So, the sentence is composed of two clauses, after all. But unlike the clauses in the previous example sentence, only one of these clauses can stand alone as a sentence.

This class will begin.
*When the bell rings.[1]

1. An asterisk (*) has been used throughout this book to identify words, phrases, and sentences that do not conform to the principles of standard usage.

Unlike the conjunction *and* in the previous example, which did not belong to either clause, the word *when* definitely belongs to the second clause in the sentence above. It cannot be removed from the clause without destroying the intended meaning of the original sentence.

The examples that you have seen demonstrate the two major types of clauses. *An **independent** clause (or **main clause**) expresses a complete thought and can stand alone as a sentence. A **dependent clause** (or **subordinate clause**) does not express a complete thought and cannot stand alone as a sentence.*

the crowd cheered (independent clause)
the band played (independent clause)

this class will begin (independent clause)
when the bell rings (dependent clause)

A dependent clause, you see, must depend upon (or "hang from") an independent clause in order for it to be included in a sentence.

All the words in an independent clause function as a sentence; the words in a dependent clause, however, function together and act as a single part of speech. Dependent clauses can act as adjectives, adverbs, or nouns.

ADJECTIVE CLAUSES

When a dependent clause modifies a noun or a pronoun in a sentence, it is called an *adjective clause* (or a *dependent adjective clause*).

The people who live here are very poor.

The sentence above is composed of two clauses, each having its own subject and its own predicate.

1. the people are very poor (independent clause)
2. who live here (dependent clause)

The dependent clause in this sentence may not, at first glance, appear to have a subject. But the pronoun *who* is, indeed, the subject of this clause and refers to the noun *people* for its meaning. The clause is a dependent clause, however, because, although it has a subject and a predicate, it cannot stand alone as a sentence; it must be attached to an independent clause.

The dependent clause *who live here* functions as a unit to modify the noun *people* and answer the question "Which people?" It acts just like a one-word adjective or an adjective phrase, but it is an adjective clause because it contains a subject and a predicate.

The people *who live here* are very poor. (adjective clause)
The *native* people are very poor. (adjective)
The people *on this island* are very poor. (adjective phrase)

Almost all adjective clauses begin with one of the *relative pronouns: who, whom, whose, which,* or *that.* Like all pronouns, relative pronouns take the place of nouns in a sentence, and they get their meaning from those nouns. But relative pronouns also have two other functions in a sentence:

1. they connect (or relate) an adjective clause to the rest of the sentence, and
2. they function as a subject, an object, or a modifier within the adjective clause.

In the previous example the relative pronoun *who* connected the adjective clause to the noun in the independent clause (*people*), and it functioned as the subject of the adjective clause.

He is the man whom I admire most.[2]

he is the man (independent clause)
whom I admire most (dependent clause)

2. This sentence is diagramed on page 113.

105

In the example above, the relative pronoun *whom* introduces the adjective clause and refers to the noun *man*, the word that the adjective clause modifies. But what function does *whom* have within its own clause? By rewriting this adjective clause as follows

I admire *whom* most

you can see that the subject of the clause is *I*, and that *whom* receives the action of the verb *admire*. Therefore, *whom* functions as a direct object within its own clause.

When *whose* is used as a relative pronoun to introduce an adjective clause, it functions as a modifier within that clause.

The person whose name is drawn will win a new car.[3]

the person will win a new car (independent clause)
whose name is drawn (dependent clause)

The dependent clause in the sentence above is an adjective clause modifying the noun *person*. It is introduced by the relative pronoun *whose,* which functions as an adjective modifying the noun *name.*

Occasionally a relative pronoun will be preceded by a preposition.

My father is the person *to whom* the credit should go.

my father is the person (independent clause)
to whom the credit should go (dependent clause)

The dependent clause functions as an adjective to modify the noun *person.* By rewriting this adjective clause in the following way

the credit should go *to whom*

you can see that the relative pronoun *whom* is the object of the preposition *to.* The prepositional phrase *to whom* functions as an adverb to modify the verb phrase *should go* and answer the question "Where?"

When a relative pronoun functions as a direct object within its own adjective clause, it can frequently be removed from the sentence without altering the meaning of the sentence. In the following sentence the relative pronoun *that* functions as a direct object within its dependent clause.

I have the results that you wanted.

I have the results (independent clause)

(D.O.) (Sub.) (Verb)
that   you   wanted (dependent clause, recast: you wanted that)
I have the results you wanted. (relative pronoun removed)

ADVERB CLAUSES

When a dependent clause functions as an adverb to modify a verb, an adjective, or an adverb in a sentence, it is called an *adverb clause* (or a *dependent adverb clause*). An example sentence used earlier contained an adverb clause.

This class will begin when the bell rings.

In this sentence, *when the bell rings* is a dependent clause because it contains a subject and a predicate, and it cannot stand alone as a sentence. It is an adverb clause because it functions as a unit to modify the verb phrase *will begin* and answer the question "When?" In this way the clause acts just like a one-word adverb or an adverb phrase.

This class will begin *when the bell rings.*[4] (adverb clause)

3. This sentence is diagramed on page 113.

4. This sentence is diagramed on page 113.

This class will begin *promptly*. (adverb)

This class will begin *in one minute*. (adverb phrase)

Just as adjective clauses usually begin with a relative pronoun, adverb clauses usually begin with a subordinating conjunction. Unlike relative pronouns, subordinating conjunctions are merely connecting words and do not have a function within the adverb clause. (For a look at subordinating conjunctions and a list of the most common ones, see Chapter 4, page 66.)

Notice that each of the italicized adverb clauses in the following sentences contains a subject and a predicate, and each answers a question commonly answered by adverbs.

I once felt poor *because I had no shoes*. (*Why* did I feel poor?)

He ran *as though his life depended on it*. (*How* did he run?)

A lion hunts *wherever it chooses*. (*Where* does a lion hunt?)

Before you leave today, please clean your locker. (*When* should you clean your locker?)

NOUN CLAUSES

A dependent clause can also function as a noun in a sentence, and, therefore, it can act as a subject or as an object within the independent clause to which it is attached.

I understand *that you want to see me*.

In the sentence above, the dependent clause *that you want to see me* has a subject (*you*) and a predicate (*want to see me*), but cannot stand alone as a sentence. The independent clause in this sentence is not merely the words *I understand,* but the entire sentence itself. The words *I understand* are only part of the sentence base; there is also a direct object that answers the question "I understand *what?*"

(Sub.)	(Verb)	(Dir. Obj.)
I	understand	*(something)*

The dependent clause *that you want to see me* functions as a noun and serves as the direct object of the verb *understand.*

In the following sentence, the noun clause (or dependent noun clause) functions as the subject of the independent clause.

Whoever wins this game will win the series.[5]

The noun clause, then, is the subject of the entire sentence; it acts just like the noun *Jim* would in its place.

Jim will win the series.

In fact, noun clauses can always be replaced by the words *someone* or *something* without changing the structure of the sentence.

Where you go is none of my business. (noun clause = subject)

(Something) is none of my business.

I will go with *whoever wants me.*[6] (noun clause = object of preposition)

I will go with (someone).

VERBALS AND VERBAL PHRASES

Some words in our language seen to act as two different parts of speech at the same time. These words are grouped under the general heading "verbals" because they are all formed from verbs and, in certain ways, they act like verbs in a sentence. Still, verbals are different from the verbs we

5. This sentence is diagramed on page 112.
6. This sentence is diagramed on page 113.

107

have seen so far because verbals are used as adjectives, nouns, or adverbs in a sentence. There are three types of verbals: participles, gerunds, and infinitives.

PARTICIPLES

Among the verb forms that were discussed in Chapter 4 were the *present participle* and the *past participle*. By preceding these forms with various helping verbs, you can express different verb tenses and tones. the present participle of the verb *fall,* for instance, is *falling*; its past participle is *fallen.*

The plane *was falling* rapidly.
The angel *had fallen* from grace.

These participles cannot be used as the only verb in a sentence because such a sentence would not convey a complete thought.

*The plane *falling* rapidly.
*The angel *fallen* from grace.

The present and past participles can be used by themselves as adjectives to modify a noun or a pronoun.

The *falling* plane vanished from sight. (modifies the noun *plane*)
The *fallen* angel could now only dream. (modifies the noun *angel*)

The verbals known as participles, then, are verb forms that are used as adjectives in a sentence.
Because a participle is part verb, it can be modified by adverbs, and it can have its own complements.

Dropping a quarter into the machine, John selected his favorite tune.[7]

The subject of the entire sentence above is the noun *John.* The entire group of words that precedes this subject acts as a unit to modify *John.* Because this group of words includes a participle and because all the words in this group work together to function as an adjective, the group is known as a *participle phrase.* (Some people prefer the word *participial* [five syllables], but I believe that *participle* is easier to pronounce and to understand.) Notice that the participle in this phrase (*dropping*) has a direct object (*quarter*) that answers the question "Dropping *what?*" The participle is also modified by the adverb phrase *in the machine.*

GERUNDS

Just as a participle is a verb form that functions as an adjective, another type of verbal, called a *gerund,* is a verb form that functions as a noun.

Running is very difficult for some people.

The subject of the sentence above is *running.* This word is a form of the verb *run;* it acts as a subject even though only nouns and pronouns can serve as subjects in a sentence. In this sentence, then, *running* is a gerund because it is part verb and part noun.

Gerunds can be easily recognized because they always end in *-ing.* Although present participles also end in *-ing,* they act as adjectives while gerunds act as nouns. Notice how the underlined gerunds in the following sentences act in all the ways that nouns can.

Her favorite pastime was *knitting.* (predicate noun)
I prefer *baking.* (direct object)
George gave *teaching* his best effort. (indirect object)
You must refrain from *talking.* (object of preposition)

7. This sentence is diagramed on page 111.

Because they are verb forms, gerunds can have complements and can be modified by adverbs and adverb phrases.

> *Finding the perfect gift in a catalog* can be difficult.[8]

The italicized part of the sentence above is a *gerund phrase*. All the words in this phrase act together as a noun and function as the subject of the sentence. The gerund in this phrase (*finding*) has a direct object (*gift*) that answers the question "Finding *what?*" This gerund is also modified by the adverb phrase *in a catalog*.

INFINITIVES

The third type of verbal is called an *infinitive*. Infinitives usually begin with the word *to* and are verb forms that can be used as nouns, adjectives, or adverbs.

> *To fly* was his only goal.
> An opportunity *to advance* came soon.
> She is eager *to succeed*.

In the first example sentence above, the infinitive *to fly* is used as a noun and functions as the subject of the sentence. In the second sentence the infinitive *to advance* modifies the noun *opportunity* and, therefore, is an adjective. In the third sentence the infinitive *to succeed* functions as an adverb modifying the predicate adjective *eager*.

Like participles and gerunds, infinitives can have complements and can be modified. The infinitive, its complements, and its modifiers all function together as an *infinitive phrase*.

> I will try *to call you in the morning*.[9]

In the sentence above, the infinitive phrase *to call you in the morning* functions as a noun and is a direct object answering "I will try *what?*" Within that infinitive phrase, the pronoun *you* is also a direct object. It is the direct object of the infinitive *to call* and answers the question ". . . to call *whom?*" The prepositional phrase *in the morning* is an adverb phrase modifying the infinitive *to call* and answering the question "When?"

Unlike participles and gerunds, an infinitive may have a subject. When it has a subject, the infinitive is no longer part of an infinitive phrase, but rather, it is part of an *infinitive clause*.

> The guard advised *them to turn back*.[10]

In this example sentence the group of words *them to turn back* is an adverb clause. The group works together as a unit and functions as the direct object of the verb *advised* ("The guard advised *what?*"). But it is different from an infinitive phrase in that the infinitive has a subject (*them*). (Strange as it may seem, when a pronoun acts as the subject of an infinitive, that pronoun should be in its *object* form.) Infinitive clauses are generally used as alternatives for clauses that begin with *that*.

> The guard advised *that they turn back*.
> The guard advised *them to turn back*.

APPOSITIVE PHRASES

When a group of words follows a noun and acts as a unit to explain or identify that noun, the group is called an *appositive phrase*.

> Mr. Corwin, my favorite teacher, is moving to Milwaukee.[11]

---

8. This sentence is diagramed on page 112.
9. This sentence is diagramed on page 112.
10. This sentence is diagramed on page 112.
11. This sentence is diagramed on page 112.

In the sentence above, the phrase *my favorite teacher* is an appositive phrase identifying the preceding noun, *Mr. Corwin.* The appositive phrase restates the meaning of the preceding noun in different words.

Appositive phrases are set off from the rest of the sentence by commas. Even when only one word is used to restate the meaning of a previous noun, that word (called an *appositive*) is set off by commas (or other marks, such as dashes or parentheses).

> The present capital of Illinois, *Springfield,* is not the only capital the state has had.

When a one-word appositive is used to restrict the meaning of the previous noun, rather than merely restate that meaning, it is not set off by punctuation. Compare the following sentences.

> Jim's wife, *Kay,* is a terrific cook.
> Joseph Kennedy's son *John* was elected to Congress at age 30.

It must be assumed that *Jim,* in the first sentence above, has only one wife, and so *Kay* merely restates the meaning of *wife* and is set off by commas. Because Joseph Kennedy had several sons, however, the noun *John* serves to point out *which* son is being referred to in the second sentence. It is not set off by commas because it does not restate the meaning of *son*—it restricts that meaning.

SENTENCE FRAGMENTS

Among the most frequent errors in written English is the *sentence fragment.* A complete sentence, you will recall, has a subject and a predicate and expresses a complete thought. A sentence fragment, on the other hand, is not a complete sentence, but it begins with a capital letter and ends with a period just as though it were.

Many sentence fragments are the result of a writer's mistaking phrases and dependent clauses for complete sentences. A prepositional phrase, for example, acts as a unit but does *not* express a complete thought; it cannot stand alone as a sentence.

> We couldn't get used to being home again.
> *After our wonderful vacation.

The sentence fragment marked with an asterisk is a prepositional phrase—not a complete sentence. This mistake can be easily corrected—as can most fragments of this type—by joining the phrase to the preceding sentence.

> We couldn't get used to being home again after our wonderful vacation.

Participle, gerund, and infinitive phrases are often mistakenly written as sentences. Although each verbal phrase contains a verb form and may contain a complement, none contains a subject, and so none can express a complete thought.

> We worked well into the night. *Scrubbing all the floors and washing all the windows. (fragment = participle phrase)
> This was all I dreamed about. *Playing in the World Series. (fragment = gerund phrase)
> Some people work themselves to death. *Just to get enough money for retirement. (fragment = infinitive phrase)

Most verbal phrases that are written as sentences can be corrected in two ways. They can be joined to a preceding sentence, or they can be made into complete sentences themselves by adding a subject and another verb.

> We worked well into the night, *scrubbing all the floors and washing all the windows.*
> *Playing in the World Series* was all I dreamed about.

Some people work themselves to death. They work *just to get enough money for retirement.*

Appositive phrases also frequently appear as sentence fragments. This error can be corrected by making the appositive phrase follow the noun it identifies, and separating the two with a comma.

The ashes came from Mount St. Helens. *The only volcano on the mainland to errupt in this century. (fragment = appositive phrase)

The ashes came from Mount St. Helens, *the only volcano on the mainland to erupt in this century.*

The most common sentence fragment of all, however, is a dependent clause that has been mistakenly written as a complete sentence. The reason that this is such a frequent error is that dependent clauses do satisfy one of the requirements of a complete sentence: They contain a subject and a predicate. But dependent clauses cannot stand alone as sentences; they depend for their meaning upon the independent clauses to which they must be attached.

The adjective clauses that most often appear as sentence fragments begin with the relative pronouns *who, which,* and *that.* If you frequently use sentence fragments in your writing, be especially careful when you write a sentence beginning with one of these words.

I went to look at the apartment. *Which was in the suburbs. (fragment = adjective clause)

I went to look at the apartment, *which was in the suburbs.*

Many people fail to understand that while *coordinating* conjunctions (such as *and* and *but*) may occasionally be used at the start of a complete sentence, *subordinating* conjunctions may not

(unless the sentence contains an independent clause). Words like *because, although, if, since,* and *when* almost always introduce dependent adverb clauses, and adverb clauses cannot stand alone as complete sentences.

We would not let Reggie drive home. *Because he had been drinking. (fragment = adverb clause)

If you join the adverb clause to the front of the independent clause, you must separate the clauses with a comma. If you join it to the end of the independent clause, no comma is necessary.

Because he had been drinking, we would not let Reggie drive home.

We would not let Reggie drive home *because he had been drinking.*

DIAGRAMING PHRASES AND CLAUSES

Diagraming prepositional phrases was shown at the end of Chapter 6 (pages 92-93). Verbal phrases are diagramed in a similar way, except that the participle, gerund, or infinitive is written in the space occupied by the preposition *and* its object. If the verbal has a complement, that complement is shown on the horizontal line containing the verbal.

Dropping a quarter into the machine, John selected his favorite tune. (participle phrase)

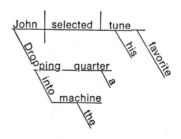

If a gerund phrase or an infinitive phrase functions as a noun, it is diagrammed by placing the entire phrase on stilts that rest on the place where the noun would appear.

Finding the perfect gift in a catalog can be difficult. (gerund phrase)

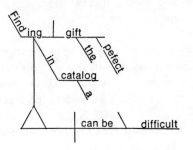

I will try *to call you in the morning*. (infinitive phrase)

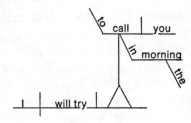

The subject of an infinitive clause is placed on a horizontal line to the left of the infinitive.

The guard advised *them to turn back*. (infinitive clause)

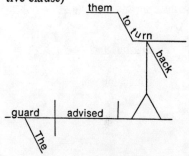

An appositive phrase is diagrammed by placing the noun that functions as the appositive in parentheses next to the noun it explains or identifies. All the modifiers of the appositive appear below it in the diagram.

Mr. Corwin, *my favorite teacher,* is moving to Milwaukee. (appositive phrase)

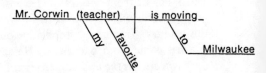

All clauses, both independent and dependent, are diagrammed as though they were separate sentences. Because every clause has a subject and a verb, these two parts appear on the same horizontal line and are separated by a short vertical line. If the clause includes a complement, that complement appears to the right of the subject and the verb. All modifiers appear on lines beneath the words they modify.

If a dependent clause functions as a noun in a sentence, the entire noun clause is placed on stilts that extend from the places normally occupied by nouns.

Whoever wins this game will win the series. (noun clause used as subject)

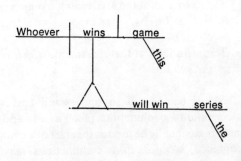

I will go with *whoever wants me.* (noun clause used as object of preposition)

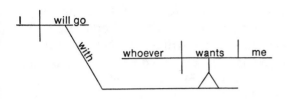

Adjective and adverb clauses are diagramed below the independent clauses to which they are attached. The relationship between the independent clause and the dependent clause is shown by a broken line that connects the two. For an adjective clause, the broken line extends from the relative pronoun in the adjective clause to the noun in the independent clause that gives the relative pronoun its meaning. First, diagram the independent clause, and diagram the adjective clause beneath it. Then connect the relative pronoun to its antecedent with a broken line.

He is the man *whom I admire most.* (adjective clause modifying the noun *man*)

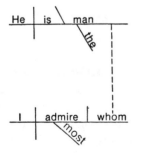

The person *whose name is drawn* will win a new car. (adjective clause modifying the noun *person*)

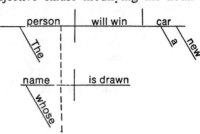

For adverb clauses, the broken line extends from the verb in the adverb clause to the word that the clause modifies. The subordinating conjunction that begins the adverb clause is written on the broken line.

This class will begin *when the bell rings.* (adverb clause modifying the verb phrase *will begin*)

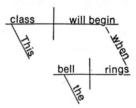

Remember: Diagraming can be interesting and challenging, but it should not be used as a test of one's skill in language. The purpose of any sentence diagram is only to show the relationships between various sentence parts. When used in this way, sentence diagrams can be valuable aids to visualizing and understanding sentence structure.

CLASSIFYING SENTENCES BY STRUCTURE

Every English sentence can be classified as belonging to one of four groups, depending upon its structure. A *simple sentence* contains only one independent clause and no dependent clauses. A simple sentence may be quite involved and may include compound subjects, compound verbs, and a variety of phrases. Still, it is a "simple" sentence because it cannot be broken down into separate clauses.

> The police officers and the fire fighters worked as a team and prevented a disaster. (simple sentence)

The example sentence above contains a compound subject (*officers . . . fighters*) and a compound verb (*worked . . . prevented*), but it is a simple sentence because it contains only one independent clause and no dependent clauses.

A *compound sentence* contains two or more independent clauses but no dependent clauses. The following sentence is a compound sentence because it is composed of two independent clauses that are joined by the conjunction *but*.

> I had heard the rumors, but I refused to believe them. (compound sentence)

A *complex sentence* contains only one independent clause and at least one dependent clause. The following complex sentence is composed of an introductory adverb clause followed by an independent clause.

> Wherever she was, there was Eden. (complex sentence)

A *compound-complex sentence* contains two or more independent clauses and at least one dependent clause.

> Paul Revere, who is remembered for his famous ride, engraved the plates for our first currency, and he built the boilers for Robert Fulton's steamboat. (compound-complex sentence.)

HELPING YOUR CHILDREN WRITE MORE MATURE SENTENCES

By understanding how phrases, clauses, and compound structures function in a sentence, you can help your children use these elements in their writing. It is not necessary—or advisable—that children learn the names of the various phrases and clauses, but it is very healthy for children—even young children—to learn to *use* these structures in their speaking and writing. Children have just as much of a need to be understood as adults do, and a child who is able to express his thoughts and feelings to others has a better chance of refining those thoughts and discussing those feelings than does a child who is unable or reluctant to communicate with others.

The writing of young children (and, to some extent, their speaking, as well) begins with short, simple sentences that are frequently run together.

> *We went to a baseball game and it was in Milwaukee and I brought my glove and I caught a foul ball.

Even when a sentence like this is broken down into separate independent clauses and properly punctuated, the writing still appears to be that of a child. It is "immature" writing because it demonstrates that the writer does not have the ability to show the relationships between various ideas; he cannot, therefore, effectively communicate these ideas to others. This is not to say that short sentences and short clauses have no place in good writing. Indeed, these structures can be very effective when they are used to achieve contrast and to convey a dramatic or forceful ideal. But the "mature" writer *has the ability* to use a variety

114

of structures and to select the types of sentences that will best convey his exact meaning and will create the precise effect he desires.

Our goal, then, is to help our children write more mature sentences. Long sentences are not necessarily mature sentences, as the previous example of run-on independent clauses should demonstrate. Highly involved and complicated sentence structures are not the goal of the good writer, either. (This, however, is a lesson that many social scientists and bureaucrats have yet to learn.) But children can and should be challenged to write with more complexity and to assemble multiple ideas in varied and complex ways. Once a person *has the ability* to structure his thoughts into various configurations, then, and only then, can he begin to develop that sense of taste, judgment, and style that marks the mature, polished writer.

Some very fine work has been done over the last two decades in finding methods that help children become accustomed to using compound subjects and predicates, verbals and verbal phrases, prepositional phrases, appositives, and dependent clauses in their writing. Most of this work falls under the label "sentence combining," but the label is a bit misleading in that the system also helps the writer develop an ability to vary the order of ideas within a sentence. In this section I will briefly sketch the methods that are most commonly employed in sentence combining. The section is not, however, intended to be a thorough study of the topic. Once you understand the principles involved, you can then decide which structures to practice with your own children, and you can create "signals" or "indicators" that will direct your children toward using additional types of sentences in their writing.

The basic principle behind sentence combining is that, through a series of written "signals" or "indicators," two or more complete thoughts can be combined into one complete sentence, or a single complete sentence can be recast in a particular way. For example, the following sentence can be recast by changing the position of the first word.

Nevertheless, the defendant was found guilty.

In order to signal that you want the child to move one part of the sentence to another position, you should write the indicator **"MOVE"** in parentheses at the end of the sentence. (Indicators in this book will always be given in bold face as well as in parentheses.) In order to show the child which part of the sentence should be moved, underline the word *nevertheless.*

Nevertheless, the defendant was found guilty. **(MOVE)**

Once the child understands the meaning of the underlining and the meaning of the indicator, he might then write the following sentence:

The defendant was found guilty, nevertheless.

This may, in fact, be exactly the sentence you wanted him to construct. But if he should, instead, come up with

The defendant was, nevertheless, found guilty.

praise him for his creativity and encourage him to try other combinations. Even if his commas are not properly placed—even if they do not appear at all—let him know that he accomplished his task and created a complete sentence. Then take the time to explain to him about how commas are used to set off interrupting elements from the rest of the sentence.

Now try using the same (**MOVE**) indicator with groups of words. Some prepositional phrases, verbal phrases, and dependent clauses can appear at more than one position in a sentence. Make sure that the sentence you select can be recast in at least one way, and then underline the group of words that you want your child to move within the sentence.

In an hour we will leave for camp. (**MOVE**)
We will leave for camp in an hour.

Television, first thought to be merely a toy, is today a necessity for many people. (**MOVE**)
First thought to be merely a toy, television is today a necessity for many people.

The entire project failed because no one would lend a hand. (**MOVE**)
Because no one would lend a hand, the entire project failed.

Always remember that you must have a recast version in mind *before* telling the child to create one.

Another method for changing the structure of a single sentence is to recast the sentence using the expletive *there* at its beginning. Children will quickly notice that the verb or verb phrase in the original sentence will have to be moved when *there* is added. To signal this change, place the indicator (**THERE**) at the end of the sentence.

Nine planets are in our solar system. (**THERE**)
There are nine planets in our solar system.

If you want to change a sentence by removing *there,* you can use the indicator (~~THERE~~) or draw a line through *there* in the original sentence.

There are many unsafe toys on the market today. (~~THERE~~)
or: ~~There~~ are many unsafe toys on the market today.

Many unsafe toys are on the market today.

The indicator (**THERE**) can be combined with the indicator (**MOVE**) as well. The expletive *there* may then appear at the middle of the new sentence rather than at the beginning. The part of the original sentence you want moved should be underlined.

Many people were attending an outdoor concert when the tornado hit. (**THERE**) (**MOVE**)
When the tornado hit, there were many people attending an outdoor concert.

The child will first add *there* to the beginning of the original sentence, and then see that in order to accomplish the second change, *there* must be moved to another position in the sentence.

Changing a sentence from the active to the passive voice may be done by using the indicator (**BY + *BE* FORM**). This requires changing the positions of the subject and the direct object, adding a form of *be,* and placing the preposition *by* in front of the original subject.

Thomas Edison invented the phonograph. (**BY + *BE* FORM**)

The phonograph was invented by Thomas Edison.

Air pollution kills thousands of people each year. (**BY** + *BE* FORM)
Thousands of people are killed by air pollution each year.

Remember: It is much more important that the child is able to recast sentences in this way than it is that he understands the terminology involved in the change.

Passive sentences, of course, can also be recast to active ones by reversing the process. The incidator (~~**BY** + *BE* FORM~~) can be used to signal this change.

The play was performed by a touring troupe. (~~**BY** + *BE* FORM~~)
A touring troupe performed the play.

So much for recasting single sentences. Other indicators can be used to help the child combine two or more complete sentences into one. For example, the indicator (**, CONJ.**) signals that two separate independent clauses should be joined by a comma and the coordinating conjunctions *and, but, or, nor, for, yet,* or *so.*

She had won a new car.
She didn't know how to drive. (**, CONJ.**)
She had won a new car, but she didn't know how to drive.

Johnny Evers was the second baseman.
Frank Chance played first. (**, CONJ.**)
Johnny Evers was the second baseman, and Frank Chance played first.

The ideas from several sentences can be joined in a series by using the (**, CONJ.**) indicator along with the comma indicator (**,**).

Ideas that are repeated in the several sentences should be marked for deletion by drawing a line through them.

The quarterback dropped back in the pocket.
~~The quarterback~~ faked a pass. (**,**)
~~The quarterback~~ ran up the middle for a touchdown (**, CONJ.**)
The quarterback dropped back in the pocket, faked a pass, and ran up the middle for a touchdown.

If you want the child to replace one of the nouns with a pronoun, cross out that noun and add the indicator (**PRO.**) at the end of the sentence.

Sharon twisted her ankle.
~~Sharon~~ still managed to finish the race. (**, CONJ.**) (**PRO.**)
Sharon twisted her ankle, but she still managed to finish the race.

More elaborate and complex changes may require using "hints" that will help the child see the structure of the sentence you have in mind. To help a child see that a phrase or clause containing several words can replace a single word, and can act as a unit in a sentence, use the word **SOMETHING** in your "hint." For example, if you want your child to combine two sentences by using a gerund phrase, use the indicators (**'S**) + (**ING**) and cross out the pronoun that the gerund phrase will replace.

Jerry played in the band. (**'S**) + (**ING**)
~~It~~ made his family proud.
Jerry's playing in the band made his family proud.

Because this change is a rather difficult one

117

for most children to grasp at first, you might give them a hint by using the word **SOMETHING.**

SOMETHING made his family proud.

A similar combination requires changing an adverb to an adjective as well as using a gerund phrase. Use the indicator (~~LY~~) to show than an *-ly* ending must be dropped, and use the (**MOVE**) indicator to show that the newly formed adjective should precede the gerund. Then give the child a hint as to the structure of the sentence you have in mind.

Jim bragged *constantly.* ('S) + (ING) (~~LY~~) (**MOVE**)
~~It~~ cost him many friends.
Hint: **SOMETHING** cost him many friends.
Jim's constant bragging cost him many friends.

Much more elaborate combinations, even ones that join three, four, or five separate sentences are possible. Indicators such as (**THAT**), (**WHO**) (**WHERE**) (**WHY**), (**HOW**, (**WHAT**), etc., can be used to signal the words you want included in a dependent clause. For example, the indicator (**WHO**) is used below to signal that the second sentence is to become a dependent clause that begins with the relative pronoun *who.*

The police finally apprehended the burglar.
~~The burglar~~ was responsible for many thefts in our neighborhood. (**WHO**)
The police finally apprehended the burglar who was responsible for many thefts in our neighborhood.

No matter what indicators you use and no matter how complex you want the resulting sentences to be, remember that your child will not come up with the exact combination you have in mind every time. The purpose of this whole exercise is to challenge the child to attempt something that he might not do otherwise. Gradually he will become familiar with these more complex structures, and he will feel comfortable using them to express his own ideas.

The indicators themselves are only a means to an end. All the styles of sentence combining have one thing in common: They use indicators and hints to guide the child, but, in the end, they remove the aids and allow the child to combine the ideas in any way he wishes. If you choose to try sentence combining with your child, you, too, must direct your efforts toward *removing* the aids. Once the child understands the many ways that ideas can be expressed, he will be writing mature sentences by himself, and the aids will only limit his creativity and no longer be "aids" at all.

9. COMMON PROBLEMS WITH PHRASES AND CLAUSES

Sentences that include phrases and clauses are more complicated than those that do not, and the more involved or complex a sentence is, the more chance there is for error. If our only goal is to write and speak without making any usage mistakes, then we would be better off to avoid phrases and clauses altogether and use only the short, independent clauses that characterize the language of children. If, on the other hand, our goal is to write and speak in well-formed, mature sentences that express exactly what we want to say in exactly the way we want to be understood, then we must accept the risks and try to reduce them wherever possible.

To me, the most stimulating idea about studying the proper use of phrases and clauses is that this area of spoken and written English, more than any other, separates the skilled from the inept, the expert from the imposter. By focusing your study of phrases and clauses on the relatively few areas in which errors most often occur, you can not only become confident in your own use of complex structures, but you can tell when someone is trying to deceive you with sentences that appear learned but are fraught with error.

THE PERSONAL PRONOUN AS OBJECT OF A PREPOSITION

Because personal pronouns have different subject, object, and possessive forms, they are the source of many usage errors, several of which have been previously discussed. It is not surprising, then, that personal pronouns should also be involved in some of the most common mistakes people make when using phrases and clauses.

Once again, let's go over the differences between the subject forms and the object forms of personal pronouns.

Subject Forms	Singular	Plural
First Person	I	we
Second Person	you	you
Third Person	he	they
	she	
	it	

Object Forms	Singular	Plural
First Person	me	us
Second Person	you	you
Third Person	him	them
	her	
	it	

For some reason (and I honestly cannot

119

explain what that reason is), the subject forms *I, we, he, she,* and *they* sound more "scholarly," more "polished" to many people than do the object forms *me, us, him, her,* and *them.* Consequently, some writers, and many speakers, will use these subject forms as a means of *appearing* learned when, in fact, the misuse of the forms only serves to characterize the user as lacking in learning or, quite possibly, as being a charlatan.

When a personal pronoun functions as the object of a preposition, it should be in its object form. Very few speakers or writers, even those whose intent is to appear learned, substitute a subject form when a preposition has only one object. Phrases like **to I, *behind she,* or **on he*[1] do not sound scholarly at all and are seldom seen or heard as replacements for *to me, behind her,* and *on him.* But when a preposition has more than one object, one of which is a personal pronoun, errors abound.

> **An invitation was sent *to Jerry and I.*
> (standard: Jerry and *me*)
> **The ball landed *behind Kelly and she.*
> (standard: Kelly and *her*)
> **The restrictions that were placed *on Tony and he* seemed unfair. (standard: on Tony and *him*)

Each of the italicized prepositional phrases in the sentences above has a compound object. The sentences are nonstandard because the personal pronoun in each phrase is a subject form instead of an object form.

The most common mistake of this type occurs in the phrase. **between you and I.*

> **Just *between you and I,* I'll bet he is lying.
> **The differences *between you and I* are minor.

This error is so prevalent in both speaking and writing that it almost begins to sound and look correct. It is not uncommon, in fact, to find *two* subject forms used after *between:* **The relationship *between he and I* is a close one. But *between* is a preposition, and a pronoun that acts as an object of that preposition must be in its object form.

If you concentrate on tuning your ear to the sound of *between you and me,* and if you use the word *between* as a signal flare that alerts you to the possibility that a potential danger lurks nearby, you will be prepared to follow that preposition with object forms, and the sound of **between you and I* will become unnatural and irritating.

> Just *between you and me,* I'll bet he is lying.
> The differences *between you and me* are minor.
> The relationship *between him and me* is a close one.

WHO, WHOM, WHOEVER, WHOMEVER

There are few problems more vexing than choosing between *who* and *whom, whoever* and *whomever.* The reason that I have chosen to deal with these problems in a chapter that concerns phrases and clauses is that the choice of *who* or *whom, whoever* or *whomever* becomes difficult only when these pronouns are used in prepositional phrases and dependent clauses.

---

[1]An asterisk (*) has been used throughout this book to identify words, phrases, and sentences that do not conform to the principles of standard usage.

The two critical points you must remember in using these pronouns correctly are

1. *who* and *whoever* are subject forms; *whom* and *whomever* are object forms, and
2. the choice of whether to use a subject or an object form depends upon how the pronoun functions *within its clause.*

The pronouns *who* and *whoever* can function as subjects and predicate pronouns; *whom* and *whomever* can function as objects of a preposition, direct object, and indirect objects.

Who is at the door? (subject)
Who will it be? (predicate pronoun: It will be *who.*)
To *whom* were you talking? (object of preposition)
Whom did you see? (direct object: You did see *whom.*)

Using the correct form in sentences like the ones above is somewhat easy because each of these sentences has only one clause, and the function of the pronoun in that clause is quite obvious.

But now consider the following sentences.

I don't know (who, whom) she will choose.
I don't know (who, whom) will be chosen.
You should vote for (whoever, whomever) is best qualified.
Tom is the player (who, whom) I want on my team.

Each of these sentences contains a dependent clause as well as an independent clause. When the pronouns *who, whom, whoever,* or *whomever* are part of a dependent clause, you

must determine how they function *within that clause.* For example, the entire dependent clause may function as an object, but the pronoun in question might be the subject *of that dependent clause.* Therefore, the pronoun must be a subject form.

Let's look at each of the previous example sentences separately to see the function of each dependent clause and the function of the relative pronoun within that clause.

I don't know (who, whom) she will choose.

The entire dependent clause *(who, whom) she will choose* acts as the direct object of the verb in the main clause. It answers the question "I don't know *what?*" Within that dependent clause, the relative pronoun also functions as a direct object. This can be seen by recasting the clause as follows:

[Sub.] [Verb] [Dir. Obj.]
She will choose (who, whom).

Because the pronoun functions as a direct object *within its clause,* it must be in its object form: I don't know *whom* she will choose.

I don't know (who, whom) will be chosen.

Here again, the entire dependent clause *(who, whom) will be chosen* functions as a direct object. But in this sentence the relative pronoun acts as the subject of that dependent clause:

[Sub.]   [Verb]
(who, whom) will be chosen.

Therefore, the pronoun must be in its subject form: I don't know *who* will be chosen.

You should vote for (whoever, whomever) is best qualified.

Even though the pronoun in question follows the preposition *for,* it is not the object of that preposition. The sentence does not say that you should vote "for (whoever, whomever)" but that you should vote "for (whoever, whomever) is best qualified." The entire dependent clause *(whoever, whomever) is best qualified* is the object of the preposition *for.* Within this dependent clause, the relative pronoun acts as the subject and, therefore, must be in its subject form: You should vote for *whoever* is best qualified.

Tom is the player (who, whom) I want on my team.

The main clause in this sentence is *Tom is the player.* The dependent clause modifies and describes the noun *player.* This dependent clause can be recast as follows:

I want (who, whom) on my team.

Within this dependent clause, then, the pronoun in question acts as the direct object of the verb *want.* Because it is a direct object, the pronoun must be in its object form: Tom is the player *whom* I want on my team.

Knowing how a relative pronoun functions within its clause is important, but the process involved in this discovery can sometimes be quite time consuming, and you simply cannot afford that time to stop in mid-sentence and figure out whether the pronoun acts as a subject or as an object. One tip that may help you in choosing the correct form is to link *who*

and *whoever* with the pronoun *he,* and to link *whom* and *whomever* with the pronoun *him.* (The letter *m* in the object forms, and its absence in the subject forms, provides a good memory aid.) Now, when you arrive at the part of the sentence in which the choice of *who* or *whom, whoever* or *whomever* has to be made, **consider only the words that follow the relative pronoun.** If the pronoun *he* makes sense when inserted into those following words, then the subject form *who* or *whoever* will be correct. If the pronoun *him* makes sense, then choose *whom* or *whomever.*

Lets try this system with the previous example sentences.

I don't know (who, whom) she will choose.

Disregard everything that precedes the pronoun in question, and determine whether *he* or *him* makes sense in the part that follows it.
THINK: She will choose *him* (not: *she will choose *he*)
Therefore, remembering that *him* is linked to *whom,* choose the object form *whom* and proceed with your sentence: I don't know *whom* she will choose.

I don't know (who, whom) will be chosen.

By considering only the words that follow the relative pronoun, you can tell that *he* makes sense and that *him* does not.
THINK: *he* will be chosen (not: *him* will be chosen)
Therefore: I don't know *who* will be chosen.

You should vote for (whoever, whomever) is best qualified.

THINK: *he* is best qualified (not: **him* is best qualified)

Therefore, because *whoever* is linked with *he*, the sentence should read: You should vote for *whoever* is best qualified.

> Tom is the player (who, whom) I want on my team.

THINK: I want *him* on my team (not: **I want *he* on my team)

Therefore: Tom is the player *whom* I want on my team.

Even in conversation, you can pause long enough before choosing *who* or *whom, whoever* or *whomever* to consider *he* and *him* in the clause you are planning. Because the pause will be quite brief, your listeners will assume that you are concentrating on the substance of what you are about to say, not on its form. (You might fill the void with a short "ahhh" or "uhhh," but please don't resort to "you know.") With a little practice you will be able to choose the proper form without even a noticeable break in your speech.

ELLIPTICAL CLAUSES

Some adverb clauses that are used to show comparisons do not contain a subject and a verb. The part of the clause that is missing, however, is understood by the listener or reader.

> She is taller than I.

The adverb clause *than I,* in the sentence above, does not have a verb. The writer has avoided the repetitious sound that would occur if the clause had been written out completely.

> She is taller than I (am).
> or, She is taller than I (am tall).

These incomplete clauses, often called *elliptical clauses,* frequently include the words *than* and *as.* When a personal pronoun is used in an elliptical clause, the form of that pronoun can tell the reader what words have been omitted.

> Dad always liked Chuck better than *me.*

The meaning conveyed by this elliptical clause is

> Dad always liked Chuck better than (Dad liked) me.

When the subject form *I* is used instead of the object form *me,* the meaning of the sentence is completely different.

> Dad always liked Chuck better than *I.*
> Dad always liked Chuck better than I (liked Chuck).

Because the choice of pronoun can change the meaning of an elliptical clause, and the meaning of the entire sentence, you must be careful to use the form that would be required if the entire clause had been written out.

> They are not as happy as (we, us).
> They are not as happy as *we* (are).
>
> Tony helped him as much as (I, me).
> Tony helped him as much as *I* (helped him).
> Tony helped him as much as (Tony helped) *me.*

THAT VS. WHICH

The question of whether to use *that* or *which* to introduce an adjective clause has been largely ignored in recent years. And yet, the distinction between these two relative pronouns is so meaningful and useful that I wish it would be resurrected and taught in today's English classes. The difference between these words is not merely a matter of propriety, but a matter of *meaning* and *accuracy* in communication. I feel so strongly about the all-too-common use of these words as synonyms that, perhaps, I should have included the topic as one of my "pet peeves."

Many people today are under the mistaken belief that *which* is the more learned form of *that*. (A friend once characterized my job of editing textbooks as "changing *that*'s to *which*'s.") To these people the word *that* has a familiar and pedestrian ring to it, much as the object forms of personal pronouns are considered "inferior" to their subject forms.

Actually, the distinction between *that* and *which* rests on the meaning of the clauses these words introduce. Some adjective clauses define or limit the meaning of their antecedent; others merely add additional, nonessential information about their antecedent. Compare the following sentences.

> Regulations have been proposed to govern television commercials *that are frequently watched by children*.
> These regulations do not cover prime-time commercials, *which are not aimed at children*.

In the first sentence the italicized adjective clause *that are frequently watched by children* limits the meaning of its antecedent, *commercials*. It is essential to the meaning of the sentence because the regulations do *not* govern all television commercials—only those that are frequently watched by children. In the second sentence, however, the adjective clause *which are not aimed at children* is not essential. This clause does not limit the meaning of *commercials* but, instead, adds additional information about those commercials. This clause gives a reason for the statement that precedes it (*which = because they*).

Essential clauses (like the one in the first example sentence) are also referred to as "restrictive clauses," or "defining clauses." These clauses should be introduced by the relative pronoun *that*. *Nonessential clauses* (also referred to as "nonrestrictive clauses" or "nondefining clauses") should be introduced by the relative pronoun *which*. Notice also that nonessential clauses are separated from the rest of the sentence by a comma. If a nonessential clause (that is, one beginning with *which*) appears in the middle of a sentence, a comma should be placed both before and after the clause.

> The Battle of Bunker Hill, which was lost by the American troops, was actually fought on Breed's Hill.

The use of the comma, then, becomes a generally reliable test for whether a clause is essential or nonessential, and, consequently, whether that clause should begin with *that* or *which*. If a comma seems proper before the clause, or if the clause could be preceded by a brief pause in voice, then it is likely that the clause is nonessential and should begin with *which*. If a comma or a pause is not appropriate, then the clause is probably essential and should begin with *that*.

> I have one briar pipe (no comma, no pause) *that* I smoke every day. (meaning: I may have several briar pipes, but I smoke one of them every day.)
> I have one briar pipe (comma, pause), *which* I smoke every day. (meaning: I have only one briar pipe, and I smoke that pipe every day.)

VERBS FOLLOWING "ONE OF THOSE"

A somewhat minor problem, but one that plagues speakers and writers who are quite knowledgeable about usage, occurs when an adjective clause follows the phrase "one of those." Should the verb in the clause be singular or plural?

> He is one of those teachers who (is, are) going to Europe this summer.

The subject of the adjective clause *who (is, are) going to Europe this summer* is the relative pronoun *who*. The verb in the clause must agree in number with its subject, but is *who* singular or plural? Most people, especially those who have some knowledge of subject/verb agreement, opt for the singular verb form *is going* because they assume that the antecedent of *who* is the singular pronoun *one*. But the sentence does not say "one is going to Europe." Rather, this sentence can be faithfully recast as follows:

> Of the teachers who are going to Europe this summer, he is one.

Now it is obvious that the antecedent of *who*

is the plural noun *teachers*; the plural verb *are going* is then in agreement with its plural subject.

> He is one of those teachers who *are* going to Europe this summer.

Notice that the italicized plural verbs in the following sentences are necessary because their subjects refer to plural nouns.

> She is another of the numerous homemakers who *are* returning to the job market. (homemakers *are* returning)
> Nellie Fox was one of the best bunters that *have* ever played the game. (bunters *have* played)

MISPLACED CLAUSES AND VERBAL PHRASES

There are very few topics within the study of grammar and usage that generate much humor. There is one, however, that can offer children and adults alike a very welcome change from the parching rigors usually associated with language study. Although this topic can be the source of some humor, it is still a very necessary and useful one for the person who is concerned about clarity in writing.

When modifiers—especially modifying phrases and clauses—are misplaced in a sentence, the meaning of the sentence can be wholly different from what the writer intended.

> *Having caused a disturbance in class, the principal sent me to the office.
> *Hanging by a slender thread, Mr. Potts watched the spider.

The first example sentence above appears to say that the principal had caused a disturbance in class. Similarly, the second sentence tells us that Mr. Potts hung by a slender thread in order to watch the spider. Misplaced modifiers like these can create a wide variance between what the writer *thinks* he is saying and what his sentence actually says.

The most commonly misplaced modifiers are verbal phrases that appear at the beginning of a sentence. Although participle, gerund, and infinitive phrases can, and frequently do, appear in this position, their meaning will not be clear unless the word that they modify immediately follows them in the sentence.

> **Being old and damaged,* I didn't think the car was worth buying.

The italicized phrase in the sentence above appears to modify the word that follows it: *I.* The writer could have made his meaning clear by placing the noun *car* immediately after the participle phrase.

> Being old and damaged, the car, to me, wasn't worth buying.

When a modifying phrase does not clearly refer to the word it is intended to modify, or when that word does not appear in the sentence at all, the phrase is said to be *dangling.*

> **Having never played chess before,* the loss was to be expected.

The italicized phrase in this sentence is dangling because the word it should modify is only in the writer's mind—not in the sentence

itself. The error can be corrected by including the pronoun *I* and placing it immediately after the participle phrase.

> *Having never played chess before,* I expected to lose.

Verbal phrases are not the only constructions that can be easily misplaced. Adverb and adjective clauses also frequently appear to modify words different from those the writer intended.

> **Even before he was born,* Brant's father decreed that his son would be a lawyer.

This sentence appears to say that, even before Brant's father was born, Brant's father wanted Brant to be a lawyer. What the writer had in mind could have been conveyed by recasting the sentence in the following way.

> Even before Brant was born, his father had decreed that Brant would be a lawyer.

The misplaced clause in the following sentence also leads to misinterpretation.

> *The fans were still buzzing about the game they had seen *as they filed out of the stadium.*

In all probability the fans didn't see the game at all as they filed out; they only talked about the game as they filed out. The italicized clause should be moved closer to the verb it modifies.

> *As they filed out of the stadium,* the fans were still buzzing about the game they had seen.

POSSESSIVE BEFORE A GERUND

A gerund, you will recall, is a verbal noun. A gerund is a verb form that ends in *-ing* but functions as a noun in a sentence. Like other nouns, gerunds can be modified by nouns and pronouns that are in their possessive forms. In fact, a noun or pronoun that precedes a gerund in a sentence *must* be in its possessive form.

> *Writing* can be a lonely profession. (gerund as subject)
> *Tom's writing* has improved lately. (gerund modified by possessive noun)
> *His writing* is really quite good. (gerund modified by possessive pronoun)

The previous sentences offer no problem. However, when a gerund functions as a direct object or as the object of a preposition, a possessive form that precedes it may not sound so proper.

> We were surprised at *Tom's behaving* that way.

The possessive noun *Tom's* is proper before the gerund *behaving*. It would be nonstandard to write the sentence without the possessive form.

> *We were surprised at *Tom* behaving that way.

This sentence is nonstandard because we were not surprised at *Tom,* but, rather, at Tom's *behaving.* Replacing the gerund with a similar noun, *behavior,* shows this meaning clearly.

> We were surprised at *Tom's behavior.*

You must train your ear to listen for possessive nouns and pronouns that precede a gerund in a sentence.

> *I couldn't understand *Fred firing* his best employee.
> I couldn't understand *Fred's firing* his best employee.

> *He apparently didn't like *me asking* for a raise.
> He apparently didn't like *my asking* for a raise.

Usage Checklist

The sentences in the following checklist concern usage problems that are discussed in Chapter 8 and Chapter 9. Some of the sentences contain usage errors, some contain two usages—only one of which is standard, and some are perfectly standard, requiring no changes at all. The answer key at the bottom identifies the changes that each nonstandard sentence requires (shown in italic type), identifies the proper choice of the two usages given, or identifies (with the letter C) the sentences that are correct. The page numbers refer to the pages on which each particular usage problem is discussed.

1. My wife JoAnne is a flight attendant.
2. This vacation package can be quite inexpensive. Which is its biggest selling point.
3. A cab was sent for Charlie and (I, me).
4. Just between you and (I, me), this thing will never fly.
5. The distance between us and them is more than a mile.
6. Honesty is the most important characteristic in the relationship between she and I.
7. I had no idea (who, whom) would be the winner.
8. I wonder (who, whom) she will bring with her.
9. He is the man (who, whom) they want for their candidate.
10. The award will go to whoever has the most points.
11. They were simply better than (we, us).
12. This is the house (that, which) I want to buy.
13. She is one of those women who (is, are) beautiful in any light.
14. I would appreciate (you, your) sending me an application.
15. I couldn't understand (Kathy, Kathy's) blaming me for her accident.

Answers: 1. , *JoAnne,* (p. 110) 2. *inexpensive, which* (p. 111) 3. me (p. 120) 4. me (p. 120) 5. C (p. 120) 6. *her and me* (p. 120) 7. who (p. 121) 8. whom (p. 121) 9. whom (p. 121) 10. C (p. 122) 11. we (p. 123) 12. that (p. 124) 13. are (p. 125) 14. your (p. 127) 15. Kathy's (p. 127)

10. PET PEEVES

In Chapter 3 I suggested that you think of various usages not as being "correct" or "incorrect," but, rather, as being "standard" or "nonstandard" and "appropriate" or "inappropriate" for a given situation. Viewed in this way, certain nonstandard forms can be (and are) quite "correct" at times because they contribute to communication rather than detract from it. There are, however, many nonstandard usages that don't contribute anything at all to the conveyance of ideas or the acceptance of the user. The most positive thing that a user of these forms can hope for is that they will go unnoticed, for, if they are recognized at all—no matter where or when they are employed—their effect is always negative. In other words, there is simply no reason at all for *choosing* to use these nonstandard forms, and it is quite likely that they persist solely out of habit.

Most of these usages occur only in speech because the process of writing allows the user the necessary time to realize that the forms are habitual, meaningless, or even absurd. Some do find their way into writing as well, and they reflect even more unkindly on the writer as a result.

From the many nonstandard forms that fall into this category, I have chosen five that are particularly irritating to me. These "pet peeves" have been selected because they are the ones I find to be most commonly used by people who should know better. If I have omitted some that are even more repulsive to you, please understand that the selection process was particularly difficult in that there were many highly qualified nominees. May I have the envelope, please?

"YOU KNOW"

Whenever I listen to an athlete being interviewed, I wonder whether there isn't some biological connection between athletic ability and the number of times a person can use "you know" in a sentence. Most professional athletes reach a 5.0 to 5.5 "you know's per sentence" average at the height of their career; any collegiate athlete whose average is higher than his grade-point average is surely destined to achieve stardom in the pros. But then I hear teenagers, teachers, reporters, politicians, and others with little claim to athletic prowess utter sentences teeming with one "you know" after another, and I realize that the problem is only related to athletes in that athletes are more often interviewed than the rest of us and that athletes so often serve as role-models for our children.

"You know" has come to be the favorite

"filler" of the day. It is not used to mean "do you know . . . ?" but, rather, it is employed whenever a spoken sentence has a break that is long enough to fit it. It is the most common method people have for avoiding what they believe to be embarrassing pauses for thought while speaking. This is why "you know" (which is most frequently pronounced "ya know") is seldom seen in writing: Writing appears to the reader to be a constant flow of thoughts. The necessary time for reflection between words or sentences is simply invisible.

When I was in school, the most common "filler" was simply the sound "ah." Every break in speech that signified that thinking and speaking could not occur at the same time was filled with an "ah," sometimes stretching into an interminable "ahhhhhh." This "filler," in fact, became almost a badge announcing that the speaker was giving each word and sentence the benefit of careful deliberation. It is true that sentences overrun by "ah" become quite irritating to the listener, but, if one must use a "filler" at all, I prefer "ah" to "you know" hands down. "Ah" is a static "filler" in that it doesn't, by itself, say anything. "You know," on the other hand, *appears* to ask a question or make a statement. I think it is quite likely that the people who pepper their sentences with "you know" use it as an abbreviation for "I hope that you know what I am saying because I just don't have the verbal skill to express it more clearly."

I honestly don't mind hearing or using "you know" once in a while. I find nothing objectionable about its occasional use as a "sentence starter."

You know, I've never really thought about that before.

The problem is that, once used, "you know" tends to breed uncontrollably. Soon it appears at the start of *every* sentence, and shortly thereafter it spreads throughout the sentences, even existing as twins or triplets in longer pauses.

*You know, I've never, you know, really, you know, you know, thought about that before, you know.

The fact that "you know" frequently clones itself into bunches is evidence that the user simply doesn't realize that he is saying the phrase at all. There is a hypnosis that affects a person who uses any "filler" over and over, sentence after sentence, and it is by breaking this trance, by making the person aware of each use, that the frequency of use can be diminished and the use itself eventually eliminated.

If you have a child who habitually uses "you know" in his speech, and if you have cultivated an understanding with your child such that he welcomes (or at least accepts) your corrections because he realizes that they are made with his own interest in mind, then don't let a single "you know" slip from his lips without immediately interrupting with "No, I don't; tell me about it."

Child: Joey Snider, you know . . .
Parent: No, I don't; tell me about it.
Child: Sorry. Well, he is always, you know . . .
Parent: No, I don't; tell me about it.

Child: I mean, he is always acting up in class, so today, you know . . .

Parent: No, I don't; tell me about it.

Even though you will be interrupting at a dizzying frequency during the first day or two, you must be sure that you use *exactly* the same sentence for each interruption. You need not use the one I have suggested, but the one you select must be kept intact every time. What you are trying to do is to so thoroughly embed this sentence in your child that he will begin to anticipate its coming.

If you are vigilant and do not let a "you know" slip by without a response, and if you are careful to keep the response exactly the same each time, a critical point will occur after just a few days. Your child will become so accustomed to hearing "No I don't; tell me about it" after each "you know" that he will supply the sentence himself before you can interrupt.

Child: We were all going down to the carwash, you know . . .

Parent: No, I don't; tell me about it.

Child: I mean, we were all going down to the carwash in Dale's pickup, you know—I know, "No, I don't; tell me about it"—but none of us . . .

Parent: Very good.

You must still keep the pressure constant; the use of "you know" may become less frequent, and so you must become even more sensitive to it. The crucial moment for eliminating this usage altogether is at hand. Once your child anticipates the response "No, I don't; tell me about it" *before* he utters "you know," he has the opportunity to avoid using the phrase at all. He will have become aware of a "you know" that he was about to use, but didn't.

You and your child will now find it profitable to practice the interruption silently, to yourselves, when you hear "you know" begin, multiply, and cascade from any speaker. You can even participate aloud when you are listening to someone speak over the television or radio. This type of practice is good fun and constantly reinforces the idea that every "you know" is obvious to others and easily avoided.

While I have concentrated here on my least favorite "filler," I do recognize that other, perhaps equally detestable, words and phrases are used today in the same way, and with similar frequency, as "you know." The words "like," "man," and "okay" (as well as the ever-popular "and stuff") spring quickly to mind, and it is worth noting, I think, that some people employ *all* of these forms, including "you know," as "fillers." If your child continually uses one or more of these "fillers" without realizing that he is doing so, try the same method I suggested for eliminating "you know." Develop your own phrase or sentence that you willl use as an interrupter and *stick with it*. Your child will gradually begin to recognize the "fillers" he has used, and finally he will recognize one that he was about to use. If any of these "fillers" are as noxious to you as they are to me, I am sure you will agree that their extermination is unquestionably worth the effort.

"HE GOES, SHE GOES, I GO"

Some adults and many teenagers today

have fallen into the habit of using the verb *go* to mean *say* during the telling of a story.

> *Well, after the first pitch he *goes,* "What was wrong with that?" So I *go,* "It wasn't even close to the plate." Then he *goes...*"[1]

Whenever I hear "he goes," "she goes," or "I go" at the start of a narrative, I feel like *going* myself, as far and as fast as possible. Like "you know," *go* tends to multiply so rapidly that one usage simply cannot exist all by itself: Once a story begins with a single *go* that means *say,* you can bet that this usage will persist throughout.

The use of *go* in telling stories is also like "you know" in that it is used unconsciously— people who use it don't realize they are doing so and don't understand how irritating it is to their listeners. Consequently, the method for correcting this usage will, once again, focus on making the user aware of what he is saying.

If you have developed a relationship with your child that will permit you to interrupt his stories without making him reluctant to tell those stories, then the question *"Where* did (you, he, she, they) go?" can be effectively used for your interrupter.

Child: We were just sitting on the floor and the principal goes ...
Parent: *Where* did he go?
Child: Huh? Oh, I mean the principal *said,* "Shouldn't you boys be in class?" So I go ...
Parent: *Where* did you go?
Child: So I *said* ...

If you are persistent in this effort and consistent in the form of your question, your child will soon supply the question himself after uttering a *go* that he was too slow to catch. His quickness will improve in time, and your interruptions will no longer be necessary.

What form your child chooses to use as a replacement for *go* and *goes* in telling stories can be a bit troublesome. The past tense verb form *said* works quite well because it describes an action that happened in the past. But some people try to make their stories seem more current by using a verb tense known as the *narrative present.* Verbs in the narrative present allow the speaker to describe past actions as though they were occurring in the present. The italicized verbs in the following story are in the narrative present:

> The doctor *comes* in and *says,* "What seems to be your trouble." I *say,* "I think I have amnesia, Doc," and so he *says,* "Then be sure to pay your bill before you leave."

In the following version these verbs appear in their past tense forms:

> The doctor *came* in and *said,* "What seems to be your trouble?" I *said,* "I think I have amnesia, Doc," and so he *said,* "Then be sure to pay your bill before you leave."

Stories that are told using the narrative present throughout can become somewhat irritating to the listener. This form has pitfalls for the speaker, too, in that it can be difficult

[1] An asterisk (*) is used throughout this book to identify words, phrases, and sentences that do not conform to the principles of standard usage.

to keep all the verbs consistently in the present tense. (The previous story, for example, might have begun *"The doctor *came* in and *says* . . .") Present tense verbs also offer more possibility for errors in agreement than do past tense verbs. So, although anything is better than *go* or *goes* for telling stories (with the possible exception of *went*), past tense forms (such as *said*) are better replacements than are the verbs in the narrative present (such as *say* or *says*). The narrative present can be used on occasion and for variety, but the past tense should be the form from which you depart.

One other thought and then we'll move on to the next "pet peeve." I said earlier that you must develop a relationship with your child that will permit language correction without destroying his desire to tell stories or to speak at all. In order to preserve your child's interest in speaking with you, it is best to concentrate on correcting one language flaw at a time. If your child consistently uses both "you know" and "goes" in relating a story, pick out the one usage you want to attack first, and interrupt only when that usage occurs. After that flaw has been eliminated, you can then move on to attacking the next. There will be plenty of time to accomplish this in two (or more) separate steps, and to try to correct all the errors at once causes so many interruptions that most children become disillusioned and discouraged.

"KIND OF, SORT OF"

The phrases "kind of . . ." and "sort of . . ." are quite proper when they mean "a variety or a type of" whatever they refer to. For example, "This *kind of* tree bears no fruit" and "That *sort of* mistake is inexcusable." However, when "kind of" and "sort of" are used to mean "somewhat" or "rather," they are nonstandard and worth exorcising from your own and your children's speech and writing.

> *I'm going home because I feel *kind of* ill.
> *Her hair had a *sort of* mousey look to it.

The first step toward eliminating this nonstandard usage is to convince your child that the words *rather* and *somewhat* are not "prissy" or "overly refined." Your child must understand that these words are very commonly used by people of all regions and groups. Only if your child becomes comfortable using "rather" and "somewhat" will he be able to avoid "kind of" and "sort of" without recasting an entire sentence each time.

The best interrupter to employ when you hear this nonstandard use of "kind of" or "sort of" is to ask "What kind was it?" or "What sort was it?" At first these questions will produce a look of astonishment and a question similar to "What kind of what?" It is worthy of noting that this response includes a perfectly standard use of "kind of"—that is, a use that implies "type" or "variety." Early conversations are likely to take the following form:

Child: I thought my locker had been smelling sort of strange . . .
Parent: What sort was it?
Child: Huh? What do you mean? What sort of what?
Parent: You said that your locker had been smelling *sort of* strange, and I want to know *what* sort of strange.
Child: Well, it had just been smelling strange, that's all.

Parent: How about "*rather* strange"?
Child: Okay, I thought my locker had been smelling *RATHER* strange lately . . .
Parent: Very good.

Part of the difficulty in eliminating the nonstandard use of "kind of" and "sort of" is that, even when they are used to mean "type" or "variety," they can have nonstandard forms. For example, the nouns *kind* and *sort* have the plural forms *kinds* and *sorts*. These plural forms must be used when more than one type or variety is being referred to; the singular forms are used when referring to only one type or variety.

> What *kind* of *thing* is that to say? (*kind* and *thing* are both singular)
> Those *kinds* of *remarks* can cause trouble. (*kinds* and *remarks* are both plural)

Nonstandard usages result from mixing these singular and plural forms.

> *What *kind* of *flowers* are *those*? (*kind* is singular, but *flowers* and *those* are plural)
> *These *sort* of *people* cannot be helped. (*sort* is singular, but *these* and *people* are plural)

Some people also create nonstandard forms by using the article *a* after *kind of* or *sort of.*

> *The story was a *kind of a* tragedy.

You should be alert to these nonstandard usages in your own and your children's speaking and writing, but your primary concern should remain the elimination of "kind of" and "sort of" to mean "rather" or "somewhat."

When "kind of" or "sort of" is used to modify a verb in a sentence, the expression cannot usually be replaced merely by substituting "rather" or "somewhat."

> *With this pen, the ink *kind of flows* on the paper.
> With this pen, the ink *seems to flow* on the paper.

Here again, the idea is to replace "kind of" or "sort of" with words that more precisely express your intended meaning.

In many instances, however, the "kind of" or "sort of" can be simply dropped from the sentence altogether without causing any change in the intended meaning.

> *Her testimony *sort of* makes me think I could have been mistaken.
> Her testimony makes me think I could have been mistaken.

"Has got, Have got"

Perhaps the most common of all the nonstandard forms are the phrases "has got" and "have got" to mean "has," "have," or "must." Many times the helping verb *have* appears as a contraction and is attached to a preceding noun or pronoun.

> *She *has got* to win this point.
> *I *have got* to be home early.
> *I've got* to be home early.

Notice that the word *got* can be eliminated from each of the sentences above without causing any change in the intended meaning. (The contraction *I've*, of course, must then be written as two words.) The phrases *have got to* and *has got to* can also be replaced by the helping verb *must*.

Although these nonstandard forms occasionally appear in writing, they are most frequently found in speech, and they are, I believe, a direct result of the ease with which *has* and *have* can be *spoken* as contractions. You see, the written contractions using *have* are quite common (*I've, you've we've, they've,* etc.), but those using *has* are not. Forms such as *she's, it's, Skip's,* etc., are representations of *she is, it is,* and the possessive form of *Skip*. But when these contractions are *pronounced*, they can take on the sound of the joining of *she + has, it + has,* and *Skip + has*.

Now, what does all this have to do with *got*? Well, in the standard sentences that follow, the emphasis is placed on the verbs *has* and *have*.

We *have* to hurry.
It *has* to be there by tomorrow.

But if you try to pronounce these verbs as contractions, you simply cannot place the emphasis where it belongs.

*We've to hurry.
*It's to be there by tomorrow.

Consequently, speakers who pronounce these helping verbs as contractions are forced into adding the verb *got* and placing the emphasis on that verb.

*We've *got* to hurry.
*It's *got* to be there by tomorrow.

Therefore, the first step toward eliminating

have got and *has got* from your own or your children's speech is to concentrate on pronouncing *have* and *has* as separate and distinct verbs rather than as contractions. (There is some overlapping benefit here in that the phrases *would have, should have, might have,* etc., will not be slurred into *would of, *should of, *might of,* etc.) It is still quite possible that *got* will find its way into the verb phrase even though *has* and *have* are pronounced distinctly. But this problem can then be solved by asking a question like "*Where did you get it?*" after each such usage.

Another remedy is to merely inject the helping verb *must* into any sentence in which you hear *has got* or *have got*.

Child: Each of us has got to bring . . .
Parent: Must!
Child: Each of us *must* bring a note from his parents.
Parent: Can you say that sentence any other way?
Child: Each of us is supposed to bring a note from his parents.
Parent: All right, but how about just using *has*?
Child: Each of us *has* to bring a note from his parents.
Parent: Very good.

After several sessions like this one, children frequently wonder whether *got* has any standard use at all. Its most common standard use is as the past tense of the verb *get*, which means "to receive," "to arrive" (as in "*Get* home by nine o'clock"), "to persuade" (as in "*Get* her to stay here"), and several other meanings as well. So, it is quite proper to say "I *got* hit by a stone" or "They *got* caught by the police," but those usages have nothing to do with the idea of *must*—that is, with the notion of necessity.

The past participle of *get* can be either *got* or *gotten*: *Got* is preferred in Britain—*gotten*, in the United States. By using *gotten* as the past participle of *get,* and by using *got* only for the past tense, you will improve your chances of avoiding the nonstandard **has got* and **have got* to mean "must."

> I *got* a good tan during my vacation. (past tense)
> I *have gotten* tan before, but never like this. (past participle)

Whenever possible, however, you should look for alternatives to *has gotten* and *have gotten*—verbs that express your meaning more precisely than these phrases do.

> I *have gotten* straight A's in English. (consider: *have received* or *have earned*)
> She *has gotten* more beautiful with age. (consider: *has become* or *has grown*)

"Hopefully"

This final "pet peeve" just may be the most vexing of all. Not only is it frequently used in both speaking and writing, but it is also frequently defended as being standard.

The adverb *hopefully* usually appears at the very beginning or at the very end of a sentence, and the reason for this is that if it would be placed nearer the verb (as other adverbs can be), it would have a different meaning from the one its users generally intend.

> *Hopefully, we will struggle on to victory.
> *We will struggle on to victory, hopefully.

In the preceding sentences the word *hopefully* is used to mean "I hope." For some strange reason, speakers and writers think that using "I hope" is less polished or less polite than using "hopefully." Yet the adverb *hopefully* means "full of hope," not "I hope." In the previous example, if *hopefully* is moved closer to the verb, it clearly answers the question "How?" about the verb.

> We will struggle *hopefully* on to victory.

In other words, we will not struggle *dejectedly,* but, rather, *full of hope*. Notice that the meaning "I hope" has completely disappeared.

If a speaker or writer wishes to say "I hope" or "It is hoped," then I think he should say that, and in those words. The adverb *hopefully,* on the other hand, should be reserved for those instances in which it has the meaning "full of hope." To me the most memorable example of the correct use of *hopefully* is Robert Louis Stevenson's "To travel hopefully is a better thing than to arrive."

Some authorities on language argue that *hopefully* can be used as a "sentence adverb" (see "Sentence Adverbs," Chapter 4, page 62). That is, rather than modifying any specific word in the sentence, *hopefully* can be viewed as modifying the *entire* sentence. They point out that, in this use, *hopefully* is no different from other sentence adverbs such as *frankly, certainly, actually,* etc.

> *Frankly,* I don't think it can be done.
> *Certainly,* I'll give you a hand.
> He hasn't been home in a month, *actually.*

However, *hopefully* is different from these other adverbs. In each of these other usages, the phrase for which the sentence adverb stands is much more difficult to plug into its sentence than "I hope (that)" is as a replacement for *hopefully*. For example, the sentence "*Hopefully,* we will be in a better position by then" can be easily changed into "*I hope that* we will be in a better position by then." But notice how awkward it is to replace the sentence adverb *certainly* in the following sentence:

> *Certainly,* I'd be glad to do it.
> *I am certain that* I'd be glad to do it.

Because *hopefully* is seldom used to mean "full of hope," and because it is so easy to fall into the habit of using *hopefully* to mean "I hope," I suggest that, as a general rule, you avoid using the word altogether. It adds nothing positive to your speaking or writing, and it is frequently viewed by others as a sign that you either don't know or don't care about the meaning of the words you use. Besides, like all the other "pet peeves" in this chapter, *hopefully* has a tendency to spread uncontrollably and to infect sentence after sentence. Just listen to any interview of a politician or any prediction by a weather forecaster and you will be convinced of the pervasiveness of this disease.

11. SPELLING

IMPROVING YOUR CHILD'S SPELLING

The argument "What difference does it make as long as he knows what I mean" is heard less frequently in the area of spelling than it is in the other areas of English usage. Even children understand that improper spelling characterizes the writer as "unlearned" in spite of the fact that he was able to convey his intended meaning.

A more common complaint—one that each of us has expressed at one time or another—is "Why can't words be spelled the way they sound?" or "Why must spelling be so irregular and illogical?" Indeed, English spelling seems almost arbitrary in the way it represents sounds with letters. The four-letter combination *ough,* for example, has a different sound in each of the following words: *though, tough, through, thorough, thought, cough, plough.* Then, too, English has a variety of ways for spelling the same sound. The letters and letter combinations in the following list are all pronounced with the same sound, as the examples in parentheses demonstrate.

e	(met)	*ie*	(friend)
a	(any)	*ea*	(bread)
u	(bury)	*ai*	(said)
ei	(heiffer)	*eo*	(leopard)

George Bernard Shaw demonstrated that the word *fish* could be spelled *ghoti* by using the sounds of *gh* in *laugh, o* in *women,* and *ti* in *nation.* (You and your children can have some fun inventing similar "words." Once you arrive at a spelling, however, be sure to divulge either the pronunciation or the words that contributed to that pronunciation. The child can then puzzle over how the word was formed or how it is pronounced.)

This complaint about the irregularity of English spelling will certainly be voiced by your children, and so you should have some ammunition on hand to counter it. The following thoughts may help in this regard. The reason that English spelling is so irregular and seems so confusing is that English is a mixture of many languages—some of which are no longer used by any people in the world. But English is not different from other languages in this way, nor is it the most irregular language of all. No language that is completely regular in every way has ever been discovered—or even invented. Still, people are able to communicate effectively in their own irregular languages, and they will continue to do so because they have no alternative. The English language has been used by billions of people, many of whom have cursed its irregularities but mastered them just the same. The point to remember is that these irregularities *are* English; they are not likely to vanish in our lifetime, if ever. You must accept the language as it is, warts and all, or doom yourself (and your children) to a life of constant apology.

Parents' attitudes toward spelling contribute to a child's spelling habits more than any other single factor. The parent who retains the "I never was much good at spelling" attitude gives his child a handy excuse whenever spelling lessons become difficult. Unless parents firmly believe in the importance of correct spelling, and appreciate the precision of correct spelling, they cannot expect these attitudes to take root in their children. Parents need not be perfect spellers themselves, but *they must demonstrate a concern for perfect spelling.* In this way parents avoid the "Do as I say, not as I do" posture, which we all know to be not just worthless, but counterproductive.

One of the ways that parents can create an environment in which spelling is seen to be important (and, at the same time, improve their own spelling skills) is to display a curiosity about how words are spelled and pronounced. Rather than merely accept the forms that are used in newspapers and magazines, a parent can say "That just doesn't look right to me; let's check it in the dictionary." Once the word is located, the parent and child should try to think of the ways in which similar words are spelled, or the spelling of different forms of that word. The silent *g* in *sign,* for example, seems less arbitrary when the word is related to *signal.* So, too, the silent *c* in *muscle* and the final *b* in *bomb* seem much more logical when the forms *muscular* and *bombard* are analyzed. The spelling of a word such as *treasure* might bring to mind the words *pleasure* and *measure,* while the single *l* in *traveled* might make one curious about the spelling of *traveling* and *traveler.*

Proper pronunciation is vital to proper spelling. Not only should parents display a curiosity about the pronunciations used on television and radio, they should concentrate on the way that they and their children enunciate the words used during conversation in the home. A child who constantly hears a slovenly pronunciation of *going to* and *have to,* for example, is quite likely to think that these phrases are spelled *gunna and *hafta.[1] Mispronunciation also, I think, accounts for misspellings such as *probaly for *probably,* *reconize for *recognize,* *Febuary for *February,* and *suprise for *surprise.* These words simply must be pronounced correctly in the home if the child is to stand any chance of pronouncing and spelling them correctly in school.[2]

Even young children can be made aware of the basic terminology that is used in spelling. After they have become familiar with the alphabet, children can then profit from knowing that the *vowels a, e, i, o,* and *u* are different from the *consonant* letters. They

[1] An asterisk (*) has been used throughout this book to identify words, phrases, and sentences that do not conform to the principles of standard usage.
[2] A teaching colleague and I once kept a list of outrageous spelling errors that were made by our students. In order to be included on our list, a word had to be so badly misspelled that you could not tell from the word alone exactly what word the child had tried to spell. Every misspelled word on our list was a representation of the way in which its speller pronounced that word. Here are two examples from that list; see if you can tell what words were intended: *pomb, sisieddy.* (Answers: *poem, society*)

should be told that words are made up of *syllables* and that each syllable of a word is pronounced separately. Each syllable has only one vowel sound; although a syllable may contain more than one vowel, it has only one vowel sound. (This is why the letter *y* is sometimes a vowel: It provides the vowel sound of *i* in words like *fly* and *crystal.* It is considered a consonant when it appears at the beginning of a word: *youth, year.*)

All children should be made aware of the difference between *long vowel sounds* and *short vowel sounds.* The following table shows examples of the sounds of long and short vowels.

Long Vowel Sounds	Short Vowel Sounds
long *a* (date)	short *a* (lap)
long *e* (be)	short *e* (bed)
long *i* (*y*) (f*i*nd, cr*y*)	short *i* (*y*) (s*i*t, m*y*th)
long *o* (no)	short *o* (rock)
long *u* (tr*u*th)	short *u* (c*u*t)
long *u* (h*u*ge/yu/)	short *u* (p*u*t)

(Notice that the long *u* can have two different sounds, as can the short *u.* Other vowels can also have sounds not shown for them on the table: f*a*ther, s*o*n, m*o*ve, m*a*chine, etc. Children will gradually come to know the many ways that vowel combinations, can sound. It is of primary importance, however, that they understand the basic meaning of "long" and "short" as the terms apply to vowel sounds.)

Although most consonant letters stand for only one sound, the consonants *c* and *g* have both a *hard* and a *soft* sound. The *hard c* has the sound of *k* in words like *c*arry, *c*ane, and reli*c.* The *soft c* has the sound of *s* in words like *c*eiling and *c*ent. The *hard g* has the sound that begins the words *g*oat and *g*et. The soft *g*

has the sound of *j* in words like *g*em and *g*eneral. (Some other consonant letters besides *c* and *g* can be pronounced in different ways. The consonant *s,* for example, is pronounced as a *z* in words like tie*s* and dog*s,* but has a different sound in *s*ing and cat*s.* These differences will become more important later on. For now, just be sure that the child understands the difference between "hard" and "soft" as these words apply to the sounds of *c* and *g.*)

Children should also be taught the meaning of the term *silent.* **A silent letter is a letter that appears in the spelling of a word, but is not sounded when the word is pronounced.** The letter *b* in the word *debt,* for example, is silent because only the *d, e,* and *t* are sounded. The most common silent letter of all is *e,* and it frequently appears at the end of a word: vin*e,* writ*e,* confus*e.* You may find it helpful to call this a "final *e*" instead of a "silent e" because the letter does have an effect on the sound of the word even though it is not actually pronounced. Keep in mind that the letters in combinations like *ph* (*ph*otograph) are not silent. The combination is sounded even though it is not the sound normally associated with the individual letters.

Once a child understands the meaning of the word *syllable,* he can then be taught to listen for the way that syllables are *accented.* We *accent* (or *stress*) a syllable when we pronounce it more forcefully than we do the other syllables in the word. Start out with two-syllable words that have a distinct accent: *stu'•dent, vil'•lage, pre•fer',* and *re•gret',* for example. Overaccentuate the accented syllable, and then have the child see how strange the word sounds when the accent is placed on the wrong syllable (*stu•dent', *vil•

lage', *pre'·fer, and *re'·gret). Then see if the child can tell which syllable is accented in some common three- or four-syllable words. Introduce your child to the accent marks that are used in the family's dictionary, but do not worry (or even discuss) the secondary accents for now. Just be sure that the child understands the meaning of the word *accent* as it applies to the way in which syllables are pronounced.

Each of the terms I have mentioned, *vowel, consonant, long vowel sound, short vowel sound, consonant sound, hard c* and *hard g, soft c* and *soft g, silent letter, syllable,* and *accented syllable* should be understood by every school-age child, and each can be learned with the help of a concerned parent.

Older children can also be taught the meaning of *prefix*: a word part that is placed in front of a word (or word stem), and *suffix*: a word part that is added to the end of a word (or word stem). Common prefixes such as *re-, pro-, pre-, mis-, de-, dis-, ir-, bi-,* and *un-* can be added to the front of familiar words to show how prefixes change the meaning of those words.

> *re-* + *form* = *reform*
> *pre-* + *view* = *preview*
> *mis-* + *spell* = *misspell*

Common suffixes such as *-ion, -ly, -ful, -cy, -able, -hood, -ous, -ish, -ist, -ive, -less,* and *-y* can be added to the end of familiar words to show how they affect meaning.

> *act* + *-ion* = *action*
> *near* + *-ly* = *nearly*
> *care* + *-ful* = *careful*

The term *word stem* applies to a basic word part that cannot stand alone as a word. For example, *flect* is a word stem that means "to bend." It cannot stand by itself as a word, but a prefix such as *re-* or *de-* can be added to it to create a word. By adding the prefix *re-* and the suffix *-ion* to this word stem, you can create the word *reflection.* Word stems and roots should be discussed only with more advanced spellers, and you should consult the child's text to see how and when these items are taught.

In addition to creating a good spelling environment and acquainting your children with the meaning of some basic terms, you can help them form a habit that will aid them in their spelling for the rest of their lives. This is the habit of always spelling a word one syllable at a time. Whether the child is spelling words in writing or orally, he should attack each word as though it were actually several short words joined together. He should concentrate on spelling the sounds in the first syllable, then the sounds in the second, and so on. I cannot emphasize the importance of this method too strongly. Many long and difficult words—words that seem, at first glance, impossible to spell—can be broken down into easily manageable parts (syllables) and conquered.

You can also help dispel the notion that English spelling is so irregular and has so many exceptions that it is practically impossible to master. Help your child understand that there are many facets of English spelling that are extremely regular, and that he should concentrate on the hundreds or thousands of words that are governed by a particular spelling rule rather than the comparatively few words that are exceptions to that rule. It is important to remember that more than three-quarters of the three thousand words we most frequently use are completely regular in their spelling. (The sounds in words that have regular spellings are spelled exactly the same way each time those sounds occur.) Many consonant sounds are spelled in only one way. Even consonant blends (two or more consonants acting together to form a single sound, as in *gr* or *bl*) generally have only one spelling. Vowel sounds and digraphs (two vowels acting together to form a single sound, as in *ea* or *oo*) have more variations, but there are still only a few ways to spell most of the irregular vowel sounds. By learning how the sounds of various consonants, consonant blends, vowels, and digraphs are spelled, and by concentrating on spelling each syllable one at a time, you can isolate the problem area in any word and choose from only a few possible ways that the sound in that area can be spelled.

Understanding how various sounds are spelled is the study of *phonics*. Your child's spelling text will tell you how certain letters in certain positions can be used as clues to discovering the way in which a sound should be spelled in a given word. Understanding phonics is essential to becoming a good speller. But your child can also build confidence in his spelling by always spelling each word one syllable at a time and by knowing that most of the words that we use most frequently are spelled in completely regular ways.

The spelling rules I will present now deal with words that have had prefixes or suffixes added to them. These rules comprise only a small slice of the rules and patterns that serve as guides to correct spelling. Indeed, there are many other rules than these that deal solely with prefixes and suffixes. I have chosen these few rules because they have surprisingly few

exceptions and because they govern the spelling of many words that children commonly misspell. Most of these rules are intended only for older children; the age of the child and the vocabulary of the child will determine whether you should present any of these rules at all. You may choose to cover a certain rule only when a particular need arises. If your child has made an error in spelling a word that ends in *-ful,* for example, you might cover only this rule and leave the others for later. You may also wish to acquaint your child with the "doubling principle" that is covered later in this chapter. You are the teacher, and you must be the judge of how much material your child can handle and still remain curious about language in general and spelling in particular.

The spelling of a word does not change when a prefix is added.

Prefix	+	Word	=	Result
mis-		take		mistake
dis-		appear		disappear
un-		able		unable
ac-		knowledge		acknowledge
in-		justice		injustice
re-		commend		recommend

A very common spelling mistake occurs when the last letter of a prefix is the same as the first letter of a word (or word stem) to which that prefix is added. The rule above tells you that no letters from the prefix or from the base word should be dropped, and so the double letters that result are perfectly correct. You may find it helpful to spell the base word first, then add the prefix.

Prefix	+	Word	=	Result
mis-		spell		misspell
dis-		satisfied		dissatisfied
un-		necessary		unnecessary
un-		needed		unneeded
un-		natural		unnatural
ac-		count		account
ac-		company		accompany
ap-		point		appoint
ap-		prove		approve
ar-		range		arrange
ar-		rest		arrest
il-		legal		illegal
il-		legible		illegible
ir-		regular		irregular
ir-		reverent		irreverent

The suffix -ful has only one l.

beautiful	peaceful	doubtful
useful	graceful	handful
wonderful	tasteful	harmful
hopeful	spoonful	

This rule is actually part of a larger one: **Words of more than one syllable generally end in one l, not two.**

cruel	symbol
cereal	expel
tranquil	final

(This general rule does not apply to words that are formed by adding a prefix to a one-syllable word: *recall, instill,* etc.)

When a suffix that begins with a vowel is added to a word that ends in *e*, the final *e* is usually dropped.
You can see how important this rule is—how many common words it affects—when you think about all the words you use that end in final *e*, and about all the common suffixes that begin with a vowel (*-ing, -age, -able, -er, -or, -y, -ous*).

Word	+	Suffix	=	Result
bite		-ing		biting
make		-ing		making
use		-age		usage
value		-able		valuable
knowledge		-able		knowledgable
bake		-er		baker
create		-or		creator
fame		-ous		famous

Have your child try using various suffixes at the end of the same base word (*use + -ing, -age, -er, -able*). Also, have him make a list of some more words ending in *e*—there are thousands.

There are a few common words in which the final *e* is kept when a vowel suffix is added. When a word ends in *-ce* or *-ge* and is pronounced with a soft *c* or a soft *g* sound, the *e* is necessary in order to retain the soft consonant sound. (The vowels *e, i,* and *y* are sometimes called "softening vowels" because a *c* or *g* that precedes them generally has a soft sound: pea*ce*able, chan*ge*able, advanta*ge*ous, outra*ge*ous, coura*ge*ous.) The final *e* is also kept to distinguish *holey* ("full of holes") from *holy* ("sacred") and to distinguish *dye-ing* ("to color") from *dying* ("passing away").

When the suffix *-ly* is added to a word ending in *y*, the final *y* is changed to *i.*

Word	+	Suffix	=	Result
ordinary		-ly		ordinarily
merry		-ly		merrily
happy		-ly		happily
easy		-ly		easily

When the suffix -*ly* is added to a word ending in *l*, that final *l* is kept.

Word	+	Suffix	=	Result
natural		-ly		naturally
usual		-ly		usually
general		-ly		generally
awful		-ly		awfully
legal		-ly		legally
partial		-ly		partially

If the base word ends in *le*, the *le* is generally dropped before adding the suffix -*ly*. This will pose little difficulty for you if you remember to pronounce the base word and the new word with the same number of syllables.

able, ably (two syllables)
horrible, horribly (three syllables)
probable, probably (three syllables)
possible, possibly (three syllables)
terrible, terribly (three syllables)
remarkable, remarkably (four syllables)
miserable, miserably (four syllables)

If a vowel precedes the final *y* in a word, the *y* is usually kept when a suffix is added.
The difference between this rule and the one that follows lies in the letter that appears just before the final *y*. Each of the following words has a vowel before the final *y*, and so the *y* is kept when a suffix is added.

Word	+	Suffix	=	Result
employ		-er		employer
destroy		-ing		destroying
play		-able		playable
spray		-ed		sprayed
annoy		-ance		annoyance

The most commonly used exception to this rule is the word *daily*.

If a consonant precedes the final *y* in a word, the *y* is usually changed to *i* before a suffix is added.

Word	+	Suffix	=	Result
noisy		-ly		noisily
merry		-ly		merrily
carry		-ed		carried
dry		-est		driest
lonely		-er		lonelier

When the suffix -*ing* is added, however, the final *y* never changes to *i* (*trying, worrying, crying, marrying*) because this would cause two *i*'s to appear together in the resulting word—a rare occurrence in English spelling. Note: Some words that end in *y* drop that final *y* altogether before a suffix is added (econom*y*—economist, iron*y*—ironic, etc.)

IMPROVING YOUR OWN SPELLING

No one begins life as a good speller; spelling is an acquired skill, not an inherited one. I have some friends who are only too eager to admit their own inability to spell common words correctly. These people would rather apologize for their spelling than take any action at all to correct the deficiency.

Most people believe that if a person did not adopt good spelling habits as a child, it is virtually impossible for him to become a good speller as an adult. This is just plain nonsense! I can tell you from my own experience that the shame and embarrassment of being a high-school or college student who cannot spell even simple words properly can be eliminated entirely in adulthood—and eliminated in a shorter time, with less effort, than you would ever believe possible. Although there is no magic cure for poor spelling, there are approaches to spelling that can bring about immediate and long-lasting results.

The first thing you should realize before you embark on any plan for spelling improvement is that your goal should not be *perfect* spelling. There is absolutely no need for you to be able to spell the hundreds of thousands of English words that you will never have occasion to use in your life. Instead, your goal should be to become a speller who has confidence in his own ability to correctly spell the words he is expected to spell—that is, the words that he uses in his personal and professional writing. Being able to spell a word like *diarrhea,* for example, may win a spelling bee for you, but how many spelling bees do you enter each year? (Parents of very young children, however, do find this word popping up all too frequently in letters to their own parents.) Having this limited goal for your spelling program, then, cuts your task down to a manageable size.

It is also important for you to realize the senselessness of trying to learn the spelling of each word separately. Remembering the precise arrangement of letters in each of the thousands of words you want to spell is possible only if you have a perfectly photographic memory. Spelling confidence comes from being able to rely on patterns and systems that cover hundreds of words at a time. Merely by remembering the pattern, you can confidently spell all the many words that fit that pattern.

Still another logical idea that is frequently overlooked by adults who want to improve

their spelling is that people never misspell an *entire* word. Most people misplace only a very few letters of even the most complicated words. What is the sense, then, of concentrating on all the letters in a certain word when only one or two of those letters cause you any difficulty? How much easier your task would be if you concentrated on spelling the problem area of a word and trusted the ability you already have to spell the rest of it.

This chapter alone cannot, and will not, solve all your spelling problems. If you want to learn additional spelling rules and patterns, there are many books on the market (and in a public library) that are devoted solely to the study of spelling improvement. In this chapter I will cover only one spelling rule, but that rule governs the spelling of thousands of commonly used words, and it has helped me out of more troublesome situations than any other rule I know. I will also demonstrate the use of another spelling system—a system that you can adapt to your own particular spelling needs and that you can build upon for the rest of your life.

Before I discuss this rule and system, let me reiterate a point that was made earlier in this chapter. There is nothing that contributes more directly to poor spelling than poor pronunciation. If you do not pronounce a word properly, there is little likelihood that you will spell that word properly. The word *pronunciation,* itself, is a good case in point. Because this word is the noun form of the verb *pronounce,* many people believe that its second syllable also has the sound /*ounce*/, and so they misspell it **pronounciation.*[1] If you pronounce the word properly, however, so that

---

[1]An asterisk (*) has been used throughout this book to identify words, phrases, and sentences that do not conform to the principles of standard usage.

its second syllable has the sound /*nun*/, you will have no difficulty at all in spelling it properly: pro•*nun*•ci•a•tion.

The words in the following list are frequently mispronounced and, consequently, frequently misspelled as well. When you use these words in speaking, pay particular attention to enunciating every syllable and every sound just as they appear in the spelling of the words.

Spelling	Pronunciation
accidentally	ac•ci•den•tal•ly (not: *ac•ci•dent•ly)
arctic	arc•tic (not *ar•tic)
athlete	ath•lete (not: *ath•a•lete)
cavalry	cav•al•ry (not: *cal•va•ry)
chocolate	choc•o•late (not: *choc•late)
disastrous	dis•as•trous (not: *dis•as•ter•ous)
different	dif•fer•ent (not: *diff•rent)
February	Feb•ru•ar•y (not: *Feb•u•ar•y)
government	gov•ern•ment (not: *gov•er•ment)
hindrance	hin•drance (not: *hin•der•ance)
jewelry	jew•el•ry (not: *jewl•ry)
laundry	laun•dry (not: *laun•der•y)
mischievous	mis•chie•vous (not: *mis•chie•vi•ous)
personally	per•son•al•ly (not: *per•son•ly)
practically	prac•ti•cal•ly (not: *prac•tic•ly)
probably	prob•a•bly (not: *prob•ly)
quantity	quan•ti•ty (not: *quan•i•ty)
remembrance	re•mem•brance (not: *re•mem•ber•ance)
sacrilegious	sac•ri•le•gious (not: *sac•re•li•gious)
surprise	sur•prise (not: *su•prise)
temperature	tem•per•a•ture (not: *tem•pra•ture)
valuable	val•u•a•ble (not: *val•u•ble)

THE DOUBLING RULE

Most adults, even those who call themselves poor spellers, have little difficulty with common words such as *admit, begin,* or *equip.* But when they are faced with the problem of writing longer forms of these words, their confidence vanishes—and for one simple reason: They don't know whether or not to double the final letter of the base form. Should it be *admitance* or *admittance? beginer* or *beginner? equiped* or *equipped?* The doubling rule that I will present now is very complex, but it can be learned—it can even be memorized. The best part about it is that this rule will solve your doubling problems *right now.* By studying this rule you can have confidence in your own ability to spell thousands of common words, including a hundred or so words that are among the most commonly misspelled words in our language.

I said that this rule is very complex, and so

147

I will break the rule down into pieces and then build the pieces back into the whole rule again. If you concentrate on each piece, you will have no difficulty understanding the whole.

The first thing you should know is that this doubling rule applies only to *words that end in a single consonant preceded by a single vowel*. Commit that to memory: *words that end in a single consonant preceded by a single vowel*. Before you think that this doubling rule is so limited that it can't apply to many words at all, consider the implications of the phrase you memorized. We are interested in whether or not the final letter of a base word is doubled before adding a suffix. The phrase tells us that the only words we will look at end in a single consonant. Well, there are surprisingly few words in the language that end in two consonants, and these words pose little difficulty in spelling their longer forms (*end* + *-ing*, *loss* + *-es*, *part* + *-ed*, etc.) And, although we will not look at words that end in a vowel, think about how awkward doubling a vowel would be. Only *ee* and *oo* appear in any common words; *aa, ii, uu,* and *yy* never do. Instead, the words we will consider all end in the following pattern: consonant—vowel—consonant. Some examples of words that fit this pattern are *ship, stop, refer, regret.*

Now, here is the first piece of the rule: **When a word ends in a single consonant preceded by a single vowel, double the final consonant before adding a suffix that begins with a vowel.** Again, this appears to severely limit the type of words covered, but let's look at it closely. *Only* when you add a suffix that begins with a vowel do you double the final consonant. If the suffix does not begin with a vowel, you do not double the final consonant.

ship + -ing (vowel suffix)	= shi*pp*ing
ship + -ed (vowel suffix)	= shi*pp*ed

But:

ship + -ment (consonant suffix)	= shi*p*ment

Notice how the rest of our example words fit the double rule. The final consonant in each is doubled before adding a suffix that begins with a vowel; the final consonant is not doubled if the suffix begins with a consonant.

stop + -ed (vowel suffix)	= sto*pp*ed
refer + -al (vowel suffix)	= refe*rr*al
regret + -ing (vowel suffix)	= regre*tt*ing

But:

regret + -fully (consonant suffix)	= regretfully

The first piece of the rule tells you one other thing: *If the end of the word does not fit the consonant—vowel—consonant pattern, you do NOT double the final consonant before adding a vowel suffix.* Consider the words *break* and *scream*. Both end in a single consonant, but that consonant is preceded by two vowels, not just one. Therefore, the final consonant is not doubled when you add a suffix.

```
break    +  -ing  =  breaking
scream   +  -ed   =  screamed
```

Practice the piece of the rule you have learned so far by combining the following words and suffixes.

```
spin + -ing      =  _____
fog + -y         =  _____
span + -ed       =  _____
rob + -ery       =  _____
wet + -ness      =  _____
flat + -en       =  _____
squirt + -ing    =  _____
prefer + -ed     =  _____
hot + -est       =  _____
dream + -er      =  _____
```

(Answers: spinning, foggy, spanned, robbery, wetness, flatten, squirting, preferred, hottest, dreamer)

Now go back over the list to see why the three words that did not have their final consonants doubled do not fit the conditions stated in the rule. (Note: The consonants *w* and *x* are never doubled, and most people would never consider doubling them. Therefore: plowing, growing, boxing, flexed, etc.)

The second piece of the rule applies to words that have more than one syllable. *When a word ends in a single consonant preceded by a single vowel—and is accented on the last syllable—double the final consonant before adding a suffix that begins with a vowel.* So, unless the word is accented on its last syllable, you do not double its final consonant. The word *differ,* for example, is accented on the first syllable—not the last: *dif'•fer.* Therefore, you would not double the final *r* before adding the suffixes *-ed, -ence,* or *-ing*: differed, difference, differing. The word *regret,* on the other hand, is accented on the last syllable: *re•gret'.* Therefore, you would double the final *t* before adding the suffixes *-ed, -ing,* or *-able*: regretted, regretting, regrettable.

You might think of this part of the rule as operating in reverse. For example, the words *kidnap, travel,* and *gallop* are all accented on the first syllable: *kid'•nap, trav'•el, gal'•lop.* If their longer forms (*kidnaped, kidnaping, kidnaper, traveled, traveling, traveler, galloped,* and *galloping*) were created by doubling the final consonant, they would have to be accented on another syllable. The non-standard spelling **kidnapped,* for instance, would have to be pronounced **kid•napped',* **travelling* would have to be pronounced **tra•vel'•ling,* and **gallopping* would have to be pronounced **gal•lop'•ping.* By pronouncing these words properly you will also be able to remember that the doubling rule does not apply to them. (Note: The noun *transfer* is accented on the first syllable: trans' fer, but when the same word is used as a verb, it may be accented on the second syllable: *trans•fer'.* It is this second pronunciation that governs the spelling of the longer forms *transferred* and *transferring,* both of which may also be accented on the first syllable.)

In combining the following words and suffixes, first check to see whether the suffix begins with a vowel, then see whether the ending of the word fits the pattern given in the rule, and, finally, check to see whether the word is accented on its last syllable.

refer + -ing	=	_____
admit + -ance	=	_____
profit + -able	=	_____
occur + -ed	=	_____
label + -ed	=	_____
forget + -ful	=	_____
detail + -ed	=	_____
transmit + -al	=	_____
edit + -ed	=	_____
confer + -ing	=	_____

confer (con•fer′) + -ence	=	conference (con′•fer•ence)
prefer (pre•fer′) + -ence	=	preference (pref′•er•ence)
prefer (pre•fer′) + -able	=	preferable (pref′•er•a•ble)
infer (in•fer′) + -ence	=	inference (in′•fer•ence)
refer (re•fer′) + -ee	=	(ref′•er•ee)

(Answers: referring, admittance, profitable, occurred, labeled, forgetful, detailed, transmittal, edited, conferring)

Now go back over the list to see why the five words that did not have their final letter doubled did not meet the conditions stated in the rule.

And now, here is the last piece of the puzzle. **If the accent on a word shifts to another syllable when the suffix is added, do not double the final consonant.** For example, the word *refer* meets all of the conditions previously stated in the doubling rule: It ends in a single consonant preceded by a single vowel, and it is accented on the last syllable (*re•fer′*). Therefore, you would double the final *r* before adding the vowel suffix *-ing*: referring. Notice that after this suffix has been added, the accent in the newly formed word falls on the same syllable it did in the original word—that is, on the sound /fer/: *re•fer′, re•fer′•ring*. But a strange thing happens when the suffix *-ence* is added to *refer:* The new word, *reference,* is no longer accented on the sound /fer/ (ref′•er•ence). The accent has "shifted" to another syllable and now falls on another sound. The third piece of the doubling rule tells you that when an accent shift like this occurs, *do not double the final consonant before adding the suffix.*

Now, let's put all the pieces of the doubling rule back together again. **When a word ends in a single consonant preceded by a single vowel, and is accented on the last syllable, double the final consonant before adding a suffix that begins with a vowel—unless the suffix causes the accent to shift to another syllable.** The rule sounds impossibly difficult in this form, but now that you know the three pieces from which it is built, you can understand the rule and use it to confidently spell thousands of words.

Although the doubling rule is amazingly free of exceptions, there are a few words that defy the rule just the same. The most commonly used exceptions are listed below.

*excel*lent (but: excelled, excelling)
*cancel*lation (but: canceled, canceling)
*tranquil*lity (but: tranquilizer)
*outfit*ting, outfitted
*gas*es, gaseous, gasification
*bus*es (or busses)
*metal*lic

Here are ten more words to test your knowledge of the doubling rule, but don't stop with these. Whenever you see a word (in a newspaper or a magazine, for instance) that has (or should have) undergone the doubling process, separate the base word from the suffix and determine for yourself whether the spelling given complies with the rule. This will not only provide you with constant reinforcement for the rule you have learned, but you will frequently discover that your ability in this area is better than that of many writers and proofreaders.

occur + -ence	=	_____
benefit + -ing	=	_____
develop + -ed	=	_____
control + -er	=	_____
travel + -ing	=	_____
expel + -ed	=	_____
shovel + -ed	=	_____
excel + -ent	=	_____
marvel + -ous	=	_____
counsel + -or	=	_____

(Answers: occ*urr*ence, benef*it*ing, deve*lop*ed, contro*ll*er, trave*l*ing, expe*ll*ed, shove*l*ed, exce*ll*ent, marve*l*ous, counse*l*or)

MNEMONICS

Everyone has his own personal spelling problems, and, of course, not all of these problems can be solved by the doubling rule. What is needed is a system that would allow each person to overcome the specific problems he has spelling specific words. The mnemonic system can do exactly that. The word *mnemonics* (pronounced: *nee•mon'•iks,* the first *m* is silent) comes from the name of the Greek goddess of memory, Mnemosyne (pronounced: nee•mos'•e•nee). Mnemonics applies to any system that improves or aids the memory. For example, when I began tak-

ing piano lessons, I was taught that the lines on the treble clef musical staff represented the notes E, G, B, D, and F, and that the easiest way to remember these notes and their order was to think of the sentence *Every Good Boy Deserves Fudge.* This was a mnemonic system—a memory aid that has remained with me even though everything else I learned about playing the piano has vanished. Perhaps your geography teacher taught you to remember the names of the five Great Lakes by thinking of the word *HOMES: Huron, Ontario, Michigan, Erie, Superior.* This, too, is an example of mnemonics.

The beauty of using mnemonics in spelling is that you can create your own memory aids and tailor them to help you spell those specific words that give you trouble. Mnemonics can allow you to link several difficult words together under one memory aid, it can be expanded to meet the needs of your expanding vocabulary, and it is absolutely portable: It can be called upon and relied upon wherever you go for the rest of your life.

Strangely enough, you already know at least one very handy spelling mnemonic, and you probably use it quite frequently.

> *I* before *E*
> Except after *C*
> Or when sounded like *A*
> As in *neighbor* and *weigh.*

We all learned this little poem as a means of helping us remember whether a word contains the letter combinations *ie* or *ei.* Let's take the poem apart and see how reliable a spelling aid it actually is.

The first two lines ("*I* before *E*, except after *C*") tell us that the combination *ie* is the one to choose, except when a *c* precedes these letters, in which case, the combination *cei* is correct.

IE	CEI
rel*ie*ve	re*cei*ve
bel*ie*ve	*cei*ling
th*ie*f	con*cei*ve
f*ie*rce	de*cei*ve
shr*ie*k	per*cei*ve
br*ie*f	re*cei*pt
cash*ie*r	
y*ie*ld	

The last two lines of the poem ("or when sounded like A, as in *neighbor* or *weigh*") tell us that the *ei* combination is also correct when the sound created by these vowels is the long *a* sound, as in the words *neighbor* (*nay•bor*) and *weigh* (*way*).

fr*ei*ght	w*ei*ght
v*ei*n	r*ei*gn
f*ei*gn	chow m*ei*n
sl*ei*gh	

The problem with this little poem is that it covers only two of the sounds that *ie/ei* combinations can have. The words given as examples of spellings covered by the first two lines are all pronounced with a long *e* sound for the *ie/ei* combinations: *relieve (ree•leev), receive (ree•seev),* etc. And, of course, all the words that are governed by the last two lines of the poem are all pronounced with a long *a* sound for the *ei* combination. But *ei* can also be pronounced with a long *i* sound as well. The following words, then, appear to be exceptions to the poem.

h*ei*ght	st*ei*n (of beer)
Fahrenh*ei*t	sl*ei*ght (of hand)

You might simply remember that the long *i* sound is represented by the combination *ei*, or you might change the poem to accommodate the spelling of this sound.

> *I* before *E*
> Except after *C*,
> Or when sounded like *I* or *A*,
> As in *height* and *weigh*.

The meter suffers a bit, but then the poem was never a literary masterpiece to begin with.

Even with the inclusion of the long *i* sound, however, one problem still remains: Words with the *ie/ei* combinations can also have the sound of short *i* and short *e*. The vast majority of these words are spelled with the combination *ie*.

an*cie*nt	handkerch*ie*f	profi*cie*nt
cons*cie*nce	impat*ie*nt	quot*ie*nt
defi*cie*nt	misch*ie*f	suffi*cie*nt
effi*cie*nt	misch*ie*vous	trans*ie*nt
fr*ie*nd	pat*ie*nt	

Notice that in several of these words, the combination *ie* follows the letter *c*.

As you might expect, there are exceptions to even this extensive look at the *ie/ei* mnemonic poem

Exceptions to *ie* pronounced long *e*:

l*ei*sure	s*ei*zure
prot*ei*n	w*ei*rd
s*ei*ze	finan*cie*r (*ie* follows *c*)

Exceptions to *ei* pronounced long *i*:

f*ie*ry	h*ie*rarchy

Exceptions to *ie* pronounced short *i* or short *e*:

152

forfeit	foreign	heifer
counterfeit	foreigner	
	sovereign	
	sovereignty	

Well, this excursion should show you that the "*I* before *E*" poem, although a useful memory aid, is nowhere near perfect. It can be a valuable tool if you understand that it applies only to certain ways that *ie* or *ei* can be pronounced. As a mnemonic device, it is reliable enough to be retained rather than thrown out altogther.

Some well-known mnemonics, however, *should* be thrown out altogether. These mnemonics cause more harm than good and are what I call "false mnemonics." The best example I know of a "false mnemonic" is the all-too-common method for teaching children the difference between the meaning of *princiPAL* and *princiPLE*. "Remember, children, the princi*pal* is your *pal*." Now, while this approach does teach the correct spelling of the word that means "a school administrator," it also teaches children that when the word has any other meaning, it should be spelled *princiPLE*. Because they rely on this "false mnemonic," many people misspell (with absolute confidence) the word *principal* when it refers to "the leading part in a play," "the main parts of a verb," or "the amount of a debt not including interest." Although each of these (and several other) definitions apply to the spelling *princiPAL,* they do not have anything to do with the word *pal,* and so they are commonly misspelled **princiPLE.* This "false mnemonic," then, actually creates misspellings and should, therefore, never be taught.

There is, however, a mnemonic that covers all the uses of *principal* and *principle.* If you link the spelling *principAl* with the word *mAin,* which also contains the letter *a,* and the spelling *principLE* with the word *ruLE,* which also ends in *le,* you can confidently select the correct form no matter how it is used in a sentence.

principAl	=	the mAin part in a play
	=	the mAin part of a verb
	=	the mAin part of a debt
	=	the mAin teacher in a school
principLE	=	a ruLE of conduct
	=	a ruLE of science, etc.

The *principal* (mAin) reason you were selected was that you have high *principles* (ruLEs).

Here is an example of the way in which a group of frequently confused words can be divided and conquered through the use of mnemonics. The following words are commonly misspelled because the last syllable in each is pronounced with exactly the same sound (*seed*).

supersede	succeed	intercede
	proceed	concede
	exceed	intercede
		precede
		recede
		secede

Very few people misspell any other letters in these words except the endings. The endings -*sede,* -*ceed,* and -*cede* are so similar that it is difficult to remember which ending goes with which word.

Notice, however, that only one word ends in -*sede: supersede. Supersede* happens to be the only word in the English language that ends in *-sede*. Because this word and this ending are unique, they will stand out in your mind, and you will not confuse them with the other words and endings.

The three words that end in *-ceed* can be linked together by the mnemonic *FULL SPEED AHEAD*. The word *SPEED* is the key because it ends in *-eed*, as does the ending *-ceed*. The first three letters of *SPEED* are the first letters of the three words that end in *-ceed*: *S*ucceed, *P*roceed, and *E*xceed. So, *FULL SPEED AHEAD* (and especially *SPEED*) tells you that *S*ucceed, *P*roceed, and *E*xceed all end in *-ceed*. The reason that the entire mnemonic, *FULL SPEED AHEAD*, is necessary is that this phrase allows you to differentiate between *proceed* and *precede* (which also begins with *p*); *FULL SPEED AHEAD* tells you to *proceed* (and it has nothing to do with the meaning of *precede*).

Once you realize that *supersede* is the only word that ends in *-sede*, and if you use the mnemonic *FULL SPEED AHEAD* to remember the three words that end in *-ceed* (*S*ucceed, *P*roceed, *E*xceed), you can confidently use the ending *-cede* for all the other words that end in this confusing sound.

Although this system can be reliably used for most longer forms of these words, (*exceeding, receding, preceded,* for example), you must be careful about the words *procedure* and *procedural*. These forms are exceptions because they do not have the double *e* that appears in *proceed, proceeding,* and *proceeded.*

DEVELOPING YOUR OWN MNEMONICS

As I said before, the beauty of the mnemonic system of spelling is that you can create your own memory aids to cover the specific words that give you the most difficulty. After you pinpoint the letter or letters that you want to remember in a particular word, you can devise a mnemonic that will permanently link those letters to that word. For example, if you have a problem remembering the correct spelling of the word *excellent,* the first thing you should do is examine the word to see exactly which part of it causes you confusion. Few people ever misspell the first two letters or the last two letters in this word. It is only the middle of this word that causes it to be frequently misspelled. In order to fix in your mind that the five middle letters are *CELLE,* you might invent a mnemonic like

> The prisoner in *CELL E* has an ex*CELLE*nt chance for parole.

Notice that this mnemonic identifies the troublesome letters *and* links those letters to the word you want to spell.

In certain cases you can use one mnemonic to remember the spellings of several words at a time, provided that all those words contain the same troublesome letters. I used to have a great deal of difficulty deciding whether to use the ending *-ent* or *-ant* for words such as *superintendent, persistent,* and *dependent.* In order to fix in my mind the fact that all these words (as well as several other similar words) ended in *-ent,* I linked the word *superintendent* to the word *student.* I chose *student* because it also ends in *-ent,* it is not likely that I would spell it *stud*ant*,* and I could easily associate a *student* with the *superintendent* of a school.

> The *superintendENT* is concerned about how each *studENT* performs.

154

Then I merely plugged into the mnemonic all the other words that I wanted to associate with this *-ent* ending.

> The *superintendENT* must be *persistENT* and *insistENT* because his job is *dependENT* upon how each *studENT* performs.

Later, when I encountered still other words that caused me this same difficulty (*correspondENT, confidENT, permanENT*, for instance), it was a simple matter to include these words in the same mnemonic.

Although you can, occasionally, weave several troublesome words into the same mnemonic, most of your mnemonics will be tailored to fit each particular, personal spelling demon. You must be careful, too, to avoid the "false mnemonics" that are created by failing to take into account words that have identical pronunciations but different spellings.

Just to get you started on developing your own mnemonics, here are a few that I use; perhaps they will be useful to you.

Word	Mnemonic
all right	How would you spell *ALL WRONG*?
arg*u*ment	There should be no *argument* about chewing *GUM* in class.
bulle*t*in	A *BULLET* was lodged *IN* the *bulletin* board.
category	A *catEgory* is a *sEction*.
embarra*ss*	*TWO Robbers* were *embarrassed* in *Sing Sing*.
ho*l*iday	Originally, a *hoLiday* was a *hoLy day*.
inter*r*upt	It is an *eRRor* to *inteRRupt*.
judg*m*ent	*G-Men* must show good *judGMent*.
main*te*nance	*TEN mainTENance* workers were needed to clean up the mess.
pro*fess*or	A *proFESSOR* must *proFESS OR* claim to be an expert.
pursuit	*I'm in PURSuit* of the man who stole my *PURSe*.
sep*a*rate	To *sePARate* means to move thing *aPARt*.
stationary·	When something is *stationARy*, it *stAnds* still.
stationery	*StationERy* is *papER* that is sold by a *stationER*.
vaccine	A *vaCCine* is measured in *Cubic Centimeters*.

In *The Memory Book* (published by Stein and Day, 1974) Harry Lorayne and Jerry Lucas advise that the most memorable mnemonics make use of exaggeration and action. The image you want to invent, then, should be both larger than life and moving. For example, if you have difficulty remembering tht the word *insurance* ends in *-Ance* (and not *-Ence*), you should link the word *insurance* with a familiar object that begins with the letter *a*. In your mnemonic, that object should be exaggerated and in motion. If you picture a gigantic *ape* selling insurance door-to-door, that image will come to mind every time you think of the spelling of the word *insurance*.

12. VOCABULARY

IMPROVING YOUR CHILD'S VOCABULARY

All of us admire writers and speakers who have a good command of the English language, and all of us want our children to have the ability to express themselves effectively. No matter what we may think about the importance of knowing the parts of speech or knowing the principles of subject/verb agreement, we all recognize the importance of correct spelling and the benefits of a large vocabulary. But helping our children improve their vocabulary is essentially different from helping them improve their spelling: We can *correct* their spelling errors and teach them how to avoid spelling errors, but we cannot *correct* the use of words that aren't in their vocabulary. In other words, the problem of improving our children's vocabulary is a problem of *creating,* not correcting.

How, then, do we go about helping our children encounter and acquire new words? The answer, I think, follows directly from the question: We must first help our children *encounter* new words, for only then will they have any reason to add those words to their vocabulary. When children hear a new word used in a conversation or when they see a new word in their reading, they have an incentive to understand its meaning. This incentive

does not exist when vocabulary words are presented in artificial ways, such as having children look up the definitions for five new words each day. Moreover, by hearing a new word, children become familiar with its pronunciation; by reading a new word, they become familiar with its spelling.

I recognize that many teachers and textbooks still use the "five-words-a-day" approach to vocabulary, but that method has about as much chance of enlarging a child's vocabulary as does telling a child to read the dictionary from *a* to *z*. Merely knowing the correct definitions does not in any way ensure that the child will use the new words in his speaking or writing. (I am reminded of the story about a child who learned that the word *pregnant* meant "carrying a baby." He confidently displayed this knowledge in a classroom report by saying "The fireman came out of the burning building *pregnant*.") Besides, our ability to remember unrelated definitions pales in comparison to our ability to forget.

One way that parents can help their young children encounter new words is by reading to them—not just nursery stories, but exciting adventure stories and other interesting works that can be found in the children's section of your public library. The reading level of these books should be a little above

157

the level on which the children, themselves, read, for then the vocabulary used in the books will challenge the children and will allow them to hear new words and usages. If a new or unusual word is crucial to their understanding of the story, you might ask them, after they have heard it once or twice, whether they can guess its meaning. If an explanation is needed, try to give them a synonym or two as well as the definition. The meaning of the new words (as well as the meaning of any strange synonym) will then be reinforced every time that word is used again in the story.

Children should also be encouraged at every possible opportunity to read stories, newspaper articles, or parts of their school texts to their parents. When they encounter words that are outside their vocabulary, they will stumble over the pronunciation, sounding out the words syllable by syllable, more concerned with defeating the words than with understanding their meaning. But this stumbling is essential to learning, for it indicates that the child is being challenged and that growth is taking place. (The value of home education is obvious here, for the child's failures do not cause him the embarrassment they would in school.) Only after the child has struggled through the pronunciation should the parent help him sound it out correctly. Only after that pronunciation is repeated a few times, and after the child can pronounce the word correctly as he reads the entire sentence in which it appears, only then should the parent inquire about the meaning of the word. Again, a synonym or two will help fix the word in the child's vocabulary and will help him respond when he encounters the

word later and the parent again asks about its meaning.

It is not possible, of course, for parents to be always available to act as an audience for their children's oral reading. Therefore, parents should help their children acquire the skills that will enable them to figure out for themselves the meaning of words they hear or read.

CONTEXT CLUES

The first and, perhaps, the most valuable vocabulary skill a child can acquire is the ability to understand the meaning of a word from the *context* in which it is used. The context of a word consists of the other words that surround it in the sentence, the other sentences that surround it in the paragraph, and the entire situation in which the word is used. For example, it is only by understanding how the verb *draw* is used that you can tell whether the word means "make a sketch," "pull a cart," "put backspin on a billiard ball," "extract blood," or any of the other thirty or so definitions the word can have. The meaning of the word *battery* depends upon whether the whole situation in which it is used refers to an "electric battery," a "military battery," a "baseball battery," or the "crime of battery."

Parents can help their children develop the skill of using context by resisting the urge to supply the correct definition whenever their children run to them with an unfamiliar word. Although it is more time consuming, it is also much more beneficial if parents ask their children to make an educated guess about the meaning of the unfamiliar word based upon how that word is used in context. Parents should tell their children to look at the general subject matter of surrounding sentences as well as the meaning of surrounding words. For example, a child who read the following passage might very well inquire about the meaning of the word *apathetic*.

The person who is elected president can change the course of history. You would think that no one would pass up a chance to vote in a presidential election. But Americans today are more *apathetic* than ever about voting.

Child: What does *apathetic* mean?
Parent: What do you think it means from the way it is used?
Child: Americans elect bad presidents?
Parent: Well, what does the rest of the passage say?
Child: It says that presidents are important and powerful and that everyone should vote.
Parent: But . . .
Child: But people are apathetic. Does that mean they are *lazy*?
Parent: Yes, it does, in a way. It means that they don't feel strongly one way or the other. Apathetic people are unconcerned, indifferent, or just not interested. Now, try to think up a sentence of your own that uses *apathetic* in this way.

Sometimes a synonym can be found in the same sentence in which an unfamiliar word occurs. Occasionally a sentence will use a series of synonyms, and only one will be unfamiliar. Children should be directed to look for these synonyms and use them as clues to the meaning of the unfamiliar word.

The atmosphere in the restaurant was like the food: bland, dull, *insipid*.

From the adjectives *bland* and *dull* you can make a good guess about the meaning of the word *insipid*: "lacking spirit or flavor."

Some sentences give the meaning of an unfamiliar word by telling you what the word does *not* mean. The clues, then, give you the opposite meaning or a contrasting meaning of the word you want to define.

The players were feeling *morose*, not happy and lively as you might expect them to be after a victory.

A child who is unfamiliar with the meaning of the word *morose* should be told to look at the words *happy* and *lively*, which he understands. If the players were "not happy and lively," and if these words are meant to show contrast with the word *morose*, then *morose* probably means the opposite of *happy* and *lively*. Realizing this, the child might come up with antonyms for happy and lively (*sad, glum, gloomy*), which would be synonyms for *morose*.

There are times when the writer will supply a definition for a word right alongside the unfamiliar word in the sentence. Still, some readers are so concerned about the meaning of the unfamiliar word that they fail to take advantage of the definition the writer has provided. Once again, by looking at the context of the unfamiliar word—that is, by considering the words and sentences that surround it—the meaning becomes clear.

The *effluent*, the water coming out of the pipe, must be free of all harmful chemicals.

In the sentence above, the word *effluent* is defined as "the water coming out of the pipe."

Frequently these supplied definitions and explanations are signaled by phrases like *that is, in other words, refers to,* and *for instance.* Children should be told to watch for signals like these because they indicate that the writer wants to be certain that an important word is fully understood.

PREFIXES, SUFFIXES, ROOTS

Another method that children can be taught to help them figure out the meaning of an unfamiliar word involves breaking a word down into its various parts. Long words are frequently just the combination of small word parts, such as prefixes, suffixes, and roots. By breaking a word down into its parts and by knowing the meaning of common prefixes, suffixes, and roots, a child can make a good guess about the meaning of any unfamiliar word that is the sum of its parts.

For example, your child might not be familiar with the meaning of the word *inflexible.* But if he broke the word down into its separate parts,

Prefix	Root	Suffix
in-	flex	-ible

and if he knew the meaning that each of these parts usually carries,

in- = not
flex = bend
-ible = capable of being

he might accurately guess that one meaning of *inflexible* is "not capable of being bent."

This method cannot always be depended upon to yield a correct definition, but it can help your children understand the general nature of a word, and it can help them realize that many common English words are direct descendants of words from other countries and ancient languages. The Latin word that meant "to see" (*spectare*), for example, can be found in more than 200 English words (*spec*tator, *spec*tacles, in*spect,* pro*spec*tor, etc.)

There are about a hundred common prefixes, almost as many common suffixes, and several hundred common roots—most of Latin or Greek origin. I will cover only a few examples of each here, but I encourage you to add the meanings of additional word parts to your children's vocabulary as your children encounter them in the word origins given in their dictionary.

It is also a very good idea to use these word parts in creating "word clusters." While I am showing only one or two examples of how each word part is used in a common word, you should challenge your children to think of other words they know that have this same word part. The root *flex,* for instance, should generate the words *flexible* and *reflex* as well as *inflexible.* The other listed form of this same root, *flec,* should call to mind *deflect, deflection, inflection,* and *reflection* as well as the example given—*reflect.* How many words can your children think of that begin with the prefix *bi-* and involve the meaning "two"? Go over each word with them to be sure that they understand how this prefix affects the meaning of the words.

Several of the listed roots can be combined with other roots to form common words. The root *bio* (meaning "life"), for example, can be combined with the root *logy* (meaning "science or study") to form the word *biology* (meaning "the science of life"). Roots such as these are actually "combining forms" and, therefore, are different from pure roots. While this distinction in terminology is not important for children to understand, they should not think of *bio* as a prefix, or *logy* as a suffix.

PREFIXES, SUFFIXES, AND ROOTS

Common Prefixes	*Meaning*	*Example*
a-, ab-	not, away, from	*a*moral, *ab*sent
anti-	against	*anti*freeze
ante-	before	*ante*cedent
auto-	self	*auto*mobile, *auto*matic
bene-	good, well	*bene*fit
bi-	two, twice	*bi*cycle
circum-	around	*circum*ference
co-, com-, con-	together, with	*com*municate, *con*ference
contra-, contro-	against, opposed	*contra*dict, *contro*versy
de-	down, off, away	*de*press, *de*cline
dis-, dif-	away from, out	*dis*tract, *dif*fract
ex-	out of, off, from	*ex*ternal
extra-	beyond, above	*extra*ordinary
hyper-	over, beyond	*hyper*space
hypo-	under	*hypo*dermic
il-, ir-	not	*il*legal, *ir*responsible
in-, im-	into, not	*in*ject, *im*possible
inter-	between	*inter*state
mal-	bad	*mal*practice
mis-	badly, ill	*mis*take
pan-	all	*Pan*-American
poly-	many	*poly*ester
post-	after	*post*pone
pre-	before	*pre*cede
pro-	for, forward	*pro*ceed
re-	back, again	*re*fund, *re*paint
semi-, hemi-	half	*semi*circle, *hemi*sphere
sub-	under	*sub*marine
super-	above, over	*super*ior
tele-	far, distant	*tele*vision
trans-	across	*trans*portation
ultra-	beyond, excessively	*ultra*modern
un-	not, lacking, opposing	*un*known, *un*wind

161

Common Suffixes	Meaning	Example
-able, -ible	capable of being	return*able*, vis*ible*
-ance, -ancy,	state of, act of,	appear*ance*
-ence, -ency,	quality of	presid*ency*
-ity, -tude	quality of	vital*ity*
-ant, -ent	one who, showing	ignor*ant*, persist*ent*
-er, -or	one who, that which	lectur*er*, elevat*or*
-ic	caused by, showing	alcoho*lic*, fana*tic*
-ist	one who, follower of	perfection*ist*, Zion*ist*
-less	without	taste*less*
-ize	make, cause to be	publi*cize*, memo*rize*
-ous	full of, containing	fam*ous*

Common Roots	Meaning	Example
act	do, drive	*act*ivity
ami	friend	*ami*able
ama, amor	love	*amor*ous
aud	to hear	*aud*ience
bio	life	*bio*logy
cap, capit	head	*capit*al
ceive, cept	take, seize	re*ceive*, re*cept*acle
chron, chrono	time	*chron*icle, *chrono*logy
clam	cry out	ex*clam*, *clam*or
corp	body	*corp*oration
cred	believe	in*cred*ible
culp	fault	*culp*rit
dic, dict	say, speak	*dict*ate
duc, duct	lead	con*duct*
dur	hard	*dur*able, en*dure*
equ	equal, just	*equ*itable
fac, fact	make, do	*fact*ory
fer	bear, carry	trans*fer*
fid, fide	faithful, loyal	*fide*lity
flec, flex	bend	re*flec*t, in*flex*ible
geo	earth	*geo*graphy
gram, graph	write	tele*gram*, auto*graph*
ject	throw	re*ject*
lect, leg	read	*lect*ure, *leg*ible
liber	free	*liber*ation
loc	place	*loc*ation
log, logy	word, study	bio*logy*
luc, lum	light	*luc*id, *lum*inous
meter	measuring device	thermo*meter*

162

(continued)

Common Roots	Meaning	Examples
micro	small	*micro*scope
mit, mis	send	e*mit*, *mis*sile
mob, mov, mot	move	*mob*ile, *mov*ie, *mot*or
pel, pulse	drive, urge	pro*pel*, re*pulse*
photo	light	*phot*ograph
phon, phono	sound	*phono*graph
pod	foot	*pod*iatrist
port	carry	im*port*
prob	prove	*prob*able
rupt	break	dis*rupt*
scop, scope	look, see	tele*scope*
scrib, script	touch	*scrib*ble, pre*script*ion
spect, spic	look	in*spect*, con*spic*uous
tact, tang	touch	con*tact*, *tang*ible
tend, tens,	stretch	ex*tend*, *tens*ion
tract	draw, pull	ex*tract*
uni	one	*uni*form
vers, vert	turn	re*vers*e, in*vert*
vid, vis	see	pro*vid*e, *vis*ible
voc	voice, call	*voc*al, *voc*ation
volv	turn	re*volv*er

USING THE DICTIONARY

Being able to base an educated guess about the meaning of an unfamiliar word on the context in which that word is used or on the meaning of its prefix, suffix, or root is a valuable aid to reading and to vocabulary. Still, it only helps you arrive at a general meaning for that unfamiliar word; in order to get a more specific, exact definition, you must consult a dictionary. There is no getting around it: The dictionary has been, and will continue to be, the most valuable tool ever invented for improving vocabulary. When you also consider the value that the dictionary has as a means of improving spelling and pronunciation, you begin to see why one's ability to use the dictionary helps develop one's ability to use the language. If you honestly want your children to be able to use language effectively in their speaking and writing, improving their ability to use the dictionary is the most helpful, single contribution you can make.

Dictionary skills can be taught to children by their parents, and can be practiced and reinforced every day in the home. The first step, of course, is to have a dictionary that is available for immediate use. It needn't be a brand new dictionary, and it shouldn't be so large that the child has difficulty lifting it. The second step is for parents to become thoroughly familiar with this dictionary. How are the entry words separated into syllables—by dots or by spaces? Does the key to the pronunciation symbols appear at the bottom of every page? Do you understand how to use this key to help you pronounce each symbol? Do the accent marks appear before or after each accented syllable? Do you understand what a secondary accent means? When more than one spelling or pronunciation is given, which is listed first—the one that is most commonly used by most people, or the one that is preferred by most authorities? Do you understand how to read the symbols and abbreviations that tell you the origin of a word? Do you understand the meanings of the usage labels that this dictionary uses? This is a long list of questions, and I could have added several more as well. But you, as a parent, must be able to answer these questions yourself because the questions will come up when you start acquainting your child with the dictionary.

No one expects a parent to be entirely knowledgeable about dictionaries—not even the publishers of dictionaries. Consequently, every good dictionary gives all the answers to all those questions I asked, and groups these answers all in one section. In the first few pages of the dictionary, even before you get to the letter *a,* there will be a section with a title like "A Guide to the Dictionary" or "Explanatory Notes." This is the most important section of the dictionary, and yet it is a section that is almost never read. Take a few hours, over a few days or weeks, and familiarize yourself with the material in this section. (Did you know that some dictionaries list spellings and pronunciations according to how frequently they are used, while other dictionaries list them according to which is most preferred?) The type is too small and the reading too difficult for most children to get anything

out of this section by themselves. The parent must understand the material and relate it to the child as they study and use the dictionary together.

SLANG

One final thought about improving your child's vocabulary: Improvement can come through deleting as well as expanding. All parents have certain words that they don't want their children to use. Not all these words are vulgarisms that create a negative impression about their user; many, in fact, are simply slang terms that happen to be in vogue at the time. But it is perfectly proper for parents to try to eliminate slang terms from their children's vocabulary.

The best way to do this is to allow your children to see that not all slang is, necessarily, bad. Slang provides our language with new words and with new uses for existing words. It is one of the ways that our word stock grows and changes. Some of the slang terms that were popular—and frowned upon—years ago have now been adopted into our spoken and written language, and are acceptable in standard usage. But the slang words and expressions that have made this ascension filled a need and gave us tools to express ideas that we could not precisely express in other ways. When a slang word or phrase fills this need, it will probably endure. On the other hand, slang that is imprecise and has so many different meanings that it does not contribute to accurate, effective communication generally disappears after a few years.

If you frown upon your children's use of slang words such as *hassle* and *rip-off,* your argument should be based on the fact that these words have so many different meanings that it is difficult, if not genuinely impossible, to know exactly which meaning the user intends. If someone has been "ripped-off," for instance, has he paid more than he thinks the item is worth? has he paid more than the item is actually worth? has the item been misrepresented by the seller? has he had something stolen from him? If someone is being "hassled," is he being threatened or merely irritated.

When you hear your children using imprecise slang expressions, ask them to be more specific—to tell you exactly what they mean. Your request will undoubtedly be met with "Oh, you know what I mean," but you must force the issue every time. "You know what I mean" and its shortened form, "ya know," are excuses for a poor vocabulary. These expressions say "I hope that you know what I mean because I simply don't have the ability to make my meaning more clear."

By requiring your children to use precise synonyms in explaining their slang expressions, you will gradually get them to see that slang words and phrases frequently cover up the fact that their user isn't sure of precisely what he wants to say. Challenging your children to define their slang expressions, then, also challenges them to think about the meaning of their entire message. The process is slow, to be sure, but the goal is well worth the difficulties you encounter in trying to achieve it.

IMPROVING YOUR OWN VOCABULARY

The difference between vocabulary training for children and vocabulary training for adults is a difference in goals. We want our children to become acquainted with as many words as possible primarily because we want them to be able to understand the information they read and hear. Their ability to use these new words in their own speaking and writing will take on increasing importance as they grow and experience new ideas and feelings that they want to express to others. Adults, on the other hand, already have a lifetime of experiences behind them, yet their vocabularies have generally not kept pace with their experiences. They have a nodding acquaintance with tens of thousands of words that they understand but do not use. Most adults, then, want their vocabulary training to improve their ability to express themselves.

All of us admire people whose vocabularies allow them to summon up the perfect word for use in a given situation. The impression created by a well-written letter or by a well-told story stems, in large part, from just a few well-chosen words that demonstrate a writer's or speaker's command of the language. These critical words must be perfectly mated to the audience as well as to the ideas being expressed. People who trot out words that are unknown to their audience demonstrate that their vocabulary (or, perhaps, their judgment) is inadequate for the task at hand. Had their vocabulary been large enough, they certainly would have been able to select synonyms that would express their meaning and permit that meaning to be understood by others as well. Word selection, therefore, is governed by *appropriateness,* which also governs most of the other areas of English usage.

The ability to quickly scan our memory and locate that perfect word—that one word that fits the audience as well as the situation—is what we adults want from our vocabulary training. So often we have groped for that perfect word in conversation, only to stumble upon it later, after the situation for which it was intended has irretrievably passed. The word we reluctantly use in place of the "perfect" word is never quite right: Its meaning is just different enough that we are forced to hammer it into shape by using qualifying words and phrases. Mark Twain put it best: "The difference between the right word and the almost right word is the difference between the lightning and the lightning bug."

Scholars (and graduate students) who study the works of great authors to determine the size of each author's vocabulary have counted approximately 28,000 different words in the writings of William Shakespeare. Although this figure makes Shakespeare's writing vocabulary one of the largest in history, there is another figure that tells us even more about why Shakespeare is the undisputed master of the English language. Of the 890,000 words that Shakespeare wrote (this is the *total* number of words that appear in all of Shakespeare's plays and poems), there are more than 11,000 words that appear only once! Shakespeare found the perfect occasion for each of these 11,000+ words only once in all his writing. His vocabulary gave him the ability to use the perfect word in the perfect situation, even though that situation would never arise again.

It is easier to come up with the "perfect" word when you are writing than it is when you are speaking. Writing allows you time for reflection, and most writing occasions even allow you enough time to locate the word you want in a dictionary or a thesaurus (a book of synonyms and antonyms). But you still have to have that perfect word in your vocabulary in order to know that it is perfect for a given situation. In speaking, you not only have to be acquainted with the word you want, but you have to be able to dredge it up from your vocabulary *immediately,* preferably without any noticeable hesitation.

In addition to our writing and speaking vocabularies, we have reading and listening vocabularies as well. These vocabularies include all the words that we understand when we see them used in writing or hear them used in speech. The number of words that we can recognize when we see or hear them is at least five times as large as the number of words we actually use in our own writing and speaking.

So, when you speak of "improving your vocabulary," which vocabulary do you want to improve: your writing vocabulary? your speaking vocabulary? your reading vocabulary? or your listening vocabulary? I believe that by concentrating on improving your speaking vocabulary, you will improve all your other vocabularies as well. If you learn a new word and can confidently use it in conversation, you will certainly be able to understand that word when you see it or hear it used by others. Your writing vocabulary will improve as well because most people use writing to express what they would like to say in speech. You "sound out" your sentences as you put them down on paper, and you change them because they don't "sound right," not because they don't "look right." By concentrating on your speaking vocabulary, you will improve your ability to express yourself clearly and effectively—to summon up that perfect word for the perfect occasion, and to do so without hesitation.

By focusing on a person's speaking vocabulary, I am departing from the methods used in most texts that deal with vocabulary improvement for adults. This is not to say that these other methods are worthless. Indeed, the material presented in the previous chapter can prove beneficial to adults as well as to children: Understanding the meaning of common prefixes, suffixes, and roots will make you more aware of word origins and will help you understand unfamiliar words that you encounter in your reading. But merely understanding a word's meaning does not in any way ensure that the word will come to mind when you need it in a conversation. Word lists and vocabulary quizes are aids to recognition, not to expression.

Have you ever wondered why your friends who are crossword puzzle fanatics do not all have unusually large speaking vocabularies? Part of the answer lies in the fact that crossword puzzles are artificial, unnatural means of expression. Not only are many of the words they require obscure and seldom (if ever) used in conversation, but the whole idea of being given a definition and asked for the word it defines is exactly opposite the way that vocabulary is acquired.

In order to improve your speaking vocabulary you must actually *use* new words in conversation. This, itself, sounds a bit backward, I know, but a word does not become a part of a person's speaking vocabulary until *after* it has been used. We all rely upon words that we have used before because we are comfortable with these words. We are confident that we can use them correctly and pronounce them properly; we know that we will not be embarrassed when we employ them in a conversation. A new word—that is, a word that we would like to use but have never used in conversation before—does not offer this security. We may employ the word in our writing, but we are reluctant to try it out in conversation.

In order to become comfortable with a new word, you must actually hear yourself use it properly in a conversation. If you can just get through that first use, if you can just employ the word once without having your listeners look askance when they hear it, then you will be able to confidently call upon that word again, and it will soon become one of your standbys. The problem, then, lies in how to go about using a new word for the first time.

The method that has proved successful for me, and for other adults to whom I have taught it, involves some study, some planning, and a bit of deceit. The first step is to select a word that you would like to add to your speaking vocabulary. This may be a word that you have heard a friend use, one that you have heard used on television, one that you have seen used in writing, or even one that you already use but in a different way. You must study this word thoroughly by looking up its meaning and pronunciation in the dictionary, and you must practice using this word orally by creating a few phrases or sentences of your own in which the word is appropriate.

The second step involves planning a way to weave this word into a future conversation. You do not want your use of the word to be so artificial and obvious that it draws the attention of those who hear it. You must use it in a way that seems natural to others, even though they may not use the word themselves. (Remember that the *listening* vocabulary of those to whom you are speaking will be much larger than their own speaking vocabulary.)

You must realize that you cannot just force the word into any conversation that happens to come up, and you must realize that it will do your vocabulary little good to use the word as a subject of conversation (such as "Does anyone know the meaning of the word _____?").

Some words are much easier than others to weave into a conversation because they can apply to a wide variety of topics. For example, suppose that you had heard a politician use the word *inane* (*in•ain'*) to describe a proposed tax law that he believed would do more harm than good. By studying the precise meaning of this word, you would realize that because it can be used to describe anything that is senseless or foolish, the conversation into which you weave this word need not concern economics or politics at all. In fact, you could use the word to describe a remark or a question of your own, no matter what topic was being discussed at the time. At a cocktail party, perhaps, you might introduce a thought by saying "I hope you won't think this question utterly *inane,* but I was wondering . . ." or "I must apologize for the *inane* remark I made about . . ." If you think that the word still might disturb your audience, you can soften the blow by including a synonym or two in the phrase you decide to use: "You may think this is a rather *empty-headed, inane* idea, but . . ." You should be able to put these more general vocabulary words into use sometime during the same day you undertake studying and practicing them.

There are, however, many words that are much less applicable to general conversation. These words are more specific and are less frequently used because they deal with a more limited subject. Words like *loquacious* and *taciturn,* for example, are used only to describe characteristics found in certain people; *stoicism* and *altruism* are heard only in discussions that concern philosophies. Weaving words like these into your conversations requires a bit of deceit. Not only do you have to use a relatively unusual word in a way that will not attract attention, but you also have to channel a conversation into a topic that will accommodate this word—again, without your listeners' noticing your intent.

Let's assume that you have heard someone use the word *connoisseur* (*kon•a•sur'*), a word that you understand quite well, but one that you are reluctant to pronounce in conversation. It might be the word's French origin (or spelling) that makes you fear the embarrassment of demonstrating to others your lack of training in foreign pronunciations. Yet, as unusual as the word appears, it is surprisingly easy to pronounce—as a few practice attempts aloud will quickly demonstrate.

While this pronunciation is fresh in your mind, you must invent a situation that will allow you to use the word in conversation. Suppose that your family is having its evening meal at McDonald's or Burger King, or another fast-food outlet. You might ask one of your children how the hamburger he is eating compares with those from the other franchises. If your question inspires your child to discuss the relative merits of various hamburgers he has tasted, you will have a perfect opportunity to make use of the situation: "How nice it is to have a *connoisseur* in the family" or "My, you really are a *connoisseur* of hamburgers."

Because it is somewhat difficult (even for the most deceitful of us) to find a way of employing each new word on the same day we begin to study it, I have found it helpful to attack more than one word at a time. Although my goal is to weave just one new word each day into my conversations, I carry with me a list of five words that I have studied and practiced and that I hope I can create an opportunity to use. The mere writing of these words on a list helps acquaint me with their spelling, and carrying the list in my pocket helps remind me of my goal. Each time I use one of my target words in conversation, I replace it with another; when I add a new word to my list, I am reminded of the words that I have yet to use.

Some married students of mine have recently added a competitive twist to this system for vocabulary improvement, and I pass it along with my unqualified approval. If a husband and wife decide to use this method at the same time, they may derive additional benefit by seeing whether they can detect their partner's target word for the day. Not only does this competition ensure that each partner will make every effort to weave a new word into a conversation accurately and discretely, but it also forces each partner to listen actively and attentively to the speech of the other. Anything that contributes to a couple's ability to listen attentively to each other is to be prized; if it also increases their vocabularies, so much the better.

I will bring this chapter to a close by expanding a bit on my previous statements concerning foreign words and their pronunciations. The average adult is expected to understand the meaning of widely used foreign words and phrases, even though he may be reluctant to use them himself. When most of us encounter a foreign word that we don't understand, we are likely to blame the author or speaker for using the word, rather than blame ourselves for not knowing its meaning. We are all too eager to critize those who weave foreign words into their speech and writing and to accuse them of trying to appear overly learned or of trying to place themselves above their audience. I will grant you that some writers and some speakers actually do employ foreign words simply for the lofty impression the use of these words generally creates. Good writers and good speakers, however, do not. They may, and frequently do, use foreign words and phrases, but they do so only when there is a reasonable expectation that their audience will understand the meaning of these words and phrases. The art of communicating, after all, lies in choosing language that is appropriate for its audience.

However, American adults do have a responsibility to learn the meaning and the use of foreign words that have been adopted into our language. These words may have unusual pronunciations and spellings, but they are just as much a part of our language as are any of the other words you would like to add to your vocabulary. In some cases the meaning of a foreign word or phrase is so precise and delicate that it cannot be expressed by just one, or even a few, common and familiar English words. These foreign words and phrases, then, can be valuable additions to your reading and listening vocabularies because they allow you to understand exactly what their user is trying to convey; they can enhance your writing and speaking vocabularies as well by giving you additional tools to express your ideas to others.

Most of the Latin words that adults are expected to understand appear only in writing, although a few (such as *alma mater* and *status quo,* for example) also occur in speech. Many French words and phrases, on the other hand, are quite commonly used in speaking—perhaps more so than in writing. These French additions to our language, then, should be studied more for their pronunciation than for their spelling.

A person who mispronounces a common foreign word in a conversation is not given any credit for his attempt; rather, he is seen as lacking in education or sophistication. This may not be just, but it is the common assumption nonetheless. Therefore, before you at-tempt to add any of the words and phrases in the following list to your speaking vocabulary, you must practice their pronunciations over and over again. You will find it somewhat difficult to weave many of these words into your conversations, but, again, this is the method you must follow if you want to be able to confidently call upon these words when the perfect occasion for them arises.

The following words and phrases are all of French origin, except where otherwise noted. Each can be found, along with more complete information about definitions and uses, in any standard dictionary.

Foreign Word or Phrase	Pronunciation	Meaning
a cappella (Ital.)	ah•kah•pell'•lah	Music sung without instrumental accompaniment
ad hoc (Lat.)	add•hock'	For a specific purpose or situation
aficionado (Span.)	ah•fiss•syo•nah'•do	A devoted enthusiast; a fan
al fresco (Ital.)	ahl•fres'•ko	In the open air; out of doors
avant-garde	ah•vahn•gard'	The most advanced or daring group, especially in ideas or technique
bête noire	bet•nwahr'	An object of hate or dread
blasé	blah•zay'	Indifferent; bored
bon vivant	bone•ve•vahn'	One who enjoys good living; a gourmet
canard	kah•nahrd'	A false or absurd story or rumor; a hoax
carte blanche	kart'•blahnsh'	Complete freedom to act; a blank check
chic	sheek	Elegant, stylish, or fashionable
coup de grâce	koo•deh•grahss'	The final blow that puts the suffering out of their misery
déjà vu	day•zhah•voo'	A feeling that one has already lived through an experience before
denouement	day•new•mahn'	The final unraveling or solution that clarifies the outcome of a plot or story
double entendre	doo•blahn•tahn'•dr	A word or phrase that has a double meaning
ennui	ahn•wee'	A feeling of listless weariness; boredom
en rapport (or just rapport)	ahn•rah•pour' (rah•pour')	In harmony; mutual understanding
espirit de corps	es•pree•deh•kor'	A common spirit of pride in a group or organization
fait accompli	feh•tah•kahn•plee'	A thing that has been done and is irrevocable, beyond recall

 (continued)

Vocabulary

Foreign Word or Phrase	Pronunciation	Meaning
faux pas	foe'•pah'	A mistake; a social error
hoi polloi (Gr.)	hoy•pah•loy'	The common people; the masses
laissez-faire	less•ay•fare'	The policy of governmental non-intervention
non sequitur (Lat.)	non•seck'•wih•tur	A fallacy of logic or reasoning in which a conclusion does not follow from the argument
nouveaux riches	new•vo•reesch'	People who have recently become rich
par excellence	par•ek•sell•ahnss'	Excellent beyond comparison
per se (Lat.)	pur•say'	By or of itself; essentially
potpourri	poh•poo•ree'	A mixture composed of many parts; a medley
savoir-faire	sav•wah•fair'	The ability to say or do the right thing; tact; poise
status quo (Lat.)	stay•tuss•kwo'	The condition that exists; the present state or position
tête-à-tête	tate•ah•tate'	A confidential or private chat between two people
vis-à-vis	vee•zah•vee'	In reference to; in regard to; directly opposite to
virtuoso (Ital.)	vir•chew•o'•so	An expert, especially in music

13. Glossary of Usage

Many people who are interested in language precision and in knowing and using the standard forms for written and spoken English find it rather difficult to locate any source that will tell them which forms are considered standard and which are not. One reason that this difficulty exists, I think, is that authors, editors, teachers, and language scholars enjoy seeing similar items grouped together and separated from items that are of another class or kind. Because of this, common problems in pronunciation are grouped together under "Vocabulary," commonly misspelled words appear in "Spelling," nonstandard abbreviations fall under "Punctuation," and so on. There is nothing wrong with this system at all; in fact, I have used it in this book. But it would also be very helpful if some of the most common errors and pitfalls could be collected in one place so that a reader could devote a few minutes from time to time toward developing an awareness of various nonstandard forms no matter how diverse those forms might be.

In this chapter I have tried to do exactly that. The items that appear here are by no means intended to be thought of as a complete list of common usage problems. Instead, these words, phrases, and abbreviations are simply a selection of the usage errors that I think can be easily avoided by people who may not have the time or the desire to delve into *why* the errors are considered errors. Each of these items should set off a signal flair in your mind when you hear them in conversation or see them in writing. That signal will indicate to you that a standard form exists, that a nonstandard form also exists, and that you should be aware of the difference between the two. As with other examples in this book, forms that are always nonstandard and forms that are used in nonstandard ways have been denoted by an asterisk (*).

a, an   Keep in mind that *a* is used before words that begin with a consonant *sound,* and *an* is used before words that begin with a vowel *sound.*

> Therefore: *an* hour's work
> *a* healthy attitude
> *an* unusual event
> *a* union contract

absolute constructions   These are phrases that do not have a grammatical relationship with any other word in the sentence. They generally appear at the beginning or at the end of a sentence, and they are separated from the rest of the sentence by a comma. No comma, however, should be used to separate the subject from the verb *within* an absolute construction.

> A rain dance will be held, *weather permitting.*
> *The judge having left,* no cases could be tried.
> *The judge, having left, no cases could be tried.

accept *vs.* except   *Accept* is a verb that means "to receive (something)." *Except* can be a verb, but it is most frequently used as a preposition meaning "leaving out."

> Please *accept* this gift as a token of my affection.
> He was kind to everyone *except* me.

accidentally   This adverb is formed by adding *-ly* to the adjective *accidental,* not to the noun *accident.* Therefore, it has five syllables, and each deserves to be pronounced: ak•si•den'•tahl•lee (not: *ak•si•dent'•lee).

acronym   An acronym is a word that is formed by using the first letter or letters from a series of other words. *Radar,* for example, is an acronym that was formed from "*r*adio *d*etecting *and r*anging"; *scuba* is an acronym for *s*elf-*c*ontained *u*nderwater *b*reathing *a*pparatus." The letters of true acronyms like these either spell an already existing word (*NOW* = *N*ational *O*rganization for *W*omen) or spell a word that comes to be accepted for general use (*laser*). Therefore, abbreviations such as CIA should not be referred to as acronyms.

A.D., B.C.   These abbreviations should always be capitalized, and periods should follow each letter. A.D. is properly placed before the year, while B.C. follows it. Both abbreviations can be used in references to centuries.

> The temple was built in *113* B.C., but it was destroyed in A.D. *291.*
> The story begins in *the fifth century* B.C.

*advance planning, *advance warning   These phrases are redundant because *any* planning and warning must, necessarily, be in advance.

advice *vs.* advise   These two words are different parts of speech and are also pronounced differently. *Advice* is a noun and rhymes with *ice. Advise* is a verb and rhymes with *size.*

> Take my *advice* and see a doctor.
> The doctor will *advise* you what to do.

affect *vs.* effect   The confusion between these two words results from the fact that both can be used as verbs: *affect* means "to influence or change"; *effect* means "to bring about a result."

> This change will *affect* many people.
> If we are persuasive, we may *effect* a change in policy.

Only *effect,* however, can be used as a noun to mean "a result."

> This program should have an *effect* (not: **affect*) on inflation.

after all   This phrase should always be written as two separate words.

> It didn't turn out to be exciting *after all* (not: **afterall*)

afterward *vs.* afterwards   Although *afterwards* is preferred in Britain, *afterward* is the standard form in the U.S.

allot, a lot, *alot*   The verb *allot* means "to distribute shares." The idea of "very much" or "a great deal" is expressed by the *two* words *a lot*. This idea should not be expressed by the nonstandard form **alot*.

> Thanks *a lot* (not: **alot*) for your help yesterday.
> *A lot* (not: **Alot*) of mistakes can be easily corrected.

all the farther, *all the faster   nonstandard forms for *as far as* and *as fast as*

almost, most   *Most* is considered nonstandard when it is used as a substitute for *almost*.

> **You can find it in *most* any department store.
> You can find it in *almost* any department store.

**alongside of*   This is a nonstandard form that simply means *alongside*.

> Park your car *alongside* (not: **alongside of*) the garage.

already, all ready   Written as one word, *already* is an adverb meaning "by or before a given time." The two words *all ready*, however, mean "everything or everyone is ready."

> We had *already* seen that movie three times. But we were *all ready* to see it again.

alright, *allright   These are non-standard forms for the word(s) that is more frequently misspelled than any other in the language. *All right* should always be spelled as two words, no matter how it is used. The best way to remember this is to ask yourself how you would spell *all wrong*.

alternate *vs.* alternative   *Alternate*, both as a verb (pronounced all'•ter•nate) and as an adjective or a noun (pronounced all'•ter•net), means "by turns." *Alternative*, on the other hand, means "a choice" (especially, one of two possibilities). Confusion between these words is especially common when they end in *-ly* and are used as adverbs.

> We will be staying at the Hilton or, *alternatively* (not: **alternately*), at the Ramada.

altogether, all together   Written as one word, *altogether* is an adverb meaning "completely." The two words, *all together*, on the other hand, mean "everyone in the same location."

> The family was *altogether* happy with its new home.
> The family was *all together* for the first time in years.

alumna, alumnae, alumnus, alumni   A female graduate is called an *alumna* (pronounced a•lum'•nah); two or more female graduates are *alumnae* (pronounced a•lum'•nee).A male graduate is an *alumnus*; two or more male graduates are *alumni* (pronounced a•lum'•nye). *Alumni* is also used to refer to a group that includes both male and female graduates.

AM, FM These abbreviations stand for two different methods of radio broadcasting: amplitude modulation and frequency modulation. No periods are used in these abbreviations in order to avoid confusion with A.M. and P.M. (see below). Although there is a trend toward using small letters instead of capital ones for AM and FM, the capital letters should be used in order to avoid confusion (however unlikely) with the verb *am* and the abbreviation for fathom (fm.).

A.M., P.M. These abbreviations for *ante meridian* and *post meridian* refer to times "before noon" (A.M.) and "after noon" (P.M.). They are almost always capitalized, and periods always follow each letter. Use these abbreviations only with *figures* showing times, and avoid redundancies that state ideas already expressed by the abbreviations.

> The bus leaves at *10* A.M.
> *The bus leaves at *ten* A.M.
> *The bus leaves at 10 A.M. *in the morning.*

amateur Whether this word is used as an adjective or as a noun, it should be pronounced with a distinct *t* in the third syllable (am′·a·*t*ur, not: *am′·a·*ch*ur).

> She was the finest *amateur* athlete in the country.

among *vs.* between The general rule is that *between* should be used when there are only two distinct and separate items. *Among* is used when there are more than two items.

> The table was placed *between* the two chairs.

The three pirates divided the treasure *among* themselves.

However, *between* can be used when there are more than two items, provided that each item is considered separately.

> We planted beans *between* the rows of corn.

*amongst Although this form is commonly used in Britain, here it is considered nonstandard. Stick with *among*.

amphitheater Strange as it may seem, this is the correct spelling of the word that means "an arena." The *ph* is pronounced as an *f*, and so the correct pronunciation of this word is am′·*f*i·the·a·ter (not: *am′·*pi·the·a·ter).

*and etc. The abbreviation *etc.* stands for the Latin phrase meaning "and so forth." Therefore, **and etc.* would mean "and and so forth," the *and* being obviously redundant and unnecessary.

angry at, angry with You can be *angry at* (or *angry about*) a situation or an event, but you are *angry with* a person.

> I will be very *angry with* (not: **angry at*) you if you break that.

ante-, anti- The prefix *ante-* means "before"; *anti-*, on the other hand, means "against." These prefixes are frequently confused, and this is the source of many misspellings.

> *ante*room (a room *before* another room)
> *ante*diluvian (*before* the flood)

*anti*aircraft (*against* aircraft)
*anti*freeze (*against* a freeze)

*any and all   This phrase appears to point out a necessary distinction; however, it very rarely means anything different from the ideas expressed by either *any* or *all*.

> *You must return *any and all* books that you have borrowed.
> You must return *any* books that you have borrowed.
> You must return *all* books that you have borrowed.

anyone, any one   When the meaning is "any person" or "anybody," *anyone* should be written as one word. However, when the meaning is "any single thing," it should be written as *any one*.

> *Any one* (not: *anyone) of these will do.
> *Anyone* would like that book.

*anyplace   This form is nonstandard when it is used to mean *anywhere*. Written as two words, however, *any place* has a different meaning and is quite standard.

> *I can't find it *anyplace*.
> It isn't in *any place* I have looked.

*anyways   a nonstandard form for *anyway*

*anywheres   a nonstandard form for *anywhere*

arctic   All-too-often this word is pronounced without the first *c* (ark'•tik, not: *ar'•tik).

> An *arctic* cold swept into the region.

*Aren't I?   When this phrase is used at the beginning of a question, it is usually in response to a statement that included "you aren't . . ." The problem is that **Aren't I?* actually means **Are I not?* and, therefore, contains an error in agreement. It is best to replace the phrase with the standard form *I'm not?* or another phrase that expresses the same idea (e.g., *Oh, no?*).

as *vs.* like   Standard English demands that *as* (including *as if* and *as though*) introduce clauses of comparison. *Like,* on the other hand, is a preposition that shows the relationship between two words in a sentence.

> He drives *like* an idiot!
> He plays with those toys *as* a child would.

When the word you want to use means "similar to (something else)," choose the preposition *like*. But when the second part of the comparison is a clause (remember that a clause *must* contain a verb), it is quite likely that your choice should be *as, as if,* or *as though*.

> She ran *like* a deer.
> She ran *as though* (not: *like) her life depended upon it.

assure, ensure, insure   *Assure* implies that all doubt or suspense is being removed; it usually has a personal object: We *assured* him that his job was secure. *Ensure* always implies a making certain or inevitable: This will *ensure* that the system will remain sound. *Insure* is best left to its more technical meaning—that is, implying a guarantee against loss or risk: This proce-

177

dure will *insure* against damage caused by improper handling.

as yet   This phrase is not, necessarily, improper, but the word *yet* all by itself works just as well in almost all cases.

> We haven't been able to locate it *as yet*.
> We haven't been able to locate it *yet*.

*at about   In expressions of time, the phrase **at about* is considered nonstandard. Use either *at* or *about,* whichever better expresses the isea you want to convey.

> **I'll be back *at about* nine o'clock.
> I'll be back *at* nine o'clock.
> I'll be back *about* nine o'clock.

athlete, athletic   *Athlete* has only two syllables and should be pronounced ath'•leet (not: **ath'•a•leet). Similarly, *athletic* (and *athletics*) is pronounced ath'•let•ik (not: **ath'•a•let•ik).

*at this point in time   Ever since the Watergate hearings demonstrated how language could be used to obfuscate and to muddle simple truths, this phrase has become a favorite of people who think that they will appear more learned and wise if they adorn their speech and writings with worthless and unnecessary trimmings. What possible benefit is there in saying "**at this point *in time*"? Does the user want to distinguish between "at this point *in space*" or "at this point *on a map*"? The phrases *at this point* and *at this time* are quite clear without combining them. But the simple adverbs *now* and *then* are even better.

awful   As an adjective meaning "inspiring awe" or "terrifying," *awful* is quite proper. However, it is considered nonstandard as an adverb meaning "very."

> The awful truth soon became apparent.
> *I am *awful* sorry I missed you yesterday.

Even the adverb form *awfully* should not be used as a substitute for *very*.

awhile, a while   *Awhile* is an adverb meaning "for a period of time." *While* can be a noun meaning "a period of time." The understandable confusion here can be most easily remedied by using the two words *a while* after the preposition *for*.

> Will you be able to stay *awhile*?
> Will you be able to stay *for a while*?

B.A. *vs.* A.B.   Either abbreviation is standard for Bachelor of Arts.

backward *vs.* backwards   Either form may be used as an adverb, but only *backward* should be used as an adjective.

> The line began to move *backward* (or *backwards*).
> *The *backwards* motion knocked me to the floor. (replace with *backward*)

*basic fundamentals   This phrase is redundant because all fundamentals, by definition, are "basic." Delete *basic*.

basis   This word is singular and can refer only to other singular words. Its plural form is *bases* (pronounced bay'•seez).

> These three principles are the *bases* on which our cult was founded.

beside *vs.* besides   *Beside* is a preposition (and should not be followed by the preposition *of*) that means "at the side of." *Besides* is most commonly used as an adverb meaning "in addition to" or "moreover."

> Sit *beside* me.
> He has few books *besides* the Bible.

*be sure and   Use *be sure to,* instead.

> *Be sure and call me tomorrow.
> *Be sure to* call me tomorrow.

between *vs.* among   See *among vs. between*

bring *vs.* take   The difference between these verbs depends upon the position of the speaker. *Bring* is used when something is being moved toward the area of the speaker or writer; *take* is used when something is being moved away from the area of the speaker or writer.

> Please *bring* the letter to me.
> *Bring this form with you when you go to the hospital.
> *Take* this form with you when you go to the hospital.

*broadcasted   Use the form *broadcast* for both the past tense and the past participle: Yesterday we *broadcast* a report. . . ; This station has *broadcast* several. . . .

*busted   The verb you want is either *broke* or *burst.*

> *He *busted* his bat on that swing. (replace with *broke*)

cabinet   This word has three syllables (cab'•ih•net), not two (*cab'•net).

*can't help but   The *but* creates an illogical double negative and should be dropped.

> *I *can't help but* think that he is lying.
> I can't help thinking that he is lying.

capital *vs.* capitol   The word *capital* should be used for every meaning other than "a building." Link the *o* in *capitol* with the dome of the Capitol in Washington, D.C.

> The Capitol (building) is in our nation's capital (city).

cement *vs.* concrete   *Cement* is a dry powder that is mixed with water, sand, and gravel to form *concrete.*

> *The wall was built of *cement* blocks. (replace with *concrete*)

*center around   One thing can *revolve around, cluster around,* or *rotate around* another, but it must *center on* (not: *center around), meaning "to focus or gather to a point."

> The argument *centered on* the issue of overtime pay.

champ at the bit   An impatient person (or horse) "*champs* at the bit"; do not use "*chomps at the bit."

chasm   This word, meaning "a deep gorge" or "a marked separation," is pronounced as though it began with the letter *k*: kaz'•um.

*circle around This phrase is almost always redundant. How else can something circle but "around"? If the movement cannot be described as "around," then *circle* is the wrong verb. If *circle* is proper, delete *around*.

> The planes had to circle the airport several times during the delay.

*close proximity *Proximity*, all by itself, means "closeness; the state of being very near." The addition of *close*, then, is unnecessary and redundant.

compare to *vs.* compare with When two things are the same general category, they may be *compared with* each other. A comparison of things that are not similar uses the phrase *compare to*. Keep in mind Shakespeare's line "Shall I *compare* thee *to* a summer's day?" (*thee* is different from *a summer's day*)

> If you *compare* this year's budget *with* our expenses from last year, you'll see my point. (*budget* is similar to *expenses*)

complement *vs.* compliment A *complement* is something that "completes." A *compliment* is "a flattering remark."

> This wine is a perfect *complement* to chicken or pasta.
> I must *compliment* you on your taste in wine.

Complimentary is the form that means "given free, as a courtesy."

*completely decimated, *completely annihilated Decimated means "to take the tenth part of" or, more generally, "to de-stroy a large part of." The addition of *completely,* therefore, destroys the meaning of the verb and tells the reader that the writer did not know the meaning of *decimate* to begin with. When *completely* precedes an absolute such as *annihilate,* it is simply redundant and should be removed.

contact Avoid using the verb *contact* when you specifically have in mind *write, call, meet,* etc.

congratulate Be sure to spell and pronounce this word with a *t* (not a *d*) in the second syllable (con•gra*t*'•u•late, con•gra*t*'•u•lay•shuns).

*consensus of opinion This cliché is redundant. *Consensus* implies opinion and should stand alone. Also avoid **general consensus* for the same reason. (Note: consensus, not: **concensus*)

*convinced to Do not follow any form of the verb *convince* with *to*.

> **He *convinced* me *to* try out for football.

Either replace *to* with a clause beginning with *that* or change the verb to *persuade*.

> He *convinced* me *that I should* try out for football.
> He *persuaded* me *to* try out for football.

Note: The preposition *of* can follow *convince*. I was *convinced of* her sincerity.

councilor *vs.* counselor A *council* is "an assembly" or "a group." Any member of a council is a *councilor. Counsel,* on the other hand, can be a noun that means "advice" or a verb that means "to advise." Therefore, a *counselor* is "one who gives advice."

criteria   The singular form of this word is *criterion*.

   *How effectively you express yourselves will be the only *criteria* used in judging these papers. (replace with *criterion*)

culinary   This word, meaning "relating to the kitchen or cookery," is pronounced with the sound of the letter *q* for its first syllable (cue′•lih•nar•ee).

data   This word, meaning "measurements, statistics, or other factual information," is plural. Its singular form is *datum*.

   *This one figure is the only *data* on which your calculation is based. (replace with *datum*)
   The *data* confirm what we suspected. (not: the data *confirms* . . .)

*just desserts   The phrase "He got his *just deserts*" implies a deserved reward or punishment—not an after-dinner treat. *Deserts* (no double *s*), besides being arid tracts of sand, are "those things that are deserved."

device *vs.* devise   The noun *device* (the second syllable rhymes with *ice*) means "a contrivance" or "a piece of equipment." The verb *devise* (the second syllable rhymes with *eyes*) means "to make" or "to invent."

diamond   This word has three syllables (die′•ah•mund).

diaper   This word has three syllables (die′•ah•per).

different   Watch for redundant uses of this word (especially in the phrase *different kinds*).

   *There were fifty *different* schools entered in the competition. (remove *different*)

different from *vs.* *different than   In standard usage the adjective *different* is almost always followed by the preposition *from*; you can never go wrong by using *from*, but you can easily do so by using *than*.

dilemma   The prefix *di-* should indicate to you that this word involves two of something: two objectionable alternatives. If you are describing a perplexing situation that does not entail the choice of two unsatisfactory possibilities, use a more general noun such as *problem, predicament, difficulty,* or *question.*

   *Our taxable income had put us in a real *dilemma*. (replace with *predicament*)

diphtheria   This word is pronounced dift•thir′•ee•ah. That's right, the first syllable ends with the sound of *f*, not *p*.

disgusted   May be followed by the prepositions *at* (*disgusted at* an action), *by* (*disgusted by* a person's habit or characteristic), or *with* (*disgusted with* a person).

disinterested *vs.* uninterested   *Disinterested* means "impartial; objective; not influenced by personal reasons." *Uninterested,* however, means "not interested; unconcerned." A trial judge should always be *disinterested,* but occasionally a judge might become *uninterested* in a boring case.

displeased   May be followed by the prepositions *at* (*displeased at* a thing) or *with* (*displeased with* a person).

dissent   Should be followed by the preposition *from,* not *with.*

dived *vs.* dove   Use *dived* for the past tense of the verb *dive.*

> The lifeguard *dived* into the pool instead of calling for help.

*drownded   The past tense of *drown* is pronounced with only one syllable; it is spelled *drowned.*

due to   This phrase is considered nonstandard when it is used as a preposition to mean "because of."

> *I couldn't come to the party *due to* my cold. (replace with *because of*)

Because this usage is nonstandard, *due to* should not be used at the beginning of a sentence. (The phrase *due to* does have standard uses: My illness was *due to* bacteria. Here *due* is a predicate adjective.)

*drug *vs.* dragged   The past tense of the verb *drag* is *dragged,* not: *drug or *drugged.

effect *vs.* affect   See *affect vs. effect*

eminent *vs.* imminent   *Eminent* means "high, lofty; above others in rank." *Imminent* means "about to happen."

> She was a good teacher and an *eminent* scholar. Her appointment to the faculty council is *imminent.*

enough   Guard against using this word when it is unnecessary.

> *I was fortunate *enough* to be included on the list. (delete *enough*)

ensure   See *assure, ensure, insure*

*enthused   Use the standard adjective *enthusiastic.*

envelop *vs.* envelope   *Envelop* is a verb meaning "to cover or wrap." *Envelope* is a noun that means "a wrapper."

environment   Be sure to pronounce the *n* in the third syllable (en•vi'•*ron*•ment).

*equally as   This is a redundancy that can be avoided by deleting *as.*

> *He is *equally as* qualified.

escape   Do not pronounce this word as though it were spelled *excape.

*estimated at about   The preposition *about* creates a redundancy because *estimated* implies *about.* The only preposition that should follow *estimated* is *at:* The crowd was *estimated at* three thousand people.

etc. This abbreviation should not be used at the end of a list that is introduced by *such as* or *for example*. (See also **and etc.*)

*everyplace As two separate words, *every place* is a standard phrase. But the nonstandard **everyplace* should not be used to mean *everywhere*.

> **Everyplace* I went, I found disease. (replace with *everywhere* or: In *every place* I went I found disease.)

*exactly identical *Identical* is an absolute that implies *exactly*. Avoid this redundancy by deleting *exactly*.

except *vs.* accept See *accept vs. except*

excerpt Should be followed by the preposition *from*, not *of*. (And don't forget to spell *excerpt* with a *c*.)

expect *vs.* suspect *Expect* means "to anticipate; to look forward to." *Suspect* means "to distrust; to have doubts about."

> *I *suspect* that I'll be home by five o'clock. (replace with *expect*)

farther *vs.* further *Farther* is used to describe distance, usually physical distance; *further* indicates "moreover" or "in addition to." Use *farther* whenever the situation is measurable; use *further* for everything else.

> *I do not wish to pursue this discussion any *farther*. (replace with *further*)
> *If you go *further* into the intersection, you will not be able to turn. (replace with *farther*)

feminine endings The endings *-ess*, *-ette*, and *-trix*, which used to be added to nouns to show that the person in question was a woman (**authoress*, **usherette*, **aviatrix*) have now disappeared from standard usage. *Actress* and *heroine* remain, but it is not improper to use *actor* and *hero* in their place.

fewer *vs.* less *Fewer* is used in comparisons to modify plural nouns and to refer to "numbers." *Less* usually modifies singular nouns and refers to "quantity."

> *There are *less* people at the poverty level today than at any other time in our country's history. (replace with *fewer*)

fiancé *vs.* fiancée The first refers to a man; the second refers to a woman. Both are pronounced fee•ahn'•say.

*finalize This is business jargon that can be easily replaced by more precise verbs such as *finish* or *complete*.

> *We will *finalize* our negotiations on Monday. (replace with *conclude*)

*first began A redundancy that can be avoided by deleting *first*.

*firstly, secondly, etc. Just use *first*, *second*, etc. (What would you have done when you arrived at *eleventh*?)

flammable *vs.* inflammable There is absolutely no difference between these words, and either is acceptable in standard usage. *Inflammable*, however, seems to mean *nonflammable* to some people;

therefore, use *flammable* in order to avoid this confusion.

flautist *vs.* flutist   This is one of the rare cases of a usage change occurring over a very brief time. Not long ago *flautist* (the first syllable rhymes with *now*) was the preferred spelling and pronunciation for "a person who plays the flute." Now it is *flutist* (flewt'•ist).

forbade   The past tense of *forbid* is pronounced with its second syllable rhyming with *sad.*

***for free**   Just use *free.*

***forbid from**   Use the preposition *to* instead of *from.* Think of the mnemonic (memory aid) *4bid2.*

He was *forbidden to* ride the subway.

forte   When this word means "one's strong point," it is pronounced with one syllable (fort). The musical term meaning "loud or powerful" is pronounced for'•tay.

Frankenstein   Frankenstein was the doctor who created the monster, not the name of the monster itself.

*These genetic experiments may yet produce a *Frankenstein.* (replace with *monster*)

***free gratis**   *Gratis* means "without payment," and so does *free.* This redundancy can be avoided by eliminating either word.

***from whence**   *Whence* means "from which place." **From whence,* then, would mean "from from which place."

*The beast returned to the cave *from whence* it came. (delete *from*)

***gild the lily**   This is a misquoted cliché. The correct line from Shakespeare's *King John* reads: "To gild refined gold, to paint the lily . . ."

government   Be sure to pronounce the *n* in the third syllable (guv'•ern•ment).

graduate   A person can *graduate from* a school or *be graduated from* a school— either form is standard. However, avoid the nonstandard *I *graduated* college in 1967.

granted   You take something *for granted,* not **for granite.*

gratis   See **free gratis*

grocery   Be sure to pronounce this word with three syllables (grow'•sir•ee).

guarantee   The first syllable rhymes with *care,* not with *car* (gair•an•tee').

***guesstimate**   Avoid this word entirely. If you mean "a guess," say so; if you mean "an estimate," even "a rough estimate," then say that.

hanged *vs.* hung   Use *hung* for all past-tense and past-particle uses except when referring to the death penalty. Draperies may be *hung,* but prisoners are *hanged.*

harass, harassment   Both words should be accented on their first syllable (hair'•us, hair'•us•ment).

*heighth   Avoid this spelling and pronunciation. The word you want is *height,* which rhymes with *might.*

herb   This word is pronounced with a silent *h* (*urb*).

Hobson's choice   Many people assume that this phrase identifies a dilemma—that is, a choice of two undesirable alternatives. However, the phrase originated with a stable-keeper whose carriages were lined up in a single column. The customers, then, had to take the first carriage in line because no other could be brought up until the ones in front of it had been taken away. A *Hobson's choice,* therefore, means a choice of the one offered or nothing at all.

homage   In this word the *h* is sounded (hahm'•ij).

*hopefully   See pages 136-137.

hors d'oeuvre   The *s* is silent (or•durv'). The French do not spell or pronounce the plural form with a final *s,* but we do (*hors d'oeuvres*).

hospitable   The accent falls on the first syllable (hoss'•pih•tah•bul).

identical   Should be followed by the preposition *with.*

*if and when   It is a rare sentence that can logically mean both *if* and *when.* Use only the one you mean, or recast the sentence in which the phrase is used.

> **If and when* that time comes, I'll be ready.
> *When* that time comes, I'll be ready.

imply *vs.* infer   A speaker or writer *implies* something when he suggests or hints at it. A reader or listener *infers* something when he draws a conclusion.

> **Are you *inferring* that I have not told the whole truth? (replace with *implying*)

*in back of   Replace this nonstandard phrase with the preposition *behind.* (However: *In the back of* the storeroom was a printing press.)

incidentally   This word has five syllables. Avoid the nonstandard spelling and pronunciation **incidently* (four syllables).

independent   Should be followed by the preposition *of.*

indexes   This has become the standard plural of *index;* however, *indices* is common in mathematics.

innocent   A technical point, perhaps, but defendants do not plead **innocent* in court, nor do juries find defendants **innocent.* The phrase *not guilty* is accurate for either case.

185

*input   This "fad" word should be avoided. Use *contribution* or *effort* instead.

*inside of   The *of* is unnecessary; just use *inside*.

insure   See *assure, ensure, insure*

*irregardless   This unnecessary, nonstandard redundancy should be replaced with the standard form *regardless*.

irrevocable   The accent falls on the sound *rev* in the second syllable (ir•rev'•uh•kuh•bul).

it's vs. its   *It's* is a contraction meaning "it is." *Its* is a possessive pronoun and, like all possessive pronouns, contains no apostrophe (*Its* engine had been removed). **Its'* is meaningless and always nonstandard.

jewelry   Be sure to pronounce all three syllables (joo'•ell•ree).

judgment   Be careful: This word is frequently misspelled **judgement*—a British spelling that is considered nonstandard in the U.S.

kindergarten   Do not pronounce this word **kin'•der•gar•den* or **kin'•dee•gar•ten*, but, rather, *kin'•der•gar•ten,* just as it is spelled.

*kind of a, *sort of a   The *a* in both expressions is unnecessary and should be deleted. Even without the *a*, do not use *kind of* or *sort of* to mean "somewhat" or "rather" (see pages 133-134).

lackadaisical   Do not pronounce this word with an *s* in its first syllable (lack•ah•day'•zih•kul not: **lacks*•ah•day'•zih•kul).

lend vs. loan   *Lend* is a verb; *loan* is a noun. I can *lend* you a *loan,* but I can't **loan* you anything. The past tense of *lend* is *lent,* not **loaned.*

   **Her father *loaned* her the amount she needed. (replace with *lent*)

If this sounds strange to you, how would you react to "Friends, Romans, countrymen, *loan* me your ears"?

less vs. fewer   See *fewer vs. less*

lie vs. lay   See pages 53-55.

lighted vs. lit   Use *lighted* (instead of *lit*) for both the past tense and the past participle of the verb *light.*

   Each person *lighted* one candle.
   After the fuse had been *lighted,* we all ran for cover.

Lit is becoming increasingly popular, but because other connotations (inebriated) are possible, stick with *lighted.*

like vs. as   See *as vs. like*

like vs. such as   There is very little difference between these two ways of making a comparison or showing examples. *Such* *as* seems to be a little more broad and introduces a more general category of comparable items. *Like,* on the other hand, draws a more direct comparison and connects items that closely resemble each other. As I said, whatever difference there is, is slight.

lit *vs.* lighted   See *lighted vs. lit.*

literally   *Literally* means "true to the exact meaning; not exaggerated." Many writers and speakers misuse this word, employing it merely for emphasis.

   *The audience *literally* fell over backward with laughter. (replace with *almost*)

long-lived   This word should be pronounced with its last syllable rhyming with the last syllable in *survived.*

machinations   This word, which means "concealed schemes for devious purposes," is pronounced with a *k* sound in its first syllable: mack•ih•nay′•shuns.

marshmallow   If you pronounce this word with an *a* in the second syllable (marsh′•mal•low), you will spell it that way, too.

may *vs.* can   See page 51.

media   *Media* is a plural noun and should be used to refer to only two or more types of agencies or instruments for conveying ideas: Representatives from all the *media* attended the conference. The singular form, *medium,* should be used to refer to one particular agency or instrument: This *medium*—television—relies on visual impressions.

meet *vs.* meet with   *Meet* has many definitions, most of which are well known to most speakers and writers. *Meet with,* however, has two distinct meanings of its own. It can be used to mean "join the company of" (He will *meet with* the board members in the morning) or "experience" (He *met with* an accident). Therefore, you may use *meeting* or *meeting with* in the following sentence, depending upon whether you mean "being introduced" or "assembling."

   I look forward to *meeting with* you next Tuesday.

memento   Do not spell or pronounce this word with an *o* in its first syllable: *momento.* the word is derived from the same root as the word *memo*; it has nothing to do with *moment.*

memorandum   Either plural form, *memoranda* or *memorandums,* is acceptable in standard usage today. (The plural of the informal, shortened form, *memo,* is *memos.*)

miniature   Be sure to pronounce this word with four distinct syllables: minn′•ee•ah•chur.

minuscule   Whether you accent the first syllable or the second syllable of this word, be sure to pronounce (and spell) it with a *u* (not an *i*) in its second syllable: mih'•nuss•kyool, mih•nuss'•kyool. The word is derived from the same root as *minus*—not *mini-*.

mischievous   Pronounce this word with only three syllables: miss'•cheh•vous.

mixed metaphor   A *metaphor* is a figure of speech in which a comparison is implied—that is, a metaphor shows a similarity without using the word *like* or *as:* The road was a ribbon of moonlight. A *mixed metaphor* occurs when the writer or speaker mingles two or more widely dissimilar images.

   *I don't like the situation we are in, but we must *play out the hand* and see if there is any *light at the end of the tunnel.*

moot   A *moot point* or a *moot question* is one that is "debatable" or "subject to discussion." Do not use *moot* to describe merely hypothetical, academic questions, or questions that have already been answered.

most   Do not use this word as a replacement for *almost.*

   **Most* everyone hits home runs in that park. (replace with *almost*)

muchly   Avoid this form entirely. *Much* is a perfectly acceptable adverb without the *-ly* ending.

nee   *Nee* (pronounced *nay*) means "born with the name of" and is used to indicate the maiden name of a married woman. Properly used, it is placed before only the person's family name—that is, the person's last name.

   A party was given to honor Mrs. Nancy Reagan *nee* Davis.

new innovation   An *innovation*, by definition, means "something newly introduced." The addition of *new,* therefore, is obviously redundant and should be avoided.

of   *Of* should not be used unnecessarily, as in the expression **off of,* **alongside of,* and **out of.* (*Out of* is usually nonstandard when it refers to direction; it is proper in the usages "two *out of* three," "*out of* a job," and "walked *out of* the office.")

often   The *t* in this word is silent: off'•n.

onto   This is a combination of two prepositions that seems similar to *into,* but, instead, is nonstandard. Use either *on* or *to,* whichever makes more sense in a given situation.

   *We climbed up *onto* the catwalk and jumped. (replace with *on* or *to*) The two words *on to* can be used when *on* is an adverb: Each generation has passed these stories *on to* its children.

ophthalmologist   As any "doctor who specializes in disorders of the eye" will tell you, this word has the sound of *f*—not *p*—in its first syllable: ahf•thal•moll•uh•jist.

opposite   Should be followed by the preposition *of* or no preposition at all.

Her room was *opposite* mine in the dorm.

oral   *Oral* is not a synonym for *verbal*. *Oral* means "spoken," whereas *verbal* means "pertaining to words, spoken or written."

orphan   A child can be an orphan if only one of his parents has died.

*over with   Another case of two prepositions where one will do. Delete *with*.

outside of   Do not use this phrase to mean "except for."

*Outside of its cost, your proposal seems acceptable to me.

Outside of can be used to mean "outside," but what benefit is there to adding the *of*? It is best to avoid the phrase entirely.

oxymoron   An *oxymoron* (pronounced ahk•sih•mor'•on) is a figure of speech that uses two seemingly contradictory terms. "Her eyes burned with a *cold fire*." "They had a *bittersweet* romance." The following expressions seem to me to have some of this same quality: "jumbo shrimp," "fresh frozen vegetables," "military intelligence," "Young Republicans."

paraphernalia   This word, meaning "a group of articles," is pronounced and spelled with an *r* in its third syllable: pair•ah•*fer*•naa'•lee•ah.

passed *vs.* past   As a general rule, use *passed* as a verb and *past* as an adjective or a noun.

The car *passed* us at a high rate of speed. By studying the *past,* you can appreciate the wonders of *past* civilizations.

phenomena   This is a plural form meaning "two or more visible, extraordinary occurrences." When referring to only one such occurrence, use the singular form *phenomenon*.

pianist   This word may be pronounced pee•an'•ist or pee'•an•ist; either is considered standard today.

place   This verb should be followed by the preposition *in*—not *into*.

*Be sure to *place* those dishes *into* that box carefully. (replace with *in*)

-place   Do not use this ending to form nonstandard words such as *noplace (meaning *nowhere*), *someplace (meaning *somewhere*), *everyplace (meaning *everywhere*), or *anyplace (meaning *anywhere*). However, these nonstandard forms can be used as two separate words, but not to indicate the meanings given above: There is *no place* like home.

*I can't find that report *anyplace*. (replace with *anywhere*)

plethora   This word, meaning "an excessive amount," is accented on its first syllable: pleth'•er•ah.

podium   A podium is not something that a speaker stands *behind*; rather, it is a platform that a speaker stands *upon*. A speaker may use a *lectern* to support his notes, but he stands upon a podium. *Podium* comes from the Latin root *pod* (meaning "foot"), which refers to the legs on which a podium stands.

pompon   If you mean the flower or the tufts or balls of crepe paper that cheerleaders hold, the word you want ends in an *n*: *pompon*. A *pom-pom,* on the other hand, is an automatic, antiaircraft cannon.

poorly   Do not use this word to mean "in poor health."

> *I have been feeling rather *poorly* since you left. (replace with *bad* or *ill*)

portmanteau words   The name comes from a line in Lewis Carroll's *Through the Looking Glass* and describes words that have been manufactured by combining two existing words. Like a portmanteau (a large, hinged suitcase that folds out displaying two compartments), the parts of these words work together as a unit: *smog = smoke + fog, brunch = breakfast + lunch.*

presently   *Presently* may be used to mean "shortly," but it should not be used to mean "now."

> *I am *presently* working on my master's thesis. (replace with *now* or *at present*)
> I will return these books to you *presently*.

principal *vs.* principle   See page 153.

proved *vs.* *proven   Although these forms are used almost interchangeably by many people today, you might be interested in knowing that the past participle **proven* was actually a principal part of the old Scottish verb *preve*. Like our verb *weave* (principal parts: *weave, weaving, wove, woven*), the principal parts of *preve* were *preve, preving, prove, proven*. This last form, the past participle *proven,* became confused with the past participle of the verb *prove,* which was *proved.* I have marked **proven* as being nonstandard, but, if you don't mind perpetuating a mistake from the past, it is unlikely that using the form will cause you any embarrassment.

provided *vs.* providing   *Provided* can have the meaning of the conjunction *if*. *Providing* should not be used in this way.

> *They will leave tomorrow, *providing* the rain stops. (replace with *provided*)

"quote ... unquote"   These words are used by speakers to represent the quotation marks that surround a word or phrase. **Unquote,* however, is meaningless and should be replaced by *close quote* or *end quote*. Note: The word *quote,* itself, may be used as a verb (I could *quote* your exact words), but not as a noun (This is a **quote* I will always remember). Use *quotation* instead.

raise *vs.* rise   *Raise* must have an object: You must raise *something*. *Rise* does not have an object; it describes a motion upward.

*The crowd *raised* up in their seats and cheered. (replace with *rose*)

rapport   The *t* is silent: rah•pour'.

Welsh rarebit   Originally, and jokingly, called *Welsh rabbit,* this dish is today pronounced as it is spelled: rare'•bit.

realtor   This word, which means a real-estate agent, is pronounced ree'•ul•tor, not *ree'•la•tor.

***reason is because**   A construction beginning "the reason is . . ." should be followed by a noun or a noun clause—not by *because.* (You wouldn't say "the cause is because . . ." would you?)

>   *The reason the fire caused so many fatalities was because the sprinkler system failed.
>   The reason the fire caused so many fatalities was that the sprinkler system failed.

***reason why**   This is a redundancy that can be eliminated by removing *why.*

>   *The reason *why* I am so tired is that I stayed out all night. (delete *why*)

recognize   Be sure to pronounce the *g* in the second syllable: reck'•ogg•nize.

***reduce down**   A redundancy; remove *down.*

***refer back**   Except in rare cases, this phrase is redundant and can be avoided by deleting *back.*

relation *vs.* relative   It is best to stick with *relative* when referring to "a kins-man," but if you insist on *relation,* follow it with *of,* not *to.*

***reoccur**   The standard word for "to occur again" is *recur.*

restaurateur   This word, which means "the proprietor of a restaurant," is not spelled or pronounced with the *n* that appears in *restaurant* (ress•tur•ah•tur').

***return back**   A redundancy; delete *back.*

***revert back**   Always redundant; delete *back.*

***Rio Grande River**   *Rio* means "river," and so the addition of *river* at the end is redundant.

root beer   The *root* rhymes with *toot,* not with *foot.*

***Sahara Desert**   *Sahara* means "desert"; therefore, the second *desert* is redundant.

>   The *Sahara* covers more than three million square miles.

***seldom ever**   *Ever* is unnecessary in this phrase; delete it.

set *vs.* sit   *Set* always has an object: You must "put or place *something.*" *Sit* very rarely has an object; it means "to rest in a sitting position."

>   *Don't just *set* there; give me a hand. (replace with *sit*)

sic   See page 202.

shall *vs.* **will**   See page 27.

sherbet   This flavored ice is pronounced sher'•bit, not *sher'•bert.

split infinitive   This construction occurs when any word or phrase is placed between *to* and the base form of a verb in an infinitive: The guards were instructed *to thoroughly search* every cell. English teachers have frowned upon the split infinitive for more than a century. The best advice I can offer is to keep the infinitive intact unless doing so creates an ambiguous or clumsy construction. The following sentence cannot be easily recast and is best left alone: We can expect the rate of inflation *to more than double* during the next five years.

spoonfuls   This is the proper plural, not *spoonsful. Also, *teaspoonfuls, cupfuls, handfuls,* etc.

start off   *Off* is unnecessary; just use *start.*

straitjacket   The first syllable of this word does not mean "without curves (*straight*)," but, rather, "narrow, tight (*strait*)" as in the "*Straits* of Magellan." Therefore, *straitjacket* (not: *straightjacket*)

strata   This word, which means "layers," is plural; its singular form is *stratum.*

*There is discord today in every *strata* of society. (replace with *stratum*)

suite   A *suite* (pronounced *sweet,* not *suit*) is "a series of items intended to be used together": a *suite* of rooms, a *suite* of bedroom furniture.

supposing   Do not use this form to mean *suppose.*

Supposing I were to tell you what really happened; would that make you happy? (replace with *suppose*)

surprise   Be sure to spell and pronounce this word with an *r* in its first syllable: sir•prize'. Note: Surprise should also be followed by the prepositions *at* or *by.*

take *vs.* **bring**   See *bring vs. take*

temperamental   Be sure to include the *a* in spelling and pronouncing the third syllable of this word: tehm•per•*ah*•mehn'•tul.

temperature   Be sure to pronounce all four syllables: tem'•per•ah•chur.

that *vs.* **which**   See pages 124-125.

theirselves   This nonstandard form should be avoided; use *themselves.*

thusly   *Thus* is a perfectly acceptable adverb meaning "in this, or that, manner." Adding an *-ly* ending doesn't make it *more* adverbial.

toward *vs.* **towards**   *Toward* is more common in the United States; *towards* is favored in Britain.

*true facts   If the facts are not true, they are not facts. Avoid this redundancy by deleting *true*.

*try and   Replace this nonstandard phrase with the standard *try to*.

> *Try to* finish that project this week.

*unawares   Drop the *s* and use *unaware*.

underhand *vs.* **underhanded**   You can throw a baseball *underhand*, but you should use *underhanded* to describe a person's sly or treacherous manner or actions.

uninterested *vs.* **disinterested**   See *disinterested vs. uninterested*

unique   *Unique* is an absolute adjective meaning "one of a kind." Do not modify this word with *very* or use it to refer to things that are merely "strange" or "unusual."

up   This preposition is unnecessary in (and should be dropped from) the expression **choose up*, **divide up*, **finish up*, and **drink up*.

upward *vs.* **upwards**   Both as an adjective and as an adverb, *upward* is the standard form in the United States. However,

the phrase *upwards of* (meaning "more than") is still in common use.

used to   When used without the helping verb *did*, the phrase *used to* is proper: He *used to* play tennis. However, when *did* is added as part of the verb phrase, the present-tense form *use* is standard: He *did* not *use to* play tennis.

valuable   Be sure to pronounce and spell this word with an *a* in the third syllable: val'•yoo•ah•bul, not *val'•yoo•bul.

vapid   This word, which means "lacking in spirit" or "tasteless," is pronounced with a short *a* in its first syllable: *va'•pihd*, not **vay'•pihd*.

*various and sundry   *Sundry* means "diverse" or "miscellaneous." So does *various*, and so the phrase is redundant. Use just one or the other.

verbal   See *oral*

veterinarian   Be sure to pronounce and spell all six syllables: veht•ur•uh•nair'•ee•un.

via   Either pronunciation, vy'•uh or vee'•uh, is standard, but the word should be used only to mean "by way of," not to mean "by means of."

> *We went to Springfield *via* train.
> We went to Springfield *via* Peoria.

viable   Restrict your use of this overworked and frequently misused word to instances in which it has the biological meaning "capable of living and growing normally."

*We should ask whether this is truly a *viable* alternative. (replace with *workable*)

vice versa   Both pronunciations, vice′•ver•suh and vy′•suh•vur•suh, are considered standard today.

wait on   Do not use this phrase to mean *wait for*.

*I am *waiting on* you to call. (replace with *waiting for*)

ways   Do not use this form to mean *way*.

*You have traveled a long *ways*. (replace with *way*)

weaved *vs.* wove   When *weave* means "to interlace threads or strands," its past tense is *wove* (My mother *wove* a scarf for me). But when *weave* means "to make a path" or "to move from side to side," its past tense is *weaved* (The runners *weaved* their way through the park).

-wise   Watch out for and avoid "fad" words that tack this ending on commonly used nouns: **ideawise, *profitwise, *weatherwise, *jobwise, *colorwise*, etc. (One of my favorite cartoons shows two men, seated at a bar. One glares incredulously at the other and says: "Did I just hear you say *'hopefullywise'?*")

wrestle   Do not pronounce this word **rass′•ul*.

14. Punctuation and Capitalization

Most people realize, I think, that written language must be punctuated in order to avoid confusing the reader, and so they put their commas, periods, and question marks in places where pauses and changes in voice would occur had their message been spoken instead of written. But punctuation, like every other area of English, has certain customs and conventions that have little if anything to do with conveying the intended meaning of a sentence. These rules for standard punctuation, instead, convey information about the writer. Just as misspelling and improper use of pronoun forms tell the reader that the writer is (for whatever reason) unfamiliar with the standard forms of written English, so the failure to adhere to the conventions of standard punctuation can cast the writer in a similarly unfavorable light. Again, the common argument "What difference does it make as long as he knows what I mean?" does not speak to the fact that language transmits messages *about the user* at the same time it transmits his intended meaning. Our goal in using punctuation, then, is to communicate *exactly* what we want to say— about our intended message and about ourselves.

Most of the rules in this chapter are either already well known to you or do not affect the writing you generally do. Because of this, these rules are just briefly stated and carry little explanation with only an example or two. You may choose merely to glance over this material so that you will know where it can be found when a specific need arises. I have grouped a few uses of certain marks together in a section titled "Notes about Punctuation." This section identifies some of the most common punctuation errors, and it should be studied carefully so that you can avoid these errors in your own writing. The area of punctuation that I find to be most often misunderstood, the placement of marks used together, is covered in a section titled "The Most Common Problem in Using Punctuation." Close study of this section can also be a profitable expenditure of your time, for the usages it discusses occur time and again, even in everyday writing.

Some of the rules concerning standard capitalization have been woven into this chapter at points where punctuation and capitalization generally occur together in writing. Additional material about proper capitalization can be found at the end of the chapter in a section titled "Notes about Capitalization."

End Marks

The exclamation point, question mark, and period are called *end marks* because each can be used at the end of a complete sentence.

We will never give up this ship!

Haven't I met you somewhere before?

The flight will leave at noon.

Exclamation points should be reserved for those sentences that express very strong emotion. Milder imperative sentences may be followed by a period.

Come here this instant!

Be sure to come back before dinner.

Requests that are in the form of a question but do not require an answer may be followed by a period or by a question mark.

Mary, will you please close the window.

Mary, will you please close the window?

Indirect questions—that is, sentences that state that something was asked or those that ask for something but not in the form of a question—should be followed by a period.

The boss asked if I needed a vacation.

I wonder whether you can help me with this.

End marks, however, do not always appear at the end of a complete sentence. An exclamation point can follow a single word or a phrase that shows strong or sudden emotion.

What a shame!

Wow! Three in a row!

Periods are also used in abbreviations.

Mr.   Dr.   Ph.D.

Mrs.   Jr.   A.D.

Ms.   Nov.   B.C.

Some abbreviations do not require the use of periods. Familiar initials such as JFK (John Fitzgerald Kennedy) or FDR (Franklin Delano Roosevelt), abbreviations for government agencies, for unions, and for well-known companies and organizations are now commonly spelled without periods.

FTC (Federal Trade Commission)

UAW (United Auto Workers)

NBC (National Broadcasting Company)

AMA (American Medical Association)

The two-letter abbreviations for states, which are used with zip codes in addresses, do not use periods.

IL (Illinois)

ND (North Dakota)

CAPITALIZING ABBREVIATIONS

The abbreviations A.D. (meaning "in the year of our Lord") and B.C. (meaning "before Christ") are always capitalized. Standard usage, however, demands that A.D. be placed before the numeral indicating a year, and B.C. be placed after the numeral.

Her death occurred in A.D. *162.* (or: in 162.)

The coin was minted around *600* B.C.

The abbreviations that mean "before noon" (A.M.) and "after noon" (P.M.) are usually capitalized, but small letters may also be used (*a.m., p.m.*). Frequently used technical terms such as *mpg* (miles per gallon), *rpm* (revolutions per minute), *mph* (miles per hour), and abbreviations for weights and measures are written in small ("lowercase") letters. Abbreviations for metric units do not require periods.

yd. (yard)	m (meter)
lbs. (pounds)	kg (kilogram)
cu. in. (cubic inch)	ml (milliliter)

THE COMMA

The comma is a separating mark of punctuation. It provides the interruption that tells the reader how to group your words, phrases, and clauses. If you keep in mind that commas (like all other marks of punctuation) are for the aid of the reader, you will not scatter them needlessly throughout your writing.

A comma is used to separate the items in a series. Whether the items are single words or groups of words, the commas separate the items *from each other,* and so no comma should follow the last item in the series. If the last two items are joined by *and* or *or,* it is still a good idea to use a comma as well as the conjunction between the last two items.

> The club bought pens, stationery, *and* envelopes.
>
> We went over the river, through the woods, *and* on to Grandma's house.

A comma is often used to separate two or more adjectives that precede a noun. As a general rule, a comma is proper if the word *and* could logically be used in its place.

> The tall, dark, handsome stranger rode out of town. (tall *and* dark *and* handsome stranger)
>
> She chose a beautiful, dark green sweater. (not: *dark *and* green)

A comma is used to separate two independent clauses that are joined by *and, but, or, nor, for, yet,* or *so.*

> Andrea concentrated on her game, *and she won easily.*

No comma is necessary in sentences that have just a compound subject or compound predicate.

> We plant the seeds each spring and harvest the crop in the fall. (no comma)

A comma is always used after an introductory interjection, an introductory participle phrase, an introductory adverb clause, or after two or more introductory prepositional phrases.

> Well, now I'm completely confused. (introductory interjection)
>
> Waving in the breeze, our flag signaled that we had survived. (introductory participle phrase)
>
> When the boat finally arrived, no one was left on the island. (introductory adverb clause)
>
> Under each wing of the plane, there were two powerful jet engines. (two introductory prepositional phrases)

Note: Use a comma after a single introductory prepositional phrase if a comma will help prevent misreading.

In the picture above, the bandit is seen leaving the bank. (comma prevents reading: *In the picture above the bandit . . .)

A comma is used to separate a direct quotation from the rest of the sentence in which that quotation appears.

> Joan replied angrily, "I never want to see you again!"
>
> "I wonder, " he said, "what I would have done in her place."

However, if the direct quotation is used as the subject or the predicate noun of the sentence, it should not be set off by a comma.

> "You'll never be able to prove it" was his reply.
>
> Her favorite expression is "Have a nice day."

Paired commas—that is, one before and one following—are used to enclose nonessential participle phrases, nonessential clauses, nonessential appositives, parenthetical expressions, and words used in direct address. Nonessential (or nonrestrictive) elements are those that can be removed without changing the meaning of the sentence. Essential elements, on the other hand, limit the meaning of the main clause and cannot be removed without changing the meaning of the sentence. As a general rule, an essential element will answer the question "Which one?"

> The ceiling, *damaged by heat and smoke,* had to be repainted. (nonessential participle phrase)
>
> Her latest novel, *Deepest Feelings,* is destined to be a best-seller. (nonessential appositive)
>
> The setting for the novel *Deepest Feelings* is San Francisco. (essential appositive, no commas)
>
> A maple tree, which provides plenty of shade, would be perfect for our backyard. (nonessential clause)
>
> One tree *that provides plenty of shade* is the maple. (essential clause, no commas)

Parenthetical expressions and words used in direct address should be set off by commas.

> This plant, I think, needs more water.
> I don't understand, Paul, why you can't see things my way.

Commas are used to separate the parts of addresses and dates.

> The meeting will take place at 700 South Seventh Street, St. Charles, Illinois, on Friday afternoon.
> The events of Sunday, December 7, 1941, changed the lives of millions.

The commas traditionally used following the name of a state or country at the end of an address (as in the first example) and following the year at the end of a date (as in the second example) are gradually disappearing and are not mandatory in standard usage.

A comma is used to separate the salutation from the body of a friendly letter and to separate the closing from the signature.

> Dear Kay,   Sincerely,

A comma is used to separate a person's name from a degree or title that follows the name.

> Charles Weiss, Ph.D.   Richard Stolley, Jr.

A comma should also be used to help the reader avoid misinterpreting the intended meaning of a sentence, even though there may be no standard rule to cover this use.

> I saw the man who fired the shot, and ran.

THE SEMICOLON

The semicolon is a separating mark of punctuation. It indicates a stronger break than a comma, but a weaker break than an end mark.

A semicolon is used to separate two independent clauses that are not joined by *and, but, or, nor, for, yet,* or *so.*

> The players were confident that they could win the pennant; the manager was not so optimistic.

When the second independent clause begins with a transitional adverb such as *then, whoever, thus, indeed, moreover, nevertheless, furthermore, therefore,* or *consequently,* the clauses should be separated by a semicolon, and the transitional adverb should be followed by a comma.

> None of the students was of driving age; therefore, their picnic had to be near the school.

A semicolon is used to separate items in a series when one or more of those items contains a comma.

> I requested the issues dated August 22, 1943; November 4, 1945; and May 18, 1949.

THE COLON

The colon is a linking mark that acts like an arrow pointing forward: It indicates that something important follows.

A colon is used to introduce a list or a series of items.

> The basket was filled with a variety of toys: dolls, puzzles, games, and model airplanes.

When used in this way, the colon has the meaning of *for example, namely, for instance,* or *that is.* However, when these expressions are stated in the sentence, the colon should not be used. A colon should also not be used when the list of items immediately follows a verb or a preposition.

> The starting infielders will be Tinkers, Evers, Chance, and Steinfeldt. (no colon)

A colon frequently appears after the expression *as follows* or *the following.*

> The first two steps are as follows:
> 1. Insert the key into the switch.
> 2. Turn the key to the right.

(If the items in the list are not complete sentences, do not use a period after them.)

A colon is used between two complete statements when the second statement explains or restates the first.

> My first day on the job was disappointing: Not a single customer entered the store.

A colon is used between hours and minutes in expressions of time, between chapters and verses in Bible passages, and following the salutation in a business letter.

11:55 P.M.   Luke 4: 1-5   Gentlemen:

CAPITALIZATION FOLLOWING A COLON

When the items in a list following a colon are complete sentences and are preceded by numerals, each item should begin with a capital letter. When a colon separates one statement from another that explains or restates the first, the second statement should be separated from the colon by one space, and it should begin with a capital letter—providing that whatever follows the colon is a complete sentence. (Authorities differ on this second point, and so it is also standard to begin a complete sentence that follows a colon, and that amplifies the sentence preceding the colon, with a small letter.)

When a colon is used to introduce a long or formal statement or quotation, it should be followed by a capital letter.

THE DASH

The dash should be thought of as a linking mark that acts like an arrow pointing backward, directing attention to what precedes it in the sentence.

A dash is frequently used before the expressions *that is, namely,* and *for example.*

> Congress had the power to prevent the crisis —that is, they had the ability, but not the will.

A dash is used following a series that refers to a final, summarizing clause. It may also precede a phrase that emphasizes or explains a phrase within the main clause.

> Duty, honor, and glory —these were the thoughts that motivated our actions.
> We knew our mission had been a failure —a failure both in judgment and in execution.

Dashes may also appear in pairs to separate a sudden break in thought from the rest of the sentence.

> They could have —and, perhaps, they should have —warned us much earlier about the danger.

THE HYPHEN

The hyphen is a linking mark that is used to link words and parts of words into a unit.

A hyphen may be used to link a word that is begun on one line and finished on the next. When used in this way, the hyphen should be placed only between syllables—one syllable words should never be hyphenated.

Hyphenate compound numbers from twenty-one to ninety-nine, and hyphenate the numerator and denominator in a fraction—unless either part already contains a hyphen.

> forty-seven   a three-fifths majority
> twenty-one hundredths

A hyphen should be used following the prefixes *self-, ex-,* and *all-,* and following any prefix that precedes a proper noun.

> self-important   ex-president
> all-world   anti-American

Hyphenate a compound adjective that precedes the noun it modifies.

> her much-improved attitude
> a well-behaved child

Do not hyphenate a compound adjective that follows the noun it modifies.

> her condition is much improved (no hyphen)
> a child who is well behaved (no hyphen)

Do not hyphenate a compound word in which the first part of the compound ends in -*ly.*

> a widely praised book (no hyphen)
> a wholly different matter (no hyphen)

There are, perhaps, a hundred rules that govern the use of the hyphen in spelling compound words. If you are in doubt about whether a particular compound word should be hyphenated, spelled as two separate words, or spelled as a single word, consult your dictionary.

PARENTHESES

Parentheses always occur in pairs. Parentheses are used to enclose incidental matter that is not closely related to the rest of the sentence. Although paired commas and paired dashes also enclose incidental information, parentheses indicate the greatest degree of separation between the words they enclose and the rest of the sentence.

> The death of Richard J. Daley (see page 428) resulted in a scramble for political power.

CAPITALIZATION WITHIN PARENTHESES

Even though the material enclosed within parentheses is a complete sentence, a capital letter is not required at its beginning if the parentheses occur within another sentence.

> The unusually long game (it lasted four hours) produced only two runs.

If the material inside the parentheses is a question or an exclamation, the question mark or exclamation point should be included within the parentheses, but, still, no capital letter is required.

> No one knew (shouldn't someone have told them?) that the trip had been canceled.

If the material inside the parentheses is a complete sentence, *and* if that material is not part of any other sentence, then the material should begin with a capital letter and end with an end mark.

> Our reservations were for five o'clock. (We arrived late, as usual.) The restaurant, however, couldn't serve us until six.

THE APOSTROPHE

The apostrophe is used to create the possessive form of nouns, to form some plurals, and to indicate where letters have been omitted from contractions.

The possessive form of a singular noun is indicated by adding an apostorophe and *s*.

> the girl's scarf   Tess's scarf

The possessive form of plural nouns that do not end in -*s* is indicated by adding an apostrophe and *s*.

> the men's league   our children's future

The possessive form of plural nouns that end in -*s* is indicated by adding only an apostrophe.

> the prisoners' grievances
>
> my parents' advice

An apostrophe is used to form the plural of letters that are referred to as letters, numbers that are referred to as numbers, and words that are referred to as words.

> the word contains two *i*'s and two *t*'s.
>
> Your *7*'s look like *9*'s to me.
>
> Commas can be used in place of *and*'s.

Numbers representing years, however, can be made plural by adding only an *s* without an apostrophe.

> The 1960*s* (or 1960's) were as turbulent as any period in our history.

An apostrophe is also used to show that one or more letters have been omitted.

> isn't   we've   they're
>
> I'd   she's   spit 'n' polish

When an apostrophe is used to represent a century, it should appear only in a reference to a single year—not a decade.

> the spirit of '76   the flood of '09
>
> (not: *the '60s)

QUOTATION MARKS

Quotation marks are used to enclose a direct quotation—that is, someone's exact words.

> "I didn't do it," the suspect pleaded.
>
> The suspect said he didn't do it. (indirect quotation)

When a direct quotation includes another direct quotation (or a title that would be enclosed by quotation marks), the included matter is enclosed in single quotation marks.

"But you told me 'Never trust anyone,' " Harriet replied.

"We will discuss Thoreau's essay 'Civil Disobedience' tomorrow," he said.

Quotation marks are used to enclose the titles of poems, essays, songs, short stories, television programs, articles, and chapter titles of books.

"The Tonight Show" has been on television for many years.

The fight song "On Wisconsin" was originally written for the University of Minnesota.

CAPITALIZATION WITHIN QUOTATION MARKS

A direct quotation that is itself a complete sentence should begin with a capital letter. If the direct quotation is interrupted, the second part of the quotation does not require a capital letter.

Norma said, "*L*et me do that, at least until you are rested."

"*L*et me do that," Norma said, "*a*t least until you are rested."

"*L*et me do that," Norma said. " *Y*ou need a rest."

When a title is enclosed in quotation marks, the first word, the last word, and all important words should be capitalized. "Important words" include all words except *a, an, the,* and coordinating conjunctions. (The *to* in an infinitive is usually not capitalized. The first part of a hyphenated compound word is always capitalized. The second part is not capitalized unless it is a noun or a proper adjective.)

"The Will to Succeed"   "Nineteenth-Century Plays"

"Self-proclaimed Leaders of the World"

Note: Some texts advise capitalizing all prepositions that have four or more letters. Be consistent in using whatever style you choose.

UNDERLINING

Underlining is used in writing to indicate titles that would be set in italic print. Titles of books, periodicals, plays, operas, movies, and the names of ships should be underlined. Generally speaking, underlining denotes works of substantial length, while quotation marks enclose titles of shorter works.

Capitalizing the titles of underlined words follows the same rule that governs capitalizing titles enclosed by quotation marks (see page 201).

The Decline and Fall of the Roman Empire
Gone with the Wind

NOTES ABOUT PUNCTUATION

Two uses of commas seem to cause more difficulty than any of the others. The first involves the use of a comma when the conjunction *and* or *or* join the last two items in a series. Should you write X, Y, and Z or just X, Y and Z? By always using a comma *and* the conjunction in cases like these, you can avoid potential misreadings.

The quarterbacks practiced with the ends and the running backs, the offensive linemen practiced with the defensive linemen, and the defensive backs practiced with the linebackers.

The other question that frequently comes up about the use of the comma is whether a comma is appropriate following a short introductory element, such as an introductory adverb or a single introductory prepositional phrase. Should a comma be used after the first word of the following sentence?

Soon the rain stopped and the traffic cleared.

Should a comma be used after the word *tries* in the sentence below?

After three tries she finally succeeded.

The point to remember here is that a comma should not be used unless there is a good reason for using it. Both of the example sentences are perfectly clear and impossible to misread without the commas, and so there is no good reason to use a comma in either sentence. Punctuate your writing where necessary and proper, but avoid overpunctuating whenever possible.

There are also two common problems that people have in using apostrophes. The first involves the use of the apostrophe in phrases like *a day's wages, a moment's thought,* and *three hours' practice.* The apostrophe is proper in these phrases because there is a possessive relationship between the two nouns in each. this use of an apostrophe is quite common in expressions of time and space, but does not carry over into other areas. In the phrase *thirty pounds pressure,* for example, the relationship between *pounds* and *pressure* is quite different from the relationships that exist in the previous examples, and does not require an apostrophe.

When two or more people (or other nouns) own or possess an object jointly, only the last noun should be written in its possessive form.

> We are going to *Harley and Eleanor's* house for Thanksgiving.

Be careful, however, that your message is not ambigious.

> We invited Buddy and Lena's friend Rob to the party. (How many people were invited—both Buddy and Rob, or just Rob?)

Some commonly used Latin abbreviations offer problems in punctuation as well as in definition. The abbreviations in the following list are always separated from the rest of the sentence in which they occur by a comma; a comma both before and after (or another mark such as a parenthesis or a dash before the abbreviation and a comma after) is required if the abbreviation occurs in the middle of a sentence. Although it was customary in the past to underline these abbreviations (indicating italic type), it is becoming more common today to treat them just like other abbreviations.

etc.	=	and so forth (*et cetera*)
e.g.	=	for example
et al.	=	and others
ibid.	=	in the work just mentioned
i.e.	=	that is
viz.	=	namely

The store sold shirts, jackets, pants, underwear, etc., right out on the sidewalk.

The other stores on the block (viz., Sears, Wards) were closed for the day.

(Notice that the abbreviation *et al.* has only one period and that the Latin phrase *et cetera* has none.)

The Latin word *sic,* which means "so" or "in this manner" is a complete word—not an abbreviation. When you see this word in print, you should understand that it is used to indicate that the word or phrase preceding it contains a misspelling or a usage error.

> The students carried signs reading "Death to the Fashist [*sic*] Pigs."

In the section that deals with hyphenating compound words (pages 199-200) I stated that a compound adjective should be hyphenated only when it precedes the noun it modifies.

a well-known man   but: a man who is well known (no hyphen)

However, if a word precedes the compound adjective and modifies only the first part of the compound, omit the hyphen.

a little-used device   but: a very little used device (no hyphen)

It is also helpful to remember that words formed with the following prefixes are not usually hyphenated: *anti-, co-, extra-, non-, over-, pre-, pro-, post-, pseudo-, re-, semi-, sub-, un-, under-.*

nonviolent   overconfident   coeducational

If the second part of the compound is capitalized or if it is a figure, then the word should be hyphenated.

anti-Semitic   pre-1900

If the second part of the compound is, itself, more than one word or if writing the compound as a single word can cause confusion or misreading, then the prefix should be followed by a hyphen.

non-native-speaking residents
re-cover (distinguishes from *recover*)

THE MOST COMMON PROBLEM IN USING PUNCTUATION

Most people have surprisingly little diffi-
culty using individual marks of punctuation properly in their writing. But when two or more marks seem to be necessary at exactly the same point, the average writer fumbles for a solution and curses himself for not remembering how he solved this problem the last time he faced it. If a sentence ends with an abbreviation, should two periods be used, or just one? Where should the period be placed in a sentence that is enclosed by parentheses? And does a comma belong inside or outside the quotation marks? (Students who face this last problem on handwritten examinations often elect to place the comma *directly beneath* the quotation marks and hope that their teacher will give them the benefit of the doubt. Tricks like this are also common in friendly letters and handwritten memos.) The problem of placing two or more punctuation marks at the same point is by far the most common problem adults have in using punctuation.

This problem can be very easily solved by remembering a few usage rules and by using a little common sense.

Rule 1: Commas are always placed *inside quotation marks,* but always *outside parentheses.*

"I can be either a good friend or a bad enemy," the sergeant said.

The causes of the decline were many (see p. 149), and all were of equal importance.

Rule 2: Periods are always placed *inside quotation marks.*

"We can do it," she pleaded, "if we try."

203

Rule 3: Periods, question marks, and exclamation points are placed inside parentheses only when the material inside the parentheses—taken by itself—would call for one of these marks.

It took ten years for the nation to recover. (It could have easily taken twice that long.)

A batting helmet will be given to every child (age twelve or under).

Why wasn't this bill voted upon before the deadline (July 1)? (Wasn't that the deadline?)

Rule 4: Question marks and exclamation points are placed inside quotation marks only when the enclosed matter is a question or an exclamation.

The speaker asked, "Is there a doctor present?"

Why did you tell me "I'll be home by ten"?

Rule 5: Only one end mark should appear at the end of a sentence. If either of two could be used, choose the one that better expresses the idea you want to convey. A period ending an abbreviation is retained when it is followed by a question mark or an exclamation point. However, a sentence should not end with two periods.

Does the plane to Los Angeles leave at 3 P.M.?

Actually, planes to Los Angeles leave at 11 A.M. and 3 P.M.

Rule 6. A comma and an end mark should not be used together. Choose an exclamation point or a question mark over a comma, but choose a comma over a period. A period that ends an abbreviation can be used together with a comma.

"Will we make it in time?" I wondered.

"That's the last straw!" he screamed.

"I'll be there in a minute," he replied.

Planes to Chicago leave at 4 P.M., 8 P.M., and 1 A.M.

Now, there are other rules that govern multiple punctuation (for instance, semicolons and colons are placed outside quotation marks and parentheses), but they cover situations that do not occur very often in most general writing. There are also a few differences between the rules given in different textbooks. But if you use your common sense and think about what type of material is actually being enclosed by quotation marks or parentheses, and if you keep in mind that the purpose of your marks is to make your meaning clear to your reader, then you can be confident in your ability to solve any problem concerning multiple punctuation.

The instructions that appear on page 207 will tell you how to use the accompanying grid and master sentences as a handy reference for solving punctuation problems.

NOTES ABOUT CAPITALIZATION

Standard usage includes the following rules for capitalization.

1. Capitalize the first word of every sentence and the first word of a direct quotation that is a complete sentence.

She asked, "Where do you live?"
What do you mean by "around the horn"?

2. Capitalize the name of persons, titles that are used with names, and titles that are used in place of names. Titles of important officials

should be capitalized when they refer to a particular person, but not when they refer to an office.

General *MacArthur*
Reverend *O'Neil*
Tell me, *Congressman*, would you like to be a senator?
My *mother* and my *aunt Phyllis* stayed home.
Will you and *Uncle Chuck* ride with me, *Dad*?

(The title *president* is capitalized only when it appears before the name of a president of the United States or when it stands in place of the name of the current president: The *President* said today . . . , *President* Hoover cannot be blamed . . . , The *president* of the United States is usually the leader of his party.)

3. Capitalize the names of specific geographical regions, bodies of water, mountains, streets, parks, buildings, and monuments. Do not capitalize compass directions unless they refer to recognized sections of the country or world.

Twelfth Street   *Lake Mead*   the *Grand Canyon*
Many people from the *Midwest* drive *south* for vacation.

4. Capitalize the days of the week, the months of the year, official holidays, the names of historical events or periods, but do not capitalize the names of seasons.

the *Middle Ages* *Labor Day* *spring Friday*

5. Capitalize all proper nouns and proper adjectives including the names of nationalities, races, and religions.

French toast   *Oriental* rug   *Roman Catholic*

6. Capitalize the names of celestial bodies, but do not capitalize *sun, moon, earth, galaxy,* or *universe.*

Halley's Comet   *Jupiter*   the *Milky Way*

(*Earth* may be capitalized when it is referred to with other planets.)

7. Capitalize the first word, the last word, and all important words in the title of any work of art (see page 201).

8. Capitalize the name of a specific school course, but do not capitalize the name of a general area of study, unless it includes a proper name.

I enrolled in *Math* 301 and *Home Economics*, but I couldn't find a *chemistry* course I liked.

9. Capitalize the brand names and registered trademarks of products.

Diet Pepsi, Coke (but: a *cola*)
a *Xerox* copy (but: a *photocopy*)
Ping-Pong (but: *table tennis*)
Levi's (but: *blue jeans*)
Band-Aid (but: *bandage*)
Jell-o (but: *gellatin dessert*)
Dictaphone (but: *dictating machine*)

Note: Years ago the words *windbreaker, aspirin, thermos, cellophane, ginger ale,* and *escalator* were proper nouns and were spelled with a capital letter. Today they are considered *generic*—that is, they refer to a general class of products instead of the product of a specific manufacturer.

Master Sentences

1. Tim responded, "It would be my pleasure."
2. Were you the one who cried "Help!"
3. Were you the one who cried "Help"?
4. Her first question was "What is your sign?"
5. "I used to be a pilot," he explained.
6. Poe's life was quite brief (1808-1849), but his works will endure forever.
7. His most well-known poem, "The Raven," appears later in this chapter (see page 226).
8. The pitcher's mound is sixty feet, six inches from the plate. (Why this distance was chosen is still unclear.)
9. "Where are you going?" she asked.
10. Cries of "Help!" "Fire!" and "Save me!" rang through the halls.
11. She received her B.A., M.A., and Ph.D. from Harvard.
12. Today we will finish our discussion of "Thanatopsis"; tomorrow we will move on to "A Forest Hymn."
13. The actual writing took more than ten years (1967-1978); however, the book became an immediate success.
14. "That will be all!" he shouted. "We've heard enough from you already."
15. Then he added, "I do not wish to be called 'Hey You.'"
16. Ancient Athens was not a democracy. (Has there ever been a true democracy?)
17. Is our heading now SSW (south southwest)?
18. The light turned green (What a break!) just as I skidded into the intersection.
19. This is a real doubloon (a Spanish gold coin)! We're rich!
20. Will you tell him "I'm sorry"?
21. Don't you ever tell me "I forgot"!
22. Do you know how to get to Indio Blvd.?
23. You're not an M.D.! You're a Q.U.A.C.K.!
24. Why did you bellow "Is the fire going out?"
25. "Would it also be illegal to enter a crowded firehouse and yell 'Movie!' she asked.
26. Was it a bird? a plane? a missile?
27. "I've spent all day," she hemmed and hawed, "just sewing and gardening."
28. "Will it be Christmas before I hear you say, 'I'm sorry'?"
29. "I thought I heard you say 'How old are you?'"
30. The game was not very exciting (our team was behind from the opening whistle) even for the most devoted fans.
31. This poem (originally titled "Honor Among Thieves") was written in 1969.
32. The pottery dates back to 1800 B.C.
33. What a thrill it was to say "We won!"
34. We began by studying the parts of speech (nouns, verbs, etc.)

INSTRUCTIONS

When two punctuation marks can be used at the same point in a sentence you are writing, locate one of the marks in the column on the left of the grid and the other in the row across the top. The numbers that appear at the intersection of that column and that row designate the correctly punctuated master sentences in which those two marks occur at the same point. One of the numbered sentences shown (or one of the example sentences used previously) should be similar to the sentence you are writing.

	Comma ,	Semicolon ;	Period .	Question Mark ?	Exclamation Point !	Quotation Marks " " ' '	Parentheses ( )
Comma ,	Do Not Use Together	Do Not Use Together	5, 11	9, 26	10, 14	1, 5, 7, 15, 27	6
Semicolon ;	Do Not Use Together	Do Not Use Together	Do Not Use Together (except when period used in abbrev.)	Do Not Use Together	Do Not Use Together	12	13
Period .	5, 11	Do Not Use Together (except when period used in abbrev.)	Do Not Use Together (See: 1, 32, 34)	4, 20, 22, 28	21, 23	1, 12, 14, 15, 27, 28, 29	7, 8, 30, 34
Question Mark ?	9, 26	Do Not Use Together	4, 20, 22, 28	Do Not Use Together (See: 24)	2, 3, 25	3, 4, 9, 20, 25, 28, 29	16, 17
Exclamation Point !	10, 14	Do Not Use Together	21, 23	2, 3, 25	Do Not Use Together (See: 33)	2, 10, 14, 21, 25	18, 19
Quotation Marks " " ' '	1, 5, 7, 15, 27	12	1, 12, 14, 15, 27, 28, 29	3, 4, 9, 20, 25, 28, 29	2, 10, 14, 21, 25	15, 25, 28, 29	31
Parentheses ( )	6	13	7, 8, 30, 34	16, 17	18, 19	31	Do Not Use Together

15. Writing Letters

In an earlier chapter I suggested that you can improve your children's spelling by having them write at every opportunity—grocery lists, chores for the day, items to pack for a trip, etc. While these activities make children feel more comfortable about writing down individual words or a few words at a time, they do not give children practice in writing complete sentences or in using proper punctuation. I believe that the best way to give them this practice is to encourage your children to write letters. Whether they are letters to friends, letters to television personalities, letters to government officials, or thank-you notes to relatives, they all provide practice in creating clear, effective sentences and paragraphs.

You must help your children form the habit of putting their thoughts in writing because they are not likely to form this habit themselves. Children have very few opportunities that demand their writing, and, consequently, most children are unskilled in the art when these opportunities eventually surface. The one idea about writing improvement that educators today agree upon is that improved writing is the result of increased writing: The more writing a child does, the more likely it is that his writing will improve.

Writing letters provides an opportunity to write that is not artificial or stilted. The child actually has an idea of his own to express—an idea that cannot be expressed in person. By encouraging him to put his message on paper, you help him develop the patience that is a necessary part of writing, but that is foreign to most experiences in childhood. Writing requires considered thought and allows time for perfected expression; children are not likely to practice these skills on their own. You can also make suggestions and ask questions about each letter as a way of getting your child to see the questions his reader might have and the observations this reader would make about the writer. Practicing writing—just like practicing anything else—will not create improvement if the same mistakes are practiced over and over again.

Improvement in letter writing, for both children and adults, comes primarily from improvement in writing in general. People who are able to convey their ideas clearly and effectively in reports, essays, written explanations, and descriptions are more likely to write effective letters than are those with lesser writing skill. Still, many adults who are quite skilled in writing are reluctant to express themselves in a letter because they are unsure about the *form* that that letter should take. Just as people fear being embarrassed about their use of language, there is also a very common fear about the embarrassment that comes from not knowing the standard forms for certain types of letters. This fear most commonly surrounds the form of the "business" letter, and it causes writers to ask questions such as "Does my signature belong at the bottom left or the bottom right of the letter?"; "Should I say 'Dear Mrs. _____', 'Dear Miss_____', or 'Dear Ms. _____' in the salutation?"; "Which fold in the letter goes in the bottom of the envelope?" Of course, writers only ask themselves these questions; they would be embarrassed to ask anyone else because doing so would demonstrate their ignorance. And, because they can't come up with the answers themselves, they elect not to write the letter after all, explaining that it wasn't really important anyway or that it would be better to convey the message over the telephone. I sometimes wonder how much of AT&T's revenue each year is directly traceable to the fear people have about being embarrassed by their own letters.

The "business" letters that strike such fear in the average adult need not pertain to "business" at all. They are merely different from the "friendly" letters that you write to people whom you know well. When you dash off a quick letter to a friend, you know your intended audience, and you know that the form of your letter will not alter any impressions your friend may have about you. But when you write to someone with whom you have had little, if any, contact, your letter represents you; it may provide your reader with his first impression of you, and you want that impression to be good enough that your reader will give serious consideration to what you have to say. These "business" letters, then, include letters of complaint or request to a manufacturer or store, letters to your landlord about problems with your plumbing, letters of application for a job or to a school, letters to a public official—all letters whose form must, necessarily, be businesslike and professional.

The first question that arises about all letters of this type is "Must the letter be typed, or may I write it in longhand?" The impression that is created by a typewritten letter is always more businesslike than that created by a handwritten one. But not everyone has the ability (or the typewriter) to type his own letters, and so the answer to the question must be "Type your letter if at all possible, but don't use your inability to type as an excuse for not writing the letter at all." A typewritten letter ensures that your writing will be legible, but if you can make your handwriting legible to your reader, then your letter will be read and acted upon. The impression that you fail to achieve by not typing your letter can be regained by the clarity of your writing.

The model letter that follows demonstrates the standard form for business letters that are handwritten. The "cover letter" that appears on page 223 shows the proper form for business letters that are typed.

Sample of Handwritten Business Letter

320 East 81st Street
New York, N.Y. 10028
November 26, 1980

Mr. Raoul Orceyré
Orceyre's Appliances
757 Third Avenue
New York, N.Y. 10017

Dear Mr. Orceyré:

    I am writing to you about a shipping charge I was required to pay on a refrigerator that I purchased in your store. I consider this to be an overcharge, and I hope that you will be able to correct it.

    On October 20 I bought a General Electric refrigerator from your salesman, Dale Alexander. Mr. Alexander told me at that time that the refrigerator would be delivered to my home free of charge. The refrigerator arrived on November 20, but the truckdriver (from the Ace Trucking Company) would not take it off his truck unless I gave him a check for $38.40 to cover the shipping costs. I am enclosing a copy of my receipt for the refrigerator and a copy of the shipping bill. Please notice that the receipt is marked "Delivery Pre-paid."

    I feel that your store should reimburse me the amount that I paid to have the refrigerator delivered. I do not wish to have credit in this amount instead, I would appreciate your sending me a check for $38.40.

           Sincerely,
           Holly Tooker
           (. .) . . . Tooker

Enclosures

THE HEADING

If your letters are written on stationery that has your own letterhead printed at the top, there is no need for you to write any part of the heading except the date on which the letter is written. In this case the date can appear at the upper left (if you are using the block style) or at the upper right (aligned with the first letter of the closing). In either case the date should be written at least two lines above the inside address. The date should not contain any abbreviations such as figures to represent the month. Notice that your name does not appear in the heading.

THE INSIDE ADDRESS

The inside address includes the name, title, and address of the person to whom you are sending the letter. The name is usually preceded by a title (*Mr., Mrs., Miss,* or *Ms.*), and, if the person's business title is short (such as *President,* for instance), it should appear on the top line, separated from the name by a comma. Longer business titles (*Personnel Manager,* for example) should be placed on the second line. Any extremely long line in the inside address should be carried over to the following line and indented three spaces. (If the inside address runs over four lines, the business title may be eliminated.) If the letter is addressed to a particular department within a company, the company name should appear on the line above the name of the department. Never abbreviate the name of a city in the inside address; however, state names may be abbreviated. The zip code is separated from the state name by two spaces.

THE SALUTATION

Direct your letter to a specific person when-ever possible. (You can find the person's name in a business directory in your library, or you can call the company and ask to whom your letter should be sent.) Above all, spell the person's name correctly: Failure to do so creates a very bad first impression.

If you know that the person to whom you are writing is a male, the salutation should read "Dear Mr. _____." If you know that the female to whom you are writing prefers one of the titles *Mrs., Miss,* or *Ms.,* use that title in the salutation. If you do not know the title preferred by a particular female, or if you are unsure about whether the person to whom you are writing is a male or a female, use the entire name in the salutation: *Dear Kay Ogle, Dear R. L. Ortmeyer.*

If you cannot determine exactly which person should receive your letter, and if you, therefore, have included only a title, a department name, or a company name in your inside address, your salutation should read "Dear Sir" (if the letter is directed to a particular, but unknown, person), "Dear Sirs" or "Gentlemen" (if the letter is directed to a company or a group. If you are troubled by the sexist nature of these salutations, you may resort to using in your salutation the name of the office or group stated in the inside address: *Dear Personnel Manager, Dear Members of the Board.*

In any case, the salutation should be placed two lines below the inside address, flush with the left-hand margin, and it should be followed by a colon.

THE CLOSING

If the paragraphs in the body of your letter are not indented (the "block style" begins each paragraph at the left-hand margin and separates each paragraph with a line of space), the closing is placed at the left, flush with the left-hand margin. If your paragraphs are indented, the closing should appear slightly to the right of the center of the page. In either case the closing should begin two lines below the last line of the letter.

The wording of the complimentary closing you use can take many forms—all but a few of which are relatively meaningless. Phrases such as "Respectfully yours," "Yours very truly," and "Sincerely yours" certainly seem out of place at the close of a letter in which you have demanded the return of your money or have questioned the possibility of canine ancestry in the person to whom you are writing. Perhaps the only truthful and logical closing in common use today is simply "Sincerely," and this is the one I suggest you use.

THE SIGNATURE

Whether your letter is typed or handwritten, by all means make your signature legible! Your signature says a good deal about you to people you have not met, and you do not want your signature to give the impression that you are sloppy, careless, or so egotistic that you think everyone will know who you are. In a typed letter the name of the writer is typed directly below the written signature (and in exactly the same form as the written signature); it is, similarly, a good idea to print your name underneath your signature in a handwritten letter.

If your sex is not immediately apparent from your first name, or if you wish to show which feminine title (*Mrs., Miss,* or *Ms.*) you prefer, you should place the proper title in parentheses in front of your printed name.

(Mr.) J. T. Lock   (Ms.) Jane Hedges

THE BODY

Now we get to the most important part of any business letter—the body. As I said before, writing good letters involves the ability to write well, and that is not something that can be taught in just a few pages. I can, however, point out a few principles that apply to writing business letters, and I can alert you to a few of the things that characterize poorly written business letters.

The most important point to remember about writing any business letter is that the letter represents you—it acts as a substitute for your own personally delivered message. The test for any business letter, then, is to see whether it actually accomplishes this purpose—whether it accurately reflects the way you would present your message if the person to whom you are writing were seated right in front of you. Try reading your letter aloud and see whether it sounds natural to you. Can you imagine yourself saying exactly what you have written in your letter? If you have used outdated phrases and pompous expressions in your letter, your writing will sound silly when it is read aloud, and that is precisely how it will sound to your reader. Would you use phrases such as "I am in receipt of your letter of . . ." or "Thanking you in advance I remain . . ." if you were presenting your message in person? Of course not. So why would you use phrases like these to represent yourself in a letter? Perhaps you, like many people in business, government, and education today, think that phrases such as these will make you appear more learned, more professional; you may even think that this is the type of language that business people use and expect in correspondence. Nothing could be further from the truth. The fact is that only those people who have nothing important to say, or who simply do not have the ability to express themselves clearly, use these cold, unnatural, meaningless words and phrases in their writing.

Good writing in a business letter is simple, clear, specific, and to the point. No business (with the exception of the government and some social sciences) can function on obfuscation and clouded communication. Businesses depend upon the ability of their employees to understand and convey written information. That ability is not enhanced by long sentences and paragraphs that lead the reader into a maze of ideas, or by meaningless words and phrases that demonstrate their writer's inability to think clearly or to express ideas effectively.

Here is a list of trite expressions, meaningless words, and wordy phrases that should be avoided in business letters. The column on the right gives either simple words and understandable phrases that may be used as possible alternatives, or a brief comment about why the phrase across from it should be avoided.

Avoid	*Substitute*
appreciate your informing me	please tell me
at a later date	later
at the earliest possible date	as soon as possible
at the present time	at present; now
at that point in time	then
at your earliest convenience	(but it may never be truly convenient; try *soon*)
be that as it may	(meaningless; delete)
by means of	by
cognizant	aware
commence	start; begin
communication	letter
due to the fact that	because
endeavor	try
eventuate	occur or happen
finalize	(Watch out for all manufactured words that end in *-ize*; for this one use *end* or *complete*.)
for the period of	for
for the purpose of	for; to
for the reason that	because
give your consideration to	consider

(continued)

Avoid	Substitute
herewith enclosed please find	I enclose; enclosed is
please find enclosed	I am enclosing
I am forwarding to you under separate cover	I am sending you separately
I have before me a copy of	(So what? Delete this and get on with whatever you are trying to say.)
I have received your letter of	(Of course you have, otherwise you wouldn't be writing.)
in accordance with	by; under
inasmuch as	since
in terms of	in
in the event of	if
I remain	(meaningless; delete)
it has come to my attention	(Obviously, or else the letter would be unnecessary.)
it is quite possible that	probably
may or may not	may
notwithstanding the fact that	even though; although
Please be advised that	(Begin with whatever follows.)
please do not hesitate to	please
subsequent to	after
sufficient	enough
terminate	end; close
Thanking you in advance	(This implies that your request will be granted; delete.)
this is to inform you	(meaningless; delete)
transmit	send
until such time as	until
utilization	use
wish to take this opportunity to	(You have your wish, now say what you mean.)
with regard to; with reference to	about; concerning

In planning the type of business letter you want to write, think about the kinds of business letters you, yourself, have received. The ones that you paid attention to were probably short and direct; the ones you only skimmed and discarded were probably long, involved, and did not make their purpose plain. The people to whom you write are no different from you, and so they will probably react to your letters in the same way you react to the letters you receive.

The business letters you write will receive

more attention from your readers if you adhere to the following general rules.

1. **Be brief.** Keep the letter to a single page if possible.

2. **Tell the reader why you are writing in the first paragraph.** This first paragraph should contain one or two sentences at most and should let your reader know what is on your mind.

3. **Give your reader only the important facts.** Limit the facts and reasons you give to the few that most clearly support your idea. Don't allow the reader to reject your entire idea just because you have included some weak evidence that can be rejected. If you are including opinions as well as specific facts, distinguish the two by clearly labeling your opinions with phrases such as "I believe that . . ." or "In my opinion. . . ."

4. **Clearly state exactly what you want the reader to do.** The last paragraph should describe the specific action that you want taken. You cannot expect any results if your reader is at all unclear about what you expect him to do.

OTHER PARTS OF A BUSINESS LETTER

There are a few additional problems that occasionally crop up in using the proper form for a business letter. The most common of these deal with the postscript, the identification line, the enclosure mark, the heading of a second page, and the envelope.

THE POSTSCRIPT

In most cases a postscript—that is, an additional note added at the bottom of a letter—is unnecessary. It is, after all, an afterthought, and it implies that the writer did not plan the body of the letter well. In some letters, such as sales letters, for instance, a postscript can be an effective device for grabbing the attention of the reader who has only skimmed the body of the letter. When a postscript is used, it is identified by the abbreviation *P.S.,* placed two lines below the last notation on the letter, and indented five spaces from the left margin.

THE IDENTIFICATION LINE

When a letter has been dictated by one person but typed by another, the initials of each person are shown in an identification line. This identification line is placed flush with the left margin and on the same line as the last line of the signature. If Donald W. Ryals dictated a letter that was typed by Robert C. Stolley, the identification line would read: *DWR:rs.*

THE ENCLOSURE MARK

When some other information (a résumé, a copy of a bill, a photograph, etc.) is being sent with a letter and enclosed in the same envelope, an enclosure mark is placed on the letter. The word *Enclosure, Enclosures,* or the abbreviation *Enc.* is placed flush with the left-hand margin and two lines below the identification line.

THE SECOND-PAGE HEADING

If your letter runs more than one page, the second page should be a plain sheet (no letterhead), and its heading should include the name of the person to whom you are writing, the page number, and the date. This heading should appear several lines above the body of the second page and stretch to the margins.

Mrs. Gail B. Mitchell —2— May 30, 1981

THE ENVELOPE

The address on the envelope should be the same as the inside address on the letter.

(However, if a person's business title has not been included in the inside address, it may be included on the envelope.) If this address requires only three lines, the lines should be double-spaced; if the address requires four or five lines, it should be single-spaced.

The return address should include the writer's name and should not take up more than three lines.

```
M. A. Lehman
19 Williams Drive
Delaware, Ohio  43015


                    Mr. Gerald Campbell
                    Personnel Manager
                    Professional Products, Inc.
                    2603 Valkar Lane
                    Champaign, Il  61820
```

The letter should have two folds, dividing the paper into equal thirds. The bottom fold should be inserted into the bottom of the envelope so that the letter will open up in the position that it is to be read when the envelope is opened.

RÉSUMÉS AND COVER LETTERS

To most adults the need to create an effective, professional business letter becomes apparent when they are looking for a new job. All of us have been, or will be, in a situation where we would like to be considered for a position with another company. Finding a job you would like is only the first step; the help-wanted ads in newspapers and your own personal contacts can usually generate any number of opportunities for which you think you are qualified. Of far more importance than merely finding a job you would like, however, is getting that company to grant you an interview so that the company can see that you are the right person for that particular job.

Once you have located a job that you think

217

you would like to have and for which you think you are qualified, you must work to convince that company that you are the person it is seeking. The company will base its decision not upon what you write, but, rather, upon how it feels about you after an interview. Your goal, then, is to get the company to grant you that interview; your writing leads to that interview, and your interview leads to that job.

When a company has a job to offer, it simply cannot interview everyone who wants that job, and so it grants interviews only to those who it thinks are most likely to fit the company's needs. The company chooses whom to interview on the basis of what the candidates have said in their *résumés* (pronounced reh'•zoom•ays). A résumé (also called a *curriculum vitae* or *vita*) is a summary of a person's educational background and employment history. Therefore, your résumé, and the "cover letter" you send with your résumé, will represent *you* to that company and will generate every impression that company will have about you until you can make your own impression in a personal interview.

The point you want to keep uppermost in your mind is that you do not want your résumé to *exclude* you from the list of people the employer wants to interview. Résumés that are "cute" or that make wildly inflated claims or that create more questions than they answer are likely to place the applicant in an unusual and unfavorable position. The place to demonstrate that you are uniquely qualified for the position is in your personal interview—not in your résumé. Your résumé should make the employer think positively about you, but you cannot, and should not,

expect it to take the place of an interview.

The most common type of résumé is the "chronological résumé," which displays your educational and employment histories in chronological order—the most recent events are shown first and the most distant ones last. A sample of a chronological résumé is shown on pages 220-221.

While there are no "rules" for writing an effective résumé, most employment counselors agree upon the following suggestions and general guidelines.

1. You do not need to type a new résumé each time you apply for a job; a good-quality photocopy will be perfectly acceptable. The original, however, should be typed, and you should use 8½" X 11" white bond paper.

2. Your résumé should not be longer than two pages; most résumés require only a single page. Give only the information that is necessary, and do not volunteer information that could better be saved for your interview. Be honest and straightforward in all the information you supply, but stress your strengths and accomplishments instead of just stating where and when you worked.

3. Don't use the first-person "*I* did this; *I* created that, etc." Try to employ an impersonal style (as in the sample résumé); even though the subject of your sentences will not be stated, it will be understood, and your résumé will not sound egotistical.

4. Include the supervisory, budget, and sales responsibilities you had in your previous jobs. Your job title alone may not mean the same thing to different employers. Also include any of your special skills and training, such as language fluencies and company training programs.

5. Don't state a specific job objective unless you can state it clearly and precisely. You do not want your stated objective to eliminate you from consideration for other positions the company might have.

6. Don't state the salary you have received or the salary you require except in general terms. You might state a broad salary range that would be acceptable to you and add that salary is only one of the considerations you have in selecting a new position.

7. You should not try to explain the reason for each job change, and you should not state your religious or political preferences.

8. Do not enclose a picture, and do not list your references on your résumé. Your references should remain confidential until the employer asks you to furnish their names and addresses.

Sample Résumé

PERSONAL

Michael J. Kistler   Married, 3 Children
4473 Stollwood Drive   Excellent Health
Carmichael, California 95608   Born: November 4, 1945
Home Phone: (916) 811-9038   Height: 5'9" Weight: 170 lbs.

EDUCATION

Wayne University   Detroit, Michigan   BS Business Management 1967
Dale Carnegie Course   "Effective Speaking: 1975

LOCATION

No restrictions.

WORK EXPERIENCE

1976 to Present-Orange Horse Products, Sacramento, California

May 1978 to Present-Personnel Manager
    Responsible for recruiting, screening, selecting and placing
    34 hourly employees and 12 salaried employees. Developed and
    directed company's training programs. Developed and instituted
    company's evaluation program and merit-pay procedure. Directed
    all employee benefit programs.

June 1976 to May 1978-Assistant Personnel Manager
    Wrote job specifications for all hourly positions within company.
    Wrote employment advertisements and assisted in screening of all
    applicants. Devised and implemented system by which probationary
    employees were supervised before they were granted permanent
    status with company.

July 1973 to June 1976-Logo 7, Inc., Indianapolis, Indiana

    Employee relations coordinator for textile company of 24
    employees. Responsible for recruiting and supervising all
    hourly workers. Created and directed new employee orientation
    program. Developed and implemented personnel procedures and
    forms, all of which the company still uses today.

220

January 1970 to July 1973-Thompson Enterprises, Oswego, Illinois

Various jobs including writing sales promotion, product brochures, and advertising for a small mail-order company. Also responsible for locating, hiring, training, and supervising 10 regional sales representatives. The addition of these representatives doubled the company's sales in two years.

MILITARY SERVICE

U.S. Navy 1968-1970
Honorable Discharge

OUTSIDE INTERESTS

Boy Scout troop leader, Secretary-Treasurer of Boys' Baseball Association, private pilot.

References furnished upon request.

Some counselors suggest that you write more than one type of résumé and that you tailor the résumés to the types of jobs being offered. The facts in your résumé do not change, but the emphasis you give those facts can. For example, if you have been employed as a secretary and you are applying for another secretarial job, your résumé would stress your skills in office management and convention- or program-planning as well as your secretarial skills. If, however, you were also thinking about changing to another field—marketing, perhaps—you would develop another résumé, one that would emphasize the parts of your secretarial background that demonstrate you have had experiences that would be valuable in marketing: As secretary for a product manager, you assisted in writing sales promotion, in conducting market research, in developing budgets, and you are familiar with pricing and packaging strategies.

Whether you have one or more than one style of résumé, the résume itself gives a prospective employer only a brief sketch of what you have done. In order to give that employer a more personal look into who you are and why you are interested in the particular job being offered, you must enclose a "cover letter" with your résumé. The cover letter, like the résumé, is not designed to land the job for you—only to land that all-important interview. The cover letter is a business letter that is directed to a particular employer who is offering a particular job. Each cover letter should be an original—never a photocopy—and, if at all possible, it should be typed. The cover letter identifies the position you are applying for, highlights the experiences you have had that relate to the job in question, and gives the employer a reason to be interested in talking with you. A sample cover letter appears on page 223.

In creating your cover letters, it is best to keep the following points in mind.

1. Tailor each letter to fit the specific qualifications and needs stated in the employment advertisement.

2. Be brief; a cover letter should never be more than one page long.

3. Do not waste your cover letter by merely repeating the information that is contained in your enclosed résumé. The résumé should act as a complement to your cover letter.

4. Put yourself in the employer's position and answer the questions you think the employer would have about you.

5. Don't base your appeal on sympathy, and don't discuss your dissatisfaction about your present job.

Sample Cover Letter

1215 Archer Street
San Diego, California 92109
December 8, 1980

Mr. Gary L. Smith
Bishop Pipe Company
82297 Indio Blvd.
Indio, California 92201

Dear Mr. Smith:

I am writing in response to your advertisement titled "Sales Manager," which appeared in the *Los Angeles Times* on December 7.

I have been involved in selling industrial products for the past ten years, and during that time I have acquired a good deal of experience in recruiting, motivating, and supervising sales personnel. I am a good salesman myself, and my record of achievement will bear out that claim. However, I believe that I can be most valuable to the Bishop Pipe Company by teaching others the sales techniques I have learned and by using my organizational skills to create and manage a network of sales representatives.

I look forward to the opportunity of meeting with you to learn more about the specific needs you have and the contributions I can make toward filling those needs. I will call your secretary in two weeks to arrange an appointment with you so that we might discuss these matters in detail.

Sincerely,

Robert J. Karnuth

Robert J. Karnuth

Enclosure

INDEX

225